COME BACK, AFRICA

STE publishers

First published in 2004 by STE Publishers
4th Floor Sunnyside Ridge,
Sunnyside Office Park,
32 Princess of Wales Terrace,
Parktown 2143
Johannesburg, South Africa

Published in October 2004

ISBN 1-919855-17-3

Editor: Peter Davis

Editorial Consultant: Michael Rogosin

Copy Editor: Michael Collins

Proofreader: Margaret Fleetwood

Cover & Book Design: Adam Rumball

Printed and bound in South Africa by Colors Print

"A timely and remarkable piece of cinema." —Time Magazine
"Extraordinary film...splendidly played against the background of South Africa. Highest recommendation!" —Cue Magazine
"Extraordinary timeliness."—New York Post
"The volatility of the racial situation in South Africa has again conspired to make Rogosin's film topical." —New York Daily News
LIONEL ROGOSIN'S
COME BACK, AFRICA
SPECIAL LIMITED ENGAGEMENT
STARTS THURSDAY, MAY 25
THE New Yorker
B'way. & 88th St. 874 9189
A WALTER READE THEATRE

CONTENTS

FOREWORD

Lionel Rogosin in world cinema was respected and honored for his unbending passion for documenting the human suffering and misery. Films that he made were not innocent objective reportages — no, he didn't pretend to be objective: he took a stand. There were no two right sides for him. And he knew that to do that, he had to take risks, to throw himself into totally unpredictable situations.

This extraordinary volume of diaries kept during the preparations and filming of *Come Back, Africa* testifies to that passion. It reveals his inquisitive, searching mind as he tries to understand Africa going through the process of waking up. There are observations and descriptions of life and thinking in South Africa at the turn of Africa's history that should be read by anyone who wants to understand that period.

We were friends, Lionel and myself, for most of his creative life. Unlike many other film-makers who concentrated only on their film-making, Lionel extended his passion and concern for the independent, probing, different cinema by creating Bleecker Street Cinema — a screening venue that became internationally known for showing work of socially and politically engaged film-makers. When in 1959 the film independents of New York were in the process of creating what became known as the New American Cinema Group, he actively joined the group. It was a very exciting period in the new cinema and Lionel was always the centre of it.

During the late period of his life unfortunately he had a great difficulty getting financing for his work. Together with Shirley Clarke, Emile de Antonio, Morris Engel, my brother Adolfas Mekas and a number of other very unique members of the Sixties cinema, because of the radicality of their cinema, they could not find backers for their films. Eventually it became, for that reason, the Lost Generation of the American cinema. Each managed to produce only two or three films. Not withstanding that fact, those two or three films - in Lionel's case *On the Bowery* and *Come Back, Africa* remain landmarks and documents both of life and cinema of that period. And in my humble opinion this volume of Lionel's notes and diaries stands in its importance and passion next to those two films as an equal third.

Jonas Mekas

Film Credits

Produced and directed by Lionel Rogosin
Written by Lionel Rogosin with Bloke Modisane and Lewis Nkosi
Photographed by Ernest Artaria and Emil Knebel
Sound recorded by Walter Wettler
Edited by Carl Lerner
South African consultant: Boris Sackville

Additional Crew
Clapper loader, production and set building by Morris Hugh
Runner: George Malebye
Pre-production assistants: McPherson and Elinor Rogosin

Cast:
Zacharia Mgabi
Vinah Bendile
Miriam Makeba
Arnold
Aunty (Martha — shebeen queen)
Dube-Dube
George Malebye
Marumu,
Morris Hugh
Hazel Futa
Lewis Nkosi
Bloke Modisane
Can Themba
Myrtle Berman
Rams
Steven
Piet Beyleveld
Jan Hoogendyk
Alexander Sackville
Sarah Sackville

featuring the music of Chatur Lal

INTRO

CW01649765

M Hodgkin

Advanced

Finance

Michael Fardon

David Cox

OSBORNE BOOKS *GNVQ* SERIES

acknowledgements

The authors would like to thank the following people who have helped and advised in the preparation of this book: Cathy Fardon, Mike Gilbert, Kay Kelly, Jason Orton and Rob Coward of NCVQ, Susie Lee and Roger Petheram.

Thanks must also go to the following organisations for help and for providing material for use in this book: Barclays Bank Connect team, Barclaycard, The Bodyshop International PLC and NCVQ.

copyright

Published by Osborne Books Limited,
Unit 1B Everoak Estate, Bromyard Road,
St Johns, Worcester, WR2 5HN
Tel 01905 748071

Printed by the Bath Press, Avon.

British Library Cataloguing in Publication Data
A catalogue record for this book is available from the British Library

ISBN 1-872962-31-9

contents

assignments

unit coverage

introduction

the text

Advanced Finance has been compiled to cover the three mandatory Units 6, 7 and 8 of the GNVQ Advanced Business Award to the 1995 revised specifications. It has been taken from Osborne Books' *Advanced Business* (1995) which covers all eight mandatory units. The reason the financial Units have been published separately is because a substantial number of teachers and lecturers have asked for them in this format.

The Units in *Advanced Finance* have been written in consultation with NCVQ. The authors have been careful to interpret the range and evidence indicators in accordance with NCVQ intentions.

Each GNVQ Unit is covered by a separate section of the book. At the beginning of each Section is an introductory page explaining its contents and how to tackle the assignments.

In most cases each chapter covers a *single* Unit Element. The performance criteria of each Element are printed below the chapter title, and are referenced within the text throughout the book. If the chapter covers only part of an Element, this is made clear in the chapter heading. Coverage of the Elements within each Unit may not be in same order as in the course specifications: they are presented within the text in what is hoped is a logical sequence. Coverage of the GNVQ Unit Elements within the book is set out on the previous page.

The text also covers all the range statements. Tutors should consult the index at the back of the book where they will find references to items in the range.

student activities

The Student Activities in *Advanced Finance* collectively cover all the performance criteria of the mandatory units. A reference to the relevant performance criterion (or criteria) is printed in the heading of each Activity.

The Student Activities are designed as learning activities to be used inside and outside the classroom – they are complementary to the Assignments which cover the Evidence Indicators. They also enable the student to develop the three main Core Skills: Application of Number, Communication and Information Technology.

assignments

Advanced Finance contains fourteen full-length Assignments printed within the chapters (see page 6 for a list). These are designed to cover the Element Evidence Indicators set down in the course specifications. They are fully referenced to the performance criteria in each Element.

Osborne Books is well aware that most centres will have devised their own assignments based around schemes of work. The assignments in this book are therefore offered as ideas and material for development. Tutors should refer to the page which introduces each main Section of the book (eg the opposite page for GNVQ Unit 6).

external testing

In order to help students prepare for the external tests, each chapter concludes with a summary, key terms and in most cases about half-a-dozen practice multiple-choice questions. In addition, the text itself uses terms from the range as subheadings.

feedback

The publication of this book is largely due to feedback from teachers and lecturers who have asked for a comprehensive but relevant and easy-to-manage coverage of the financial and planning Units. Please let us know what you think of this book in terms of format, content and 'usability'. Your comments (of whatever type!) are greatly valued.

Michael Fardon
David Cox

July 1995

SECTION

1

GNVQ UNIT 6
FINANCIAL TRANSACTIONS, COSTING AND PRICING

introduction to content

This section examines the financial aspects of the operation of businesses. The first chapter looks at the concept of 'added value' and applies it to profit-making and the importance of maintaining the flow of money in a business. The following two chapters deal with the 'nuts and bolts' of running a business – the processes of selling and buying and the documentation involved. The section concludes with two chapters on costing and pricing decisions – working out how much a product is going to cost to produce and then seeing at what price you can profitably sell it.

assignments

Because of the more technical nature of this subject, the Assignments are more self-contained than in previous Units, and very often give you the figures you need. They are to be found on pages 26, 47, 72, 73, 94, and 114. The first assignment deals with added value and the money cycle in a garden furniture company. The second and third assignments are very practical and deal with the documents of buying and selling; they also require you to collect documents from local businesses. The assignment on costing looks at the calculation of costs by two businesses (the figures are given). The final assignment – on pricing decisions – is based on a cricket bat manufacturer.

1 Added value and the money cycle

GNVQ SPECIFICATIONS

Element 6.1

Explain added value, distribution of added value and the money cycle

performance criteria – a student must

1 explain the trading cycle of goods or services in a business and their added value
2 explain the distribution of added value
3 explain the money cycle
4 explain factors for consideration when selling
5 explain factors for consideration when buying

what this chapter covers

In this chapter we will see the importance of the money flows in and out of a business – the creation of 'added value' in a product which can then generate cash and profit for the business. We will also look at the practical side of purchasing and selling – getting a good deal and making sure that customers pay up on time.

what you will learn from this chapter

- the trading cycle involves the buying of goods and services, the 'adding of value' by the business by manufacturing, adapting or selling a product or service, and then charging a suitable price to make a profit
- the money cycle is what happens to the money in the trading cycle – it highlights the importance of making sure that there is enough money – 'cash flow' – in the business to buy the goods and services needed to enable the business to operate
- if the money runs out, the business may go 'bust' – become insolvent
- when a business sells a product it must set up procedures to make sure that it will get its money from the purchaser
- when a business buys a product it must ensure that it assesses the suppliers carefully and gets 'value for money'

the trading cycle and added value

pc 6.1.1

the trading cycle

When a business sells a product – which can be a good or a service – it involves a *trading cycle*: the product is ordered and supplied and money is received back again from sales. If all goes well, a profit should be made, if it does not, a loss is incurred.

the concept of added value

As a business spends money on raw materials, components, expertise, overheads, and so on, it is *adding value* to its product. It is putting money and resources in a product which it can then sell at a profit. To take a simple example, a farmer can sell the apples that the farm grows at, say, 45p per pound. But the farmer can also *add value* to the apples by processing them – into apple juice, cider and apple pies. These processes will cost the farmer in terms of materials and overheads, but they will also enable the farmer to charge more in the long run because *value has been added* to the product.

To see how the trading cycle and the added value concept link up, look at the diagram below. You will see that selling a product involves:

- *costs* which add value to the product
- money received from sales which is then *distributed* to cover costs and also to provide a profit for the business owner

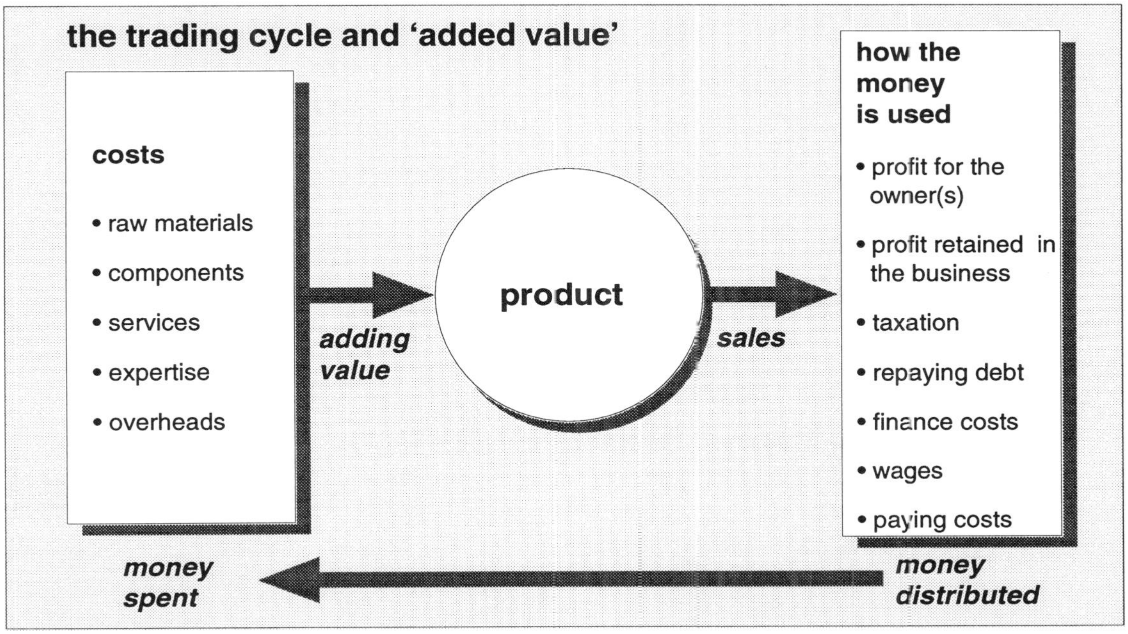

the cost of added value

If you look at the diagram on the previous page you will see that the left-hand box headed 'costs' contains a number of items. Some of these are easy to estimate. For example

- raw materials and components will cost a certain amount
- services such as advertising and insurance can be estimated
- overheads (rent, business rates, power bills) will be mostly fixed costs

cost accounting

We will see in Chapter 4 that it is possible for a *cost accountant* in a large organisation to give a manufactured item a certain 'cost' made up of its raw material cost, and the cost of the overheads involved in its production. We are not concerned in this chapter with the technicalities of working out this cost. All we need to appreciate is that this method of costing places a figure on the 'value' that is 'added' to a product as it goes through the manufacturing process. The diagram below shows that there are three main stages in the production process. At each stage, the business can place a 'cost' on an item.

adding value in the manufacturing process

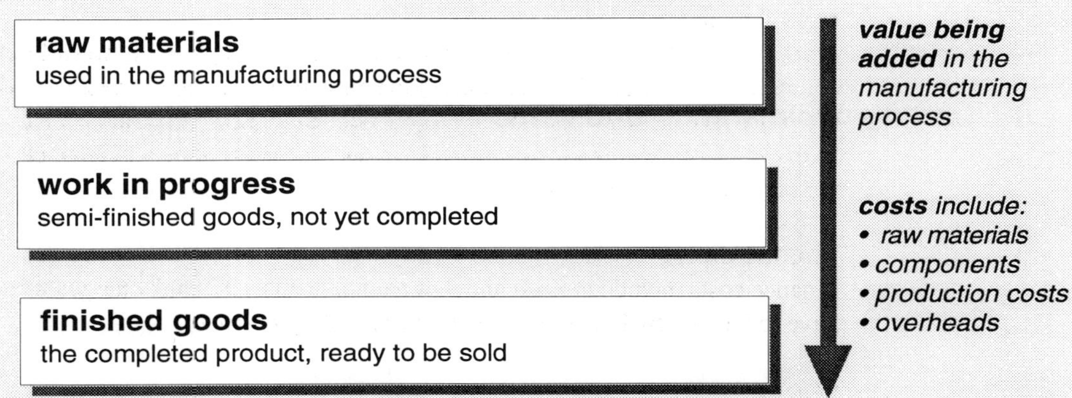

the distribution of added value

pc 6.1.2

what happens to the money?

When a business has sold its 'added value' product it will receive its money in due course. This will then be *distributed*. If you look again at the diagram on page 11, you will see in the right-hand box how the money is used.

profit for the owner(s)

Whether the business is a sole trader or a limited company, the owner(s) of the business will want to see a return on the money invested in adding value to the product. Sufficient profit should be made. For the sole trader, profit can be taken in the form of *drawings* – money taken out of the business. Shareholders' profits are distributed in the form of *dividends* on the company's shares.

profit retained in the business

It is normal and sensible practice to retain some of the profit in the business so that it can be invested in new products, equipment and research. The business should be looking ahead to develop its product range to make further profits in the future. Just because the managing director is driving around in a Mercedes does not mean that the company is successful!

taxation

Business profits are taxable – an unfortunate but unavoidable fact of business life. Sole traders and partners are taxed as individuals – they pay *income tax* on their business profits. Limited companies pay *corporation tax* on their profits. Businesses and their owners therefore have to set aside a proportion of their profits to paying tax to the Inland Revenue. Also if VAT is charged by a business on its product, the VAT will have to be paid to HM Customs & Excise (set off against VAT paid on the purchases a business makes).

repaying loans

Many businesses finance part of their operations through loans from banks and other providers of finance. Part of the cash generated by the business will therefore have to be allocated for repayment of *capital* (the actual amount borrowed) and *interest* (the cost of that finance calculated as a percentage of the amount borrowed) – see below.

finance costs

Finance costs include *interest* and *fees* paid on loans, and bank charges which have to be paid by businesses whether or not they borrow.

wages

A further cost to be borne by the business is the *wages and salaries* bill. If a business is labour-intensive, this bill can be high.

paying costs

The costs listed in the left-hand box will need paying for – the money in effect goes full circle – this is part of the *trading cycle* in operation. You will see that these costs include raw materials, services used, the business running expenses (overheads).

CASE STUDY

pc 6.1.2

Jo's Burger Bar – adding value

situation

Jo Okobase runs a successful burger bar in the town. He is a sole trader. He works in the burger bar himself and employs two part-timers. The business is financed from his own capital and by a £20,000 five-year bank loan. Jo has been working out the figures for last year's trading. He gives them to you in rough form, and you set them out as a table and a diagram to show the trading cycle and the adding of value to Jo's burgers:

Money received	£
Sales of food	100,000
Money spent (adding value)	
Raw materials – foodstuffs bought in	35,000
Business costs (insurance, gas bills)	9,000
Total of money paid out	44,000
Value added (£100,000 less £44,000)	56,000
Distribution of profit (added value)	
Profit taken out by Jo*	25,000
*(He will have to pay income tax out of this money)	
Wages	15,000
Repayment of part of bank loan from profit	4,000
Profit retained in the business	12,000
	56,000

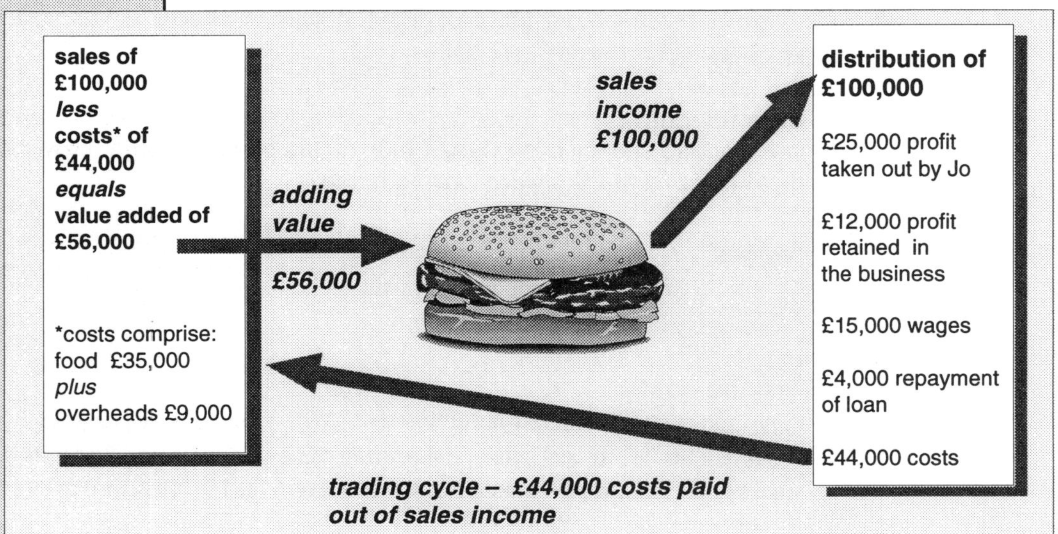

STUDENT ACTIVITY 1.1
performance criteria 6.1.1 & 2

assessing added value

Case Study

Enigma Software Limited is a small company which develops and sells computer software products in CD format. The management is very pleased with the figures for last year. They are:

Costs	£
2,500 disks at £1.00 each	2,500
Packaging and printing of manuals	5,000
Wages and salaries	50,000
Consultancy fees	25,000
Premises costs	15,000
Finance costs	7,500
Lease of computer equipment	10,000
Income	
Sales of CD packages	175,000

questions

1 Draw up a statement of profit for the company based on the statement of value added shown in the Case Study on the previous page. How much profit has Enigma Software Limited made?

2 If you were the directors of the company, what would you do with that profit? Do you have any choice? Draw up a pie chart showing how you would distribute the profit.

3 Explain in simple terms to the directors what "added value " means.

4 Calculate the percentage of the total cost represented by the raw material costs (ie the disks and the packaging). Why is it so low in comparison with the profit figure? What does this say about added value?

cash and the the money cycle

pc 6.1.3

the importance of cash

It is often said that cash is the 'lifeblood' of any business. When the cash dries up, the business fails. In this section we look in detail at how cash circulates in the business. As a first step, study the diagram below which shows the money cycle in a manufacturing business.

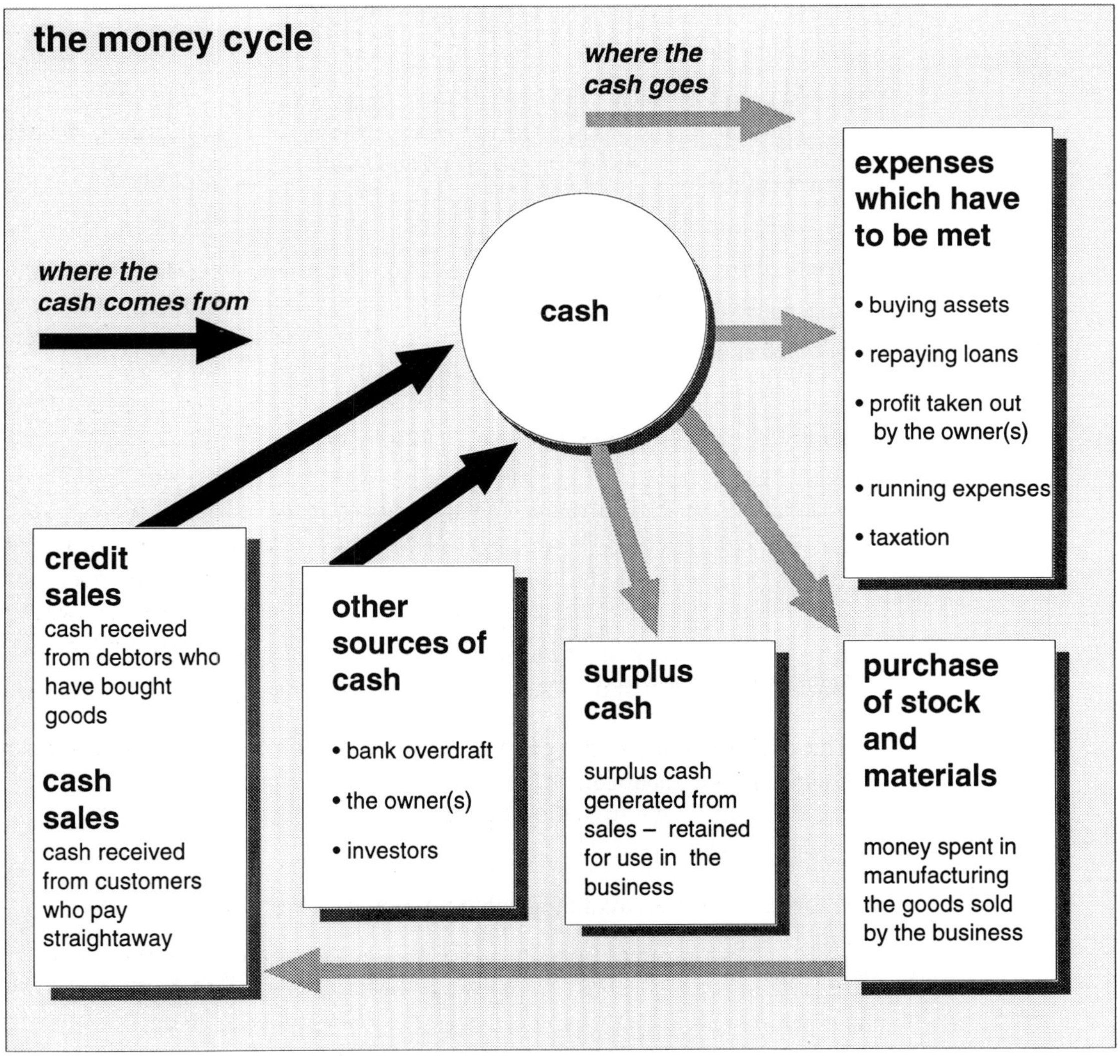

where the cash comes from

As you will see from the left-hand side of the diagram on the previous page, there are two main *sources* of cash:

- cash from the sale of the products of the business – the more the business sells, the more cash it will receive
- cash received from other sources, for example the bank overdraft, cash introduced by the owner(s) or other investors

where the cash goes

As you will see from the right-hand side of the diagram on the previous page, there are two main '*drains*' on the supply of cash:

- expenses which have to be met anyway – buying assets (equipment), repaying loans, paying the owner(s), running expenses and taxation
- paying for the product being sold – in the case of a manufacturing business this will be stocks of raw materials and related expenses

surplus/residual cash

You will also see from the diagram that a third arrow points to 'surplus cash'. If a business is trading profitably, and the money from sales is being received promptly, the amount of cash over time will exceed the amount being spent. As a result, a cash *surplus* or *residue* will build up, possibly in an interest-paying bank account. The business can be described as being 'liquid' – it can afford to pay off the amounts it owes as they fall due.

where things can go wrong – the importance of cash flow

As you will see from the diagram on the previous page, the flow of cash is vital to the running of a business. Just as the supply of electricity to a household can be cut off if the bill is not paid, with disastrous consequences, the owner of a business can face failure if the 'cash flow' is not maintained – either from sales or from the bank!

This cycle of money coming in and out of the business can be very precariously balanced. For example:

- what if sales fall well below the targets set?
- what if a big customer who owes money goes 'bust'?
- what if the bank will not lend any more money on overdraft?

In all these cases *the supply of cash will be reduced and the business may not be able to pay important bills or pay its suppliers.* Look at the danger points shown on the diagram on the next page Then read the Case Study which follows. It shows what can go wrong when the supply of cash dries up.

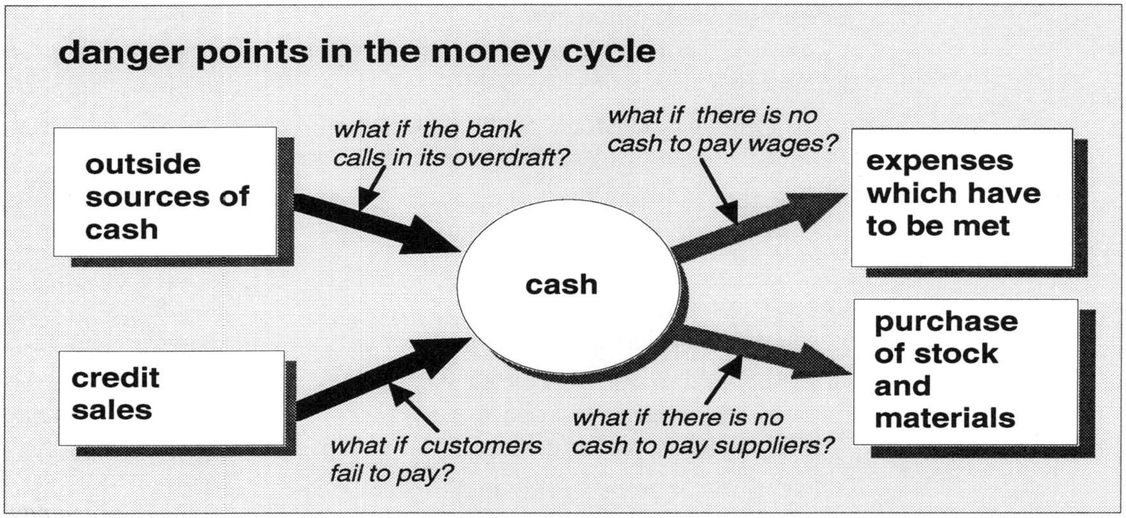

CASE STUDY

pc 6.1.3

John Spender – cash flow problems

situation

John Spender has started up in business making novelty clocks. He buys quartz clock mechanisms from a wholesaler whom he pays 30 days after he has received the goods and the invoice. He makes the casings from wood and plastic in his workshop. He employs two production workers and does all the marketing, selling and administration himself.

He is very pleased that he has been able to secure contracts to supply a major department store chain and a catalogue mail order company with his clocks. They agree to pay him 60 days after he has supplied and invoiced the goods. He has a £5,000 overdraft with the Albion Bank to provide "cash flow" for the period **after** *he has paid for his materials, but* **before** *he receives payment from his two big customers.*

This is what happens:

November

He and his production workers start to work flat out to supply the orders received – which are larger than expected. He has had to order more materials than expected, and his wages bill is bigger.

December

He has to pay for his first month's supplies. He has to borrow from the bank on overdraft to pay for them. The bank manager is reasonably happy about this, although he says the amount is larger than he was expecting from John's forecast (a document known as a Cash Flow Forecast).

January

Disaster strikes. The department store's buyer telephones to say that some of the clocks have been returned by their customers complaining that they are faulty. The department store is returning the faulty ones, and will not pay for the remainder until they have been sold. The mail order company, on the other hand, have had no problems, and he receives his first cheque from them.

February

John issues a cheque to the supplier of the quartz mechanisms, but the bank refuse to pay it, saying that the overdraft is too high – he has borrowed too much already. The supplier refuses to send any more mechanisms. John only has three weeks' supply left in stock.

March

John finds that he has to lay off his production workers – he cannot make any more clocks, and he cannot supply orders received. He has no money to pay the workers.

April

The bank makes formal demand for its overdraft – it wants its money back. The bank has a mortgage over John's house, and can sell it if John cannot repay the borrowing.

May

John's business fails. He is **insolvent** *– he owes more than he has got.*

STUDENT ACTIVITY 1.2
performance criterion 6.1.3

cash flow problems

analysis and investigation

Read through the John Spender Case Study and answer the following questions:

1. What is the document John has shown to the bank, telling them how much money he is going to need to borrow from them? Obtain and examine a copy of one of these documents – you will need it for your later studies.

2. How much did John think he was going to need to borrow?

3. Why was he going to need this money?

4 Why did the amount of cash needed exceed his forecasts initially (ie before he sent out any goods)?

5 What technical problem occurred which meant that his supply of cash began to run out?

6 Was it a good idea just to sell to two customers? How could John have solved this problem?

7 Why did the supplier of quartz mechanisms refuse to supply any more?

8 Why did John lay off his production workers? What would have happened if he had kept them on?

9 What was the final 'death blow' to John's business. What could happen to him and his family?

10 What could John have done to avoid his business failing? Discuss this in class.

insolvency – going 'bust'

pc 6.1.3

The Case Study of John Spender you have just looked at is a sorry tale of what can go wrong. As you will see, business failure is often a result of cash flow failure. It is not always entirely the fault of the business owner(s) – bad luck often has a part to play.

Insolvency is the inability to pay debts as they fall due. If the people who are owed money – the creditors – consider they can get their money back through the courts they can do so by

- making an individual (sole trader or partner) 'bankrupt'
- 'winding up' a company or asking for a company 'administration order'

The end-result of these legal processes is that the assets (belongings) of the individual or company will be sold under court supervision to pay off the creditors. Do not assume that if you make someone bankrupt (or wind up a company) that you will get all or any of your money back – there may not be any! Also, if a lender such a bank has a signed mortgage (a charge) over the property (eg John's house in the Case Study), the lender will get 'first cut' and the remaining creditors will have to follow in the queue for money.

selling procedures

pc 6.1 4

cash sales and credit sales

When a business sells a product – and by 'product' we mean a manufactured item or a service – it will either, like a shop, receive its money straightaway, or it will sell on credit, and receive the money later – it hopes! There are therefore two ways of selling:

- **cash sale** – where the money is received straightaway
- **credit sale** – where the money is to be received later

Note that a 'cash' sale does not necessarily mean that cash is used – the business may accept payment by cheque or debit card. 'Cash payment' means immediate payment. With a cash sale a *receipt* is often given to the buyer as proof of purchase, with a credit sale, an *invoice* is usually issued to the buyer. We will look at these documents in more detail in the next chapter.

checking out the buyer – 'creditworthiness'

When a business sells on credit to a business it has not dealt with before, it needs to make sure that the buyer is likely to be able to pay for the goods or services sold. The buyer must be *creditworthy*. It is all very well being able to clinch a sale for your product, but if the buyer goes bankrupt after you have delivered the goods, not only will you lose your money, you may well lose the goods as well! There are various ways in which you can 'check out' the buyer's *creditworthiness*:

- ask for a trade reference from another business which supplies the buyer
- ask for a reference from the buyer's bank

It is normal commercial practice for a buyer to supply these names and addresses to the seller.

If you are selling to a business you can obtain a credit report, for a fee, from a *credit reference agency* such as Dun and Bradstreet which collects useful business information. Many credit reference agencies nowadays are on-line by computer link.

payment terms

When a business sells goods or services, as we have seen earlier in this chapter it needs to get the money in as soon as possible. It will have to arrange the most advantageous *payment terms*. The best terms are a *cash sale* – the money is received immediately and can be used in the business straightaway.

Normally a business will issue a sales invoice stating the period of time given to the buyer to pay up. The most common period is 30 days. This does not mean, however that payment will be received then. As we will see in the next chapter, businesses often pay on a statement issued at the end of the month. An invoice issued in October will therefore normally be paid at the end of November when the statement is issued. Statistics show that the average payment period in the UK is approximately 45 days.

Some businesses offer a *cash discount* to buyers: this is a percentage reduction in the bill (often 2.5%) for quick settlement, eg within seven days. Clearly these businesses consider it is better to receive *less money* straightaway (it costs them 2.5%) rather than wait a month or so and possibly have to borrow that money from a bank and pay bank interest.

You should note that it is an unfortunate fact of business life that large buyers can demand very long payment terms from small sellers! For example if you are a farmer selling a speciality cheese to a large supermarket chain you may have to wait up to three months to be paid.

credit control

When a business sells on credit, the business buying the product and owing money to the seller is known as a *debtor*. The seller will keep a record of what is owed by each debtor in an account in its 'books', just as a bank keeps an account for each of its customers. The debtors' accounts are known collectively as the 'sales ledger' (see page 120).

An efficient business will keep an eye on its *sales ledger*, making sure that it receives the money that is owed by sending out reminders, and taking stronger measures if necessary – this process is known as *credit control*. The credit control measures a business might take include:

- **statement** – a document setting out what is owed and when it has to be paid, normally sent out monthly – many businesses pay up on receiving a statement (see page 42 for an example)
- **telephone call** – some businesses which owe money ignore statements and may need reminding by telephone
- **chaser letter – polite** for example "we shall be grateful if you will settle up as soon as possible"
- **chaser letter – formal** "kindly send your cheque by return of post"
- **solicitor's letter** – you put the matter in the hands of a solicitor who will write to the debtor threatening legal action
- **court action** – if the amount is large, you can take the matter to the civil courts if you think the debtor has got the money

Good credit control means money in the bank for the business; poor credit control means that the business can lose money – people will tend to pay as late as they can, or in some cases not at all, if they can get away with it!

bad debt

A bad debt is a debt which will not be repaid. If a business sells its products to another business which then becomes bankrupt or cannot or will not repay, the seller incurs a loss – a *bad debt*. This then becomes an expense of the seller and will reduce the level of profits. Businesses with good credit control should incur fewer bad debts.

selling procedures and the money cycle

As you will gather from the last few pages, the way in which a business sells its products and chases up debts will affect the amount of money coming into the business. An efficient business will be able to improve the flow of cash in the money cycle.

STUDENT ACTIVITY 1.3
performance criterion 6.1.4

selling procedures

(it is suggested that this Activity is carried out using the same resources as Activity 1.4)

investigation

You are to talk to local businesses or business advisers about the questions asked below and then set out your answers in writing.

1 How do you 'check out' a buyer with whom you have not has dealings before?

2 What sort of payment terms would you offer to
   (a) a new customer?
   (b) an old and trusted customer?

3 How do payment terms affect the cash position of a business?

4 What steps would you take to chase up a debt of
   (a) £45?
   (b) £4,500?

buying procedures

pc 6.1.5

assessing suppliers

When a business is buying goods or services is has to decide which supplier (or suppliers) it is to use. The decision can be a difficult one. Read through the following comments;

"This supplier offers the lowest price"

"This company seems good – it is ISO 9000 approved. But they are pricey."

"These people guarantee delivery within two days of order – that's quick."

"These people give a good price, but you have to buy in bulk."

It is said that efficient purchasing involves buying the right quantity and quality at the right time from the right supplier at the right price. This is obviously easier said than done! The following hints may prove useful when assessing suppliers:

- study product literature carefully – brochures, catalogues, publicity material from different suppliers – they will give you a good idea of the *quality* of the organisation
- look for ISO 9000 (or equivalent) approval
- compare prices carefully
- ask for firm delivery times
- enquire about discounts for quantity purchases
- enquire about discounts for cash (immediate) payment
- if possible, visit the suppliers and see whether they look efficient and well-organised

negotiating terms

It *is* possible to haggle over prices. As mentioned above, discounts may be given for bulk purchases or for early (cash) settlement. It may also be possible to get one supplier to match the price of another (just as many electrical retailers will 'match' the price of another). The important factor, however, is for a business to establish a trading relationship with a supplier with which it feels *comfortable*. It may not be the cheapest, the biggest or the fastest, but it should be the supplier which provides the buyer with the best combination of customer satisfaction, quality and reliability.

placing orders

The mechanics of placing orders will be dealt with in the next chapter. The basic document used is the *purchase order.* This can be sent to the seller through the post, or if the seller and buyer are linked by computer, by EDI (Electronic Data Interchange). The purchase order will state:

- the *specification* of the product required (the details will normally be available in the seller's catalogue or in the seller's written quotation)
- the *quantity* required
- the *price* (but not always – see page 35)
- the required *delivery date*

suppliers and the money cycle

Buyers should always try to obtain as long a credit period as possible (ie pay as late as possible). This will help the flow of cash in the money cycle. If it is possible, for example, to pay a supplier after sixty days rather than thirty, *the amount owed will be available for use in the buyer's business as cash.* Alternatively, if the buyer is borrowing from the bank on overdraft, a delay in settling a bill will mean borrowing less, and paying less interest. A buyer should, however, beware of taking liberties and making a habit of paying later than the due date – the seller may cut off credit altogether!

STUDENT ACTIVITY 1.4
performance criterion 6.1.5

buying goods

(it is suggested that this Activity is carried out using the same resources as Activity 1.3)

investigation

You are to talk to local businesses or business advisers about the questions asked below and then set out your answers in writing.

1. If you were in charge of buying for a small business, what factors relating to terms of supply would you consider when ordering a new desktop computer for running standard business applications?

2. What type of discounts may be available when you are ordering goods from suppliers?

3. How do the payment terms you negotiate affect the cash position of your business? What are the best type of payment terms?

EVIDENCE COLLECTION ASSIGNMENT 1

the trading and money cycles

Element 6.1

introduction

This assignment tests your understanding of

- the concept of the trading cycle of a business
- the concept of the money cycle of a business
- the significance of the buying and selling processes to the money cycle

task 1

pcs. 6.1.1 & 2

Helios Furniture Limited is a company which supplies garden furniture. It manufactures wooden furniture at its factory in Broadfield and also sells plastic furniture imported from Spain. It is a private limited company owned by the Norris family, and headed by Managing Director, Karl Norris.

The book-keeper has been extracting the figures for the last financial year from the computer accounting system used by Helios. The main figures are as follows:

	£
Total sales of furniture	750,000
Purchase of raw materials	205,000
Purchase of imported furniture	95,000
Payment of wages	220,000
Business expenses (overheads)	95,000

The book-keeper also mentions that £15,000 of a bank loan has been repaid during the year (this is *not* included in the business expenses figure above).

You are to calculate:

(a) the total cost of raw materials and imports

(b) the cost of the finished products (this should include wages and expenses, but exclude the loan repayment)

(c) the amount of profit the company has made

(d) the Corporation Tax payable on the year's profit (assume a rate of 25%)*

(e) the amount of dividends payable to the shareholders (10% of profit)*

*Note to Tutors – ignore Advance Corporation Tax.

task 2

pcs 6.1.1 & 2

In order to give meaning to the figures extracted in Task 1, you are to draw up a flow diagram showing the consecutive stages in the trading cycle listed below. You should illustrate the diagram with money amounts. Each of the stages could be shown as a separate 'box'.

- the cost of raw materials and imports (ie the cost of the product *before* value is added in the form of wages and other expenses)
- the total cost of the product *after* value has been added in the form of wages and other expenses
- the sales income and profit
- where the sales income goes – tax, dividends, paying costs, retained profit

The diagram should be accompanied by short notes explaining each of the stages and concluding with a paragraph explaining the meaning of "added value' in the context of the figures for Helios Furniture Limited.

task 3

pcs 6.1.1 – 3

(a) Construct a simple spreadsheet showing the money cycle of Helios Furniture Limited. Use the figures you have already extracted. The spreadsheet should contain three sections:

- cash received (assume all the goods sold have been paid for)
- cash spent – all costs and distributions of profit (added value)
- residual/surplus cash

(b) What does the spreadsheet say about the relationship between the trading cycle and the money cycle?

(c) Rework the spreadsheet assuming that one of the limited company customers of Helios has gone into liquidation, owing Helios £75,000. This amount will have to be deducted from the cash received total. What affect does this have on the residual cash?

task 4

pcs 6.1.4 & 5

(a) How can the payment terms negotiated by Helios Furniture Ltd with its customers and suppliers affect the money cycle?

(b) Why is it important – in terms of the trading and money cycles – to assess the performance of suppliers in respect of prices, quantities, quality and delivery?

(c) How can Helios Furniture Ltd guard against the scale of bad debt which was incurred in Task 3 (c)?

chapter summary and key terms

- The trading cycle involves the buying of goods and services, the 'adding of value' by the business by manufacturing, adapting or selling a product or service, and then charging a suitable price to obtain a return and a profit.
- The money cycle is what happens to the money in the trading cycle – it highlights the importance of making sure that there is enough money – 'cash flow' – in the business to buy the goods and services needed to enable the business to operate.
- If the money runs out, either through insufficient money from sales, or because the bank will not lend any more, the business may become insolvent – unable to pay its debts as they fall due.
- When a business sells a product it must set up procedures to make sure that it will get its money from the purchaser. These procedures will often include obtaining references before a a sale is made and chasing up the debt after the sale is made.
- When a business buys a product it must ensure that it assesses the seller carefully and negotiates the best terms.

key terms

added value	spending money on a product – on materials, processing, design, expertise – so that it gains value and can be sold to make a profit
trading cycle	the process of making of a product (an item or a service) and then charging for the product to make a return and a profit
money cycle	the circulation of cash in a business – turning it into a product which can be sold to produce more cash
cash flow	the eventual surplus (or shortfall) of cash which will decide whether or not a business can continue to operate
credit control	the process of 'vetting' potential customers and monitoring the receipt of money that you are owed
bad debt	a debt that will not be repaid
insolvency	the inability to pay debts as they fall due – when the amount you owe is greater than the assets you own

multiple-choice questions

1 The trading cycle is

A a list of all sales made to customers

B the cash received when credit sales have been made

C a computer method of paying for goods

D turning cash into a product and selling it for cash

Questions 2 – 4 relate to the following information:

In the trading cycle, added value

A is increased by investing in the product

B is recovered by the business

C is distributed

Which of the above statements applies to the following?

2 Purchase of services and expertise

3 Reinvestment in the business

4 Sale of the product

5 Decide whether each of these statements is True (T) or False (F)

(i) in the money cycle an increase in the bank overdraft will be a drain on cash

(ii) a weak point in the money cycle is the ability of the debtors of the business to pay

A (i) T (ii) T

B (i) T (ii) F

C (i) F (ii) T

D (i) F (ii) F

6 Credit control is used to

A list the customers to whom credit notes are issued

B ensure money is received from customers

C negotiate favourable terms with suppliers

D establish advantageous credit terms for customers

2 Documents for purchases and sales

GNVQ SPECIFICATIONS
Element 6.2
Explain financial transactions and complete supporting documents
performance criteria – a student must:

1 explain the purposes of financial transactions and documentation

2 explain the use of purchase documents and complete them clearly and accurately

3 explain the use of sales documents and complete them clearly and accurately

Note: performance criteria 4 to 7 of this Element covering documents for payments and receipts, errors and security checks, are all dealt with in the next chapter.

what this chapter covers

This chapter is very practical in nature. Having examined the background to financial transactions we will look in detail at the financial documents relating to purchases and sales, and then see how they work in practice by means of Case Study.

what you will learn from this chapter

- the recording of **financial transactions** enables the owner of a business to monitor its performance and provide information required by law
- the **purchases documents** used by a business buying goods include:
  - the *purchase order,* which places the order with the supplier
  - the *invoice*, which lists the goods and tells you what you owe
  - the *credit note*, which is sent to you if you are due a refund
  - the *goods received note*, which records the goods when they arrive
- the **sales documents** used by a business selling goods include the purchase order and invoice mentioned above – they also include:
  - the *order received note*, an internal record of the receipt of the order
  - the *delivery note*, which is sent with the goods
  - the *statement of account,* sent to the buyer summarising what is owed
  - the *remittance advice* which is sent when payment is made

financial transactions

pc. 6.2.1

recording purchases and sales

Financial transactions are transactions which involve money:

- buying goods and services
- selling goods and services
- paying expenses

As we will see in the next section of this chapter, financial transactions generate *documents* such as invoices. These establish the *mutual understanding between buyer and seller*, setting down in documentary form the terms of the agreement between them – the amount owing, the payment date, any special discounts. Both buyer and seller agree to abide by these terms, which form the basis of a *legal agreement.*

generation of accounts – accounting systems

Financial transactions are recorded in the *accounting system* of a business. An accounting system is simply the set of records kept by the business to record its income and expenses, what it owns, what it owes and what it is owed. Each type of transaction will be entered in a record known as an *account.* The accounting records may be handwritten and kept in books, they may be input onto a computer, using a commercial program such as Sage™. They may be complex or they may be simple, depending on the size and sophistication of the business. Business accounting systems are explained in more detail in Chapter 6.

monitoring business performance

A business needs to record financial transactions for very practical reasons. It will need to *monitor its performance.* It wants to know, for example:

- what its sales performance is – how much has it sold?
- what is its profit?
- how much is it owed by its customers?
- how much does it owe its suppliers?

This information is available from the accounting records and also from financial statements extracted from the accounting records. These include:

- the *profit and loss statement* (showing what profit or loss has been made)
- the *balance sheet* (showing what the business owns and owes)

If most of this information is not readily available, the owner or manager of a business will not have much idea as to what is going on. He or she will not be able to make informed decisions, and the business could run into trouble.

legal requirements of accounting records

Businesses have to keep accurate accounting records so that they can provide information to the Inland Revenue (for tax that may have to be paid) and to HM Customs and Excise (for Value Added Tax purposes). This is a very serious obligation. The tax authorities can visit a business and put the financial records "under the microscope" to see if there are any tax "fiddles" taking place.

If a business is a *limited company* it must operate in accordance with the terms of the Companies Acts 1985 and 1989 and maintain records for financial transactions, sending a copy of the profit statement, balance sheet and a directors' report every year to Companies House and to shareholders.

Now study the summary of the use of financial transactions shown below.

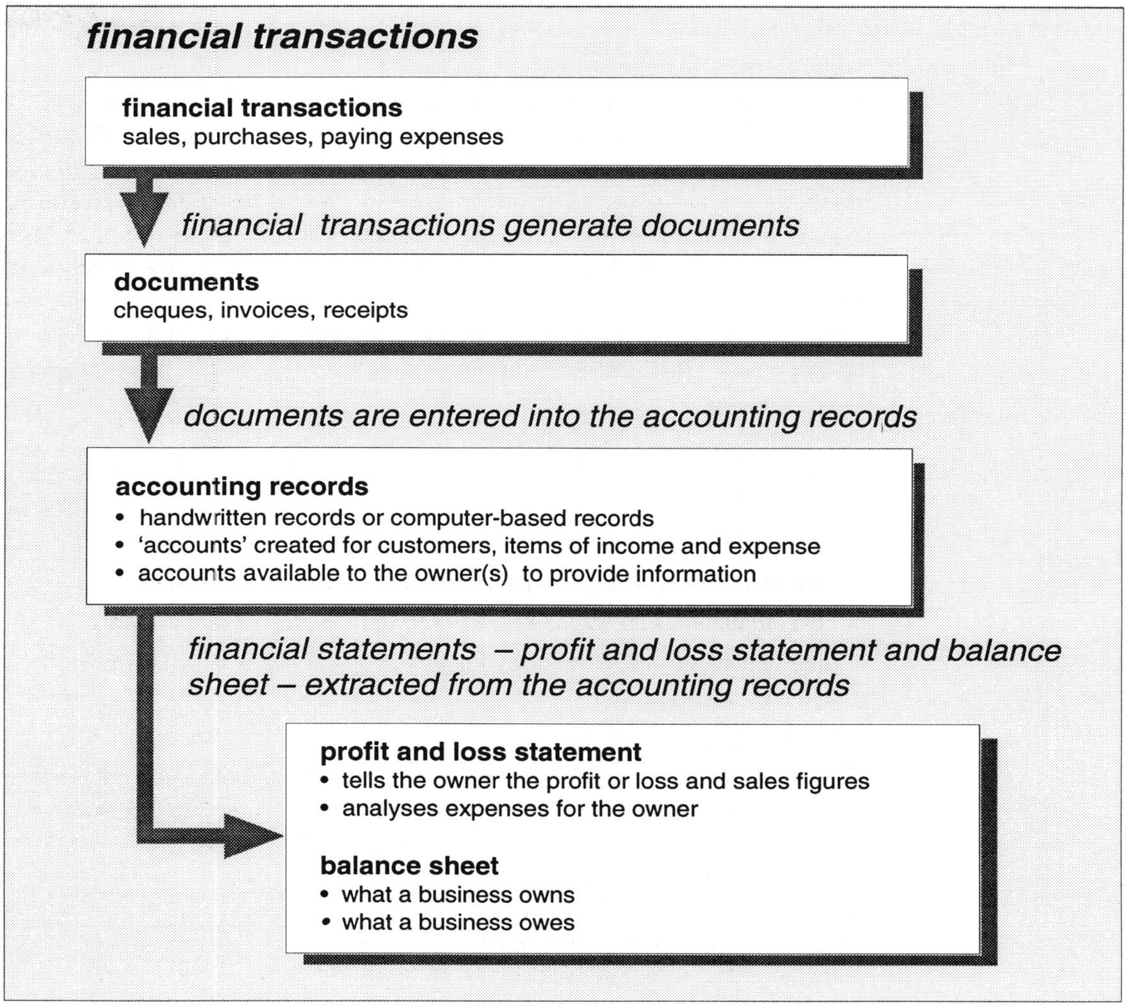

STUDENT ACTIVITY 2.1
performance criterion 6.2.1

financial transactions

You are talking to a group of people starting up in business for the first time. Write replies in the form of short notes in response to the following questions:

(a) "What exactly do you mean by financial transactions?"

(b) "What sort of information can I get from my accounting records?"

(c) "Do I really need to keep accounting records?"

purchases and sales documents

pcs 6.2.2 - 3

the documents used

When a business buys and sells goods or services it will use a number of different financial documents. A single sales transaction of course involves *both* seller *and* buyer, and therefore in this chapter we taken the view that it makes sense to look at the purchases and documents *together* (performance criteria 6.2.2 and 6.2.3). We do this by means of a Case Study involving the buyer and seller of fashion socks. Documents involved in the purchasing process include:

- the *purchase order,* which the buyer sends to the seller
- the *order received note* on which the seller records receipt of the order
- the *delivery note* which goes with the goods from the seller to the buyer
- the *goods received note*, which the buyer uses to record the goods when they arrive
- the *invoice*, which lists the goods and tells the buyer what is owed
- the *credit note*, which is sent to the buyer if any refund is due
- the *statement,* sent by the seller to remind the buyer what is owed
- the *remittance advice*, sent by the buyer when the goods are paid for

the flow of documents

Before you read the Case Study, examine the diagram set out on the next page. Down the columns representing the buyer and the seller are various activities which lead to transactions which in turn generate documents. You should appreciate that not all the activities happen all the time – the goods received note and order received note are not used by all organisations, and of course a credit note is only used when an adjustment is needed. Most of the time things run smoothly and the invoice is paid following receipt of a statement.

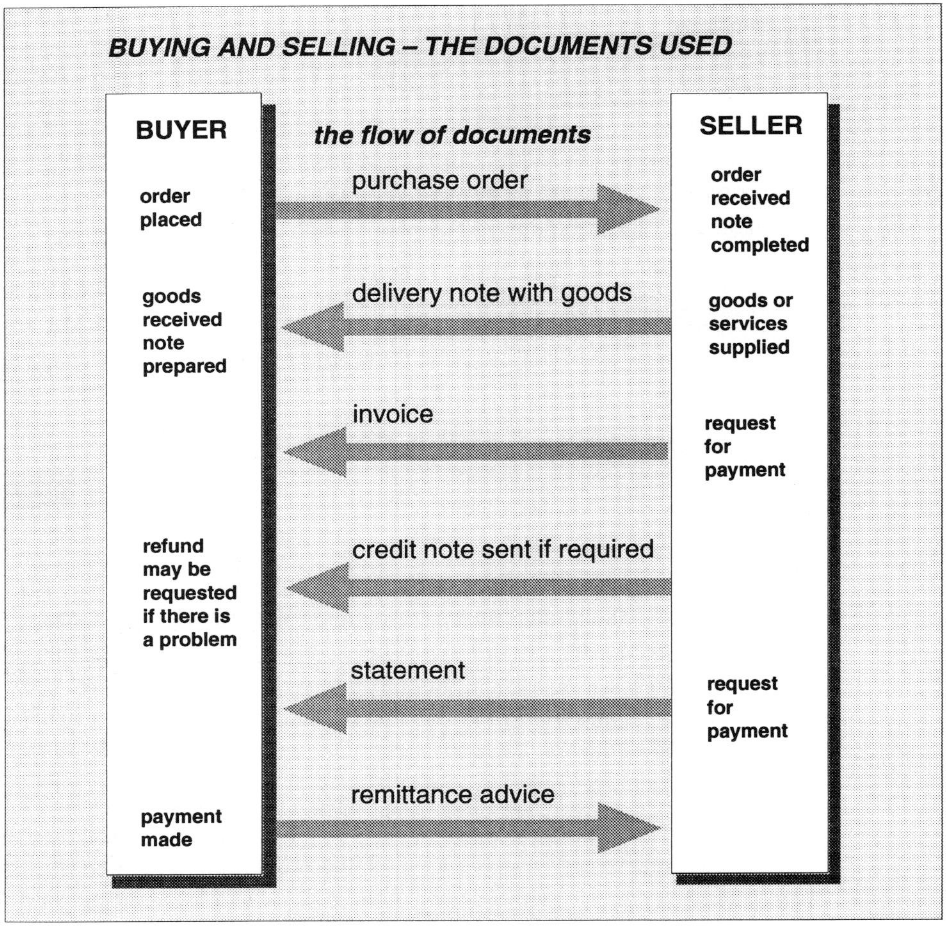

CASE STUDY

pcs 6.2.2 - 3

Cool Socks – a purchase and sales transaction

situation

Cool Socks Limited manufactures fashion socks in a variety of colours. It supplies a number of different customers, including Trends, a fashion store in Broadfield.

In this Case Study we see an order for 100 pairs of socks placed by Trends with Cool Socks. The socks are delivered, but some are found to be faulty, so a refund has to be made. Finally, payment has to be made for the socks.

The Case Study looks in detail at the purchase and sales documents involved. Now read on.

purchase order – *the goods are ordered*

In this Case Study, Trends orders some socks from Cool Socks. The buyer at Trends will post or fax the authorised purchase order shown below. The order will have been typed out in the office, or produced on a computer accounting program. The details of the socks will have been obtained from Cool Socks' catalogue, or possibly by means of a written or telephoned enquiry.

Note the following details:

- each purchase order has a specific reference number – this is useful for filing and quoting on later documents such as invoices and statements
- the catalogue number of the goods required is stated in the product code column – this number can be obtained from the supplier's catalogue
- the quantity of the goods required is stated in the quantity column – socks are obviously supplied in pairs!
- the description of the goods is set out in full
- the price does not need to be stated, although some purchase orders will include a price
- the purchase order is signed and dated by the person in charge of purchasing – without this authorisation the supplier is unlikely to supply the goods (the order will probably be returned!)

Trends
4 Friar Street
Broadfield
BR1 3RF
Tel 01908 761234 Fax 01908 761987
VAT REG GB 0745 8383 56

PURCHASE ORDER

Cool Socks Limited,
Unit 45 Elgar Estate,
Broadfield,
BR7 4ER

purchase order no 47609
date 25 09 95

product code	quantity	description
45B	100 pairs	Blue Toebar socks

AUTHORISED signature *D Signer* date *25/09/95*

order received note – *the order is recorded*

Some organisations will record an incoming purchase order when it is received on a separate internal form – a *sales order received note*; some organisations will merely put a rubber stamp on the purchase order when it is received. Some organisations do not bother with either! The details noted if this system is used are likely to be: the date of receipt, the initials of the person checking the order, and an indication that the order has been passed for processing. It may be, for example, that the goods will have to be manufactured to order.

delivery note – *the goods are delivered*

A delivery note is despatched with the goods when the order is ready. It is normally either typed in the office or printed out by a computer accounting program. In this case, the delivery note travels with the socks, and a copy will be signed by Trends on receipt. Note the following details:

- the delivery note has a numerical reference, useful for filing and later reference if there is a query
- the method of delivery is stated – here the delivery is by parcel carrier
- the delivery note quotes the purchase order number – this enables the buyer to 'tie up' the delivery with the original order
- the delivery note quotes Cool Socks' catalogue reference, the quantity supplied and the description of the goods – these details will be checked against the goods themselves and the invoice when it is received
- no price is quoted on the delivery note
- the delivery note will be signed and dated by the person receiving the goods

DELIVERY NOTE

COOL SOCKS LIMITED

Unit 45 Elgar Estate, Broadfield, BR7 4ER
Tel 01908 765314 Fax 01908 765951
VAT REG GB 0745 4672 76

Trends
4 Friar Street
Broadfield
BR1 3RF

delivery note no	68873
delivery method	Lynx Parcels
your order	47609
date	01 10 95

product code	quantity	description
45B	100 pairs	Blue Toebar socks

Received

signature......*V Williams*......name (capitals)......*V WILLIAMS*......date......*5/10/95*......

goods received note – *the goods are checked*

A goods received note (GRN) will be completed by the person in Trends who looks after the stock. Not all businesses keep GRNs, but when used they act as a useful 'checklist' that the goods received tally with the goods ordered, and are in good condition. In the case of this delivery, ten pairs of the socks have been received damaged – in this case Trends want a refund.

Note the following details:

- the document is an internal one, it will not be sent anywhere but kept within Trends
- details of the goods are noted, together with the purchase order number (which will be on the delivery note)
- the details of the carrier are noted, the consignment reference is the reference number given by the carrier to the parcel of socks
- the person at Trends examining the goods and the person double-checking them will both sign the form
- the condition of the goods – the damage to the socks – is recorded
- the document is in three copies – the one shown is the Accounts Department copy; there will also be copies for the buyer and the stockroom

Trends | **GOODS RECEIVED NOTE**

Supplier

Cool Socks Limited,
Unit 45 Elgar Estate,
Broadfield,
BR7 4ER

GRN no 1871
date 05 10 95

quantity	description	order number
100 pairs	Blue Toebar socks	47609

carrier Lynx Parcels | consignment no 8479347

received by *V Williams* | checked by *R Patel*

condition of goods		**copies to**
	good condition damaged ✓ (10 pairs) shortages	Buyer Accounts ✓ Stockroom

invoice – *payment is requested by the seller*

The invoice is the trading document which is sent by the seller to the buyer stating how much is owed by the buyer for a particular delivery of goods.

The invoice, like the delivery note, is prepared in the supplier's office, and is either typed or produced on a computer printer using a computer accounting program. Invoices produced by different organisations will vary to some extent in terms of detail, but their basic layout will always be the same. The invoice prepared by Cool Socks Ltd – illustrated on page 39 – is typical of a modern typed or computer printed document.

Note the following details, and refer to the invoice on the opposite page.

addresses

The invoice shows the address:

- of the seller/supplier of the goods – Cool Socks Limited
- where the invoice should be sent – to Trends
- where the goods are to be sent – if it is different from the invoice address

references

There are a number of important references on the invoice:

- the numerical reference of the invoice itself – 787923
- the account number allocated to Trends by the seller – 3993 – possibly for use in the seller's computer accounting program
- the original reference number on the purchase order sent by Trends – 47609 – which will enable the shop to 'tie up' the invoice with the original order

date

The date on the invoice is important because the payment date (here one month) is calculated from it. The invoice date is often described as the 'tax point' because it is the transaction date as far as VAT calculations are concerned, ie it is when the sale took place and the VAT was charged.

Note: VAT (Value Added Tax) is a tax on the supply of goods and services. At the time of writing the VAT rate is 17.5%.

Turn to page 40 for further explanation of the invoice.

INVOICE

COOL SOCKS LIMITED

Unit 45 Elgar Estate, Broadfield, BR7 4ER
Tel 01908 765314 Fax 01908 765951
VAT REG GB 0745 4672 76

invoice to

Trends
4 Friar Street
Broadfield
BR1 3RF

deliver to

as above

invoice no	787923
account	3993
your reference	47609
date/tax point	01 10 95

product code	description	quantity	price	unit	total	discount %	net
45B	Blue Toebar socks	100	2.36	pair	236.00	0.00	236.00

GOODS TOTAL	236.00
CASH DISCOUNT	0.00
SUBTOTAL	236.00
VAT	41.30
TOTAL	277.30

terms
Net monthly
Carriage paid
E & OE

points to remember– the procedure for working out the invoice total is:

1. *CALCULATE THE TOTAL COST:* *QUANTITY x PRICE = TOTAL COST*
2. *CALCULATE THE VAT:* *TOTAL COST x 17.5% = VAT*
3. *CALCULATE THE FINAL TOTAL:* *TOTAL COST + VAT = FINAL TOTAL*

the goods

As the invoice states the amount owing, it must specify accurately the goods supplied. The details – set out in columns in the body of the invoice – include:

- *product code* – this is the catalogue number which appeared on the original purchase order and on the delivery note
- *description* – the goods must be specified precisely
- *quantity* – this should agree with the quantity ordered
- *price* – this is the price of each unit shown in the next column
- *unit* is the way in which the unit is counted and charged for, eg
  – boxes of tights
  – single items, eg designer dresses
- *total* is the unit price multiplied by the number of units
- *discount %* is the percentage allowance (known as trade discount) given to customers who regularly deal with the supplier ie they receive a certain percentage (eg 10%) deducted from their bill
- *net* is the amount due to the seller after deduction of trade discount, and before VAT is added on

cash discount and VAT

Further calculations are made in the box at the bottom of the invoice:

- *Goods Total* is the net amount due to the seller (the total of the net column)
- *Cash Discount* is a percentage of the Goods Total (often a 2.5% discount) which the buyer can deduct if he or she pays straightaway rather than waiting the month allowed on the invoice – there is no cash discount in this example
- *Value Added Tax* (VAT), here calculated as 17.5% of the total after deduction of any cash discount. VAT is added to produce the invoice final total.

terms

The terms for payment are stated on the invoice. In this case these include:

- *Net monthly* – this means that full payment of the invoice (without cash discount) should be made within a month of the invoice date
- *Carriage paid* means that the price of the goods includes delivery
- *E & OE* stands for 'errors and omissions excepted' which means that if there is a error or something left off the invoice by mistake, resulting in an incorrect final price, the supplier has the right to rectify the mistake and demand the correct amount

credit note – *a refund is due to the buyer*

A credit note is a 'refund' document. It reduces the amount owed by the buyer. The goods, remember, have not yet been paid for. The credit note is prepared by the supplier and sent to the buyer. For example:

- the goods may have been damaged, lost in transit or are faulty
- not all the goods have been sent – this is referred to as 'shortages'
- the unit price on the invoice may be too high

In the case of the socks, Trends has received 10 damaged pairs. These will be sent back to Cool Socks with a *returns note* (not shown here) asking for *credit* – ie a reduction in the bill for the 10 faulty pairs. Cool Socks will have to issue the credit note for £27.73 shown below.

Note the following details:

- the invoice number of the original consignment is quoted
- the reason for the issue of the credit note is stated at the bottom of the credit note – here 'damaged' goods
- the details are otherwise exactly the same as on an invoice

CREDIT NOTE

COOL SOCKS LIMITED

Unit 45 Elgar Estate, Broadfield, BR7 4ER
Tel 01908 765314 Fax 01908 765951
VAT REG GB 0745 4672 76

to

Trends
4 Friar Street
Broadfield
BR1 3RF

credit note no	12157
account	3993
your reference	47609
our invoice	787923
date/tax point	10 10 95

product code	description	quantity	price	unit	total	discount %	net
45B	Blue Toebar socks	10	2.36	pair	23.60	0.00	23.60

Reason for credit
10 pairs of socks received damaged
(Your returns note no. R/N 2384)

GOODS TOTAL	23.60
CASH DISCOUNT	0.00
SUBTOTAL	23.60
VAT	4.13
TOTAL	27.73

statement – *the seller requests payment*

A supplier will not normally expect a buyer to pay each individual invoice as soon as it is received: this could result in the buyer having to make a number of payments during the month. Instead, a statement of account is sent by the supplier to the buyer *at the end of the month.* This statement, which can be typed out, or printed by the seller's computer accounting program, shows what is owed by the buyer to the seller. It contains details of:

- invoices issued for goods supplied – the full amount due, including VAT
- refunds made on credit notes – including VAT
- payments received from the buyer (if any)
- the final amount due

The statement issued by Cool Socks to Trends for the period covering the sale and refund is shown below.

STATEMENT OF ACCOUNT

COOL SOCKS LIMITED

Unit 45 Elgar Estate, Broadfield, BR7 4ER
Tel 01908 765314 Fax 01908 765951
VAT REG GB 0745 4672 76

TO

Trends
4 Friar Street
Broadfield
BR1 3RF

account 3993

date 31 10 95

date	details	debit £	credit £	balance £
01 10 95	Invoice 787923	277.30		277.30
10 10 95	Credit note 12157		27.73	249.57

AMOUNT NOW DUE	249.57

remittance advice – *payment is sent*

A remittance advice is a document sent by the buyer to the seller stating that payment is being made. Very often a printed remittance advice is attached to the statement sent by the seller: the idea is that this encourages the buyer to make payment!

We will look at making payments in detail in the next chapter. You should note here that payment can be made in two completely different ways

- by *cheque*, in which case the remittance advice goes with the cheque
- by *electronic transfer* (known as a BACS payment) between the bank account of the buyer and the bank account of the seller; in this case a remittance advice will be sent by post, *but no cheque is written*

We will look at both types of remittance advice.

cheque payment

Here Trends have used a 'tear-off' remittance advice sent by Cool Socks with their statement. You will see that Trends have been asked to tick the invoice they are paying. If there were more than one invoice to pay, they would tick each one that they were paying.

Note that before payment can be authorised and made, Trends must match up the Purchase Order copy, Delivery Note, Goods Received Note, invoice and any other relevant documentation to make sure in very basic terms that they re paying for what they got!

TO **COOL SOCKS LIMITED**
Unit 45 Elgar Estate, Broadfield, BR7 4ER
Tel 01908 765314 Fax 01908 765951

REMITTANCE ADVICE

FROM

Trends
4 Friar Street
Broadfield
BR1 3RF

Account 3993

Please indicate items you are paying (✓) and return this advice with your cheque

ref	outstanding	(✓)
787923	£249.57	✓
TOTAL	£249.57	

CHEQUE ENCLOSED £ 249.57

The cheque made out by Trends is shown on the next page. It will be attached to the remittance advice and will be posted to Cool Sock at the beginning of November.

Albion Bank PLC
7 The Avenue
Broadfield BR1 2AJ

Date *5 November* 19*95* — 90 47 17

Pay *Cool Socks Limited*

Two hundred and forty nine pounds 57p — £ *249.57*

A/c payee only

TRENDS

V Williams

072628 90 47 17 11719512

electronic transfer payment

If Trends made regular payments to Cool Socks, Cool Socks might suggest settlement of invoices could be made by electronic transfer between their bank accounts, using BACS (Bankers Automated Clearing System) computer transfer.

If this system is used no cheque will be written, but a remittance advice will still need to be posted to Cool Socks by Trends so that Cool Socks can tally up the payment when it appears on its bank statement. A typical electronic payment remittance advice is shown below.

BACS REMITTANCE ADVICE

FROM: Trends
4 Friar Street
Broadfield
BR1 3RF

TO: Cool Socks Limited
Unit 45 Elgar Estate,
Broadfield, BR7 4ER

05 11 95

Your ref	Our ref		Amount
787923	47609	BACS TRANSFER	249.57
		Total	249.57

THIS HAS BEEN PAID BY BACS CREDIT TRANSFER DIRECTLY INTO YOUR BANK ACCOUNT
ALBION BANK NO 11451226 SORT CODE 90 47 17

STUDENT ACTIVITY 2.2
performance criteria 6.2.2 & 3

using financial documents

Note: these tasks require you to prepare your own purchase orders and invoices. You are advised to collect samples from local businesses and to study the examples in this chapter.

task 1

Work in pairs and play the roles of buyer and seller. The buyer is a clothes shop and the seller a clothes manufacturer. You will need copies of two blank business documents: purchase order and invoice. You should use today's date and the current VAT rate, but will need to make up the following details:

- the names and addresses of buyer and seller
- catalogue numbers
- order numbers and invoice numbers

The buyer is to complete two separate purchase orders and the seller is to complete an invoice for each order. The orders are as follows:

(a) 100 pairs of tights (black) at £1.25
25 woollen jumpers (green) at £15 each
50 nighties (pink) at £8.50 each

(b) 25 dresses (red) at £15 each
30 pairs of denim jeans (black) at £17.50 each
50 pairs of tights (black) at £1.30 each

There is no trade discount available to the buyer. Add VAT at the current rate.

task 2

You work for Deansway Trading Company, a wholesaler of office stationery, which trades from The Modern Office, 79 Deansway, Stourminster WR1 2EJ. A customer, The Card Shop of 126 The Crescent, Marshall Green, WR4 5TX, orders the following on order number 9516:

(a) 5 boxes of assorted rubbers at £5 per box, catalogue no 26537
(b) 100 shorthand notebooks at £4 for a pack of 10, catalogue no 72625
(c) 250 ring binders at 50p each, catalogue no 72598

VAT is to be charged at the current rate on all items, and a 2.5 per cent cash discount is offered for full settlement within 14 days. Prepare invoice number 8234, under today's date, to be sent to the customer.

STUDENT ACTIVITY 2.3
performance criterion 6.2.6

sorting out mistakes

Examine carefully the invoice shown below and write down any errors which you can find. In each case state what the consequence of the error might be if it went undetected.

INVOICE

COOL SOCKS LIMITED

Unit 45 Elgar Estate, Broadfield, BR7 4ER
Tel 01908 765314 Fax 01908 765951
VAT REG GB 0745 4672 76

invoice to

Trends
4 Friar Street
Broadfield
BR1 3RF

deliver to

as above

invoice no	787923
account	3993
your reference	47609
date/tax point	

product code	description	quantity	price	unit	total	discount %	net
45R	Red Toebar socks	100	2.45	pair	254.00	10.00	279.40

GOODS TOTAL	279.40
CASH DISCOUNT	0.00
SUBTOTAL	279.40
VAT	48.89
TOTAL	230.51

EVIDENCE COLLECTION ASSIGNMENT 2

purchases and sales documents

Element 6.2, pcs. 1,2,3,6

introduction

This assignment tests your understanding of

- the use of purchase documents
- the use of sales documents

The assignment also gives you practice in completing these documents.

task 1

pcs. 6.2.2 & 3

You are to collect examples (where possible) of the following business documents:

- purchase order
- sales order received note
- delivery note
- goods received note
- invoice
- credit note
- statement of account (not bank statement)
- remittance advice (either cheque remittance, or BACS remittance)

Ideally these documents should be obtained from local businesses. If this is not possible, examine financial documents in a number of textbooks. The object of the exercise is to see the *variety* of presentation that exists – you may be surprised at the differences you find.

task 2

pcs. 6.2.2 & 3

This assignment involves a practical exercise in the exchange of documents between buyer and seller. The businesses involved are:

buyer
Osborne Micros Limited
Unit 1B Severnside Industrial Estate
Mereford MR1 2TR
Tel 01906 226576 Fax 01906 226342

seller
Stourford Office Supplies
Unit 12 Avon Industrial Estate
Stourford SF5 6TD
Tel 01807 765434 Fax 01807 765123

In preparation for a practical exercise you are to design a set of financial documents. The documents required are:

Osborne Micros Limited:	**Stourford Office Supplies:**
Purchase Order	Delivery Note
Goods Received Note	Order Received Note
Remittance advice (cheque or BACS)	Invoice and Credit Note
	Statement

If resources permit, use a computer to design the forms. They can be drawn in a graphics or Desk Top Publishing package. Time-saving hint! – use the same computer file for each 'set' of documents and adapt and change it for the different documents.

task 3

pcs. 6.2.1,2 & 3

Keep a blank copy of each document for your Portfolio and add to each a note which gives an explanation of its purpose and function – what it is used for.

task 4 – practical exercise

pcs. 6.2.2 & 3

(a) You work for Osborne Micros Limited, and on 13 March 1996 make out a purchase order for 100 OKISONIC Macroline 276 computer printer ribbons. The details are:

- Purchase Order No 6372
- Catalogue No 726261

Sign the purchase order with your own name.

(b) You work for Stourford Ofice Supplies and on 15 March receive the purchase order. Note the details on your sales order received note. On 15 March you are to complete an invoice and delivery note. The details are as follows:

- delivery note: number 26755, delivery method Parceline
- invoice: number 652772, account OSB 002, catalogue price £4.50, customer discount 10%, VAT at the current rate

(c) On 22 March at Stourford Office Supplies you receive a telephone call from Osborne Micros Limited pointing out that ten of the ribbons supplied on invoice 652772 are faulty. You reply that you will issue them with an adjusting credit note. You are to complete the credit note. The details are:

- credit note number 2167
- date 22 March
- customer discount and VAT rate as on the invoice

(d) Assume the role of the stock control clerk in Osborne Micros and complete the Goods Received Note relating to the faulty consignment. The details are as follows:

- date 22 March
- GRN no 2348
- Consignment no. 8759300

Sign the GRN and get someone else to countersign it .

(e) On 30 April, Stourford Office Supplies is preparing statements to send to all their customers to show the balance outstanding on each account. You are to prepare the statement for Osborne Micros Limited at that date.

Note that:

- there was no amount outstanding before invoice 652772 and credit note 2167
- another invoice (no. 652801 for £456.75) was issued on 14 April
- no payments have been received during the period

(f) Take on the role of an accounts clerk in Osborne Micros and complete the remittance advice (cheque or BACS) paying the appropriate amount to Stourford Office Supplies. Assume that you only pay items which have been outstanding for more than 30 days.You do not need to complete any payment document.

task 5

pc 6.2.6

It is obviously important that documents should be completed accurately and correctly. The situations set out below are examples of things that can go wrong. Read through the three situations and then in each case:

- identify the problem that has arisen
- suggest a practical solution which could be adopted by the business concerned
- state what might happen if the problem is not dealt with

(a) a business selling goods receives a purchase order where the catalogue number quoted and the description of the goods ordered do not tally

(b) an invoice is received from a supplier and the addition is incorrect – as a result you have been overcharged

(c) the person checking the delivery note against a consignment of goods fails to record a shortage (ie not enough goods sent) in a delivery received from a supplier

chapter summary and key terms

- Financial transactions generate documents which in turn are recorded in the accounting system of a business. The documents establish the mutual understanding and legal relationship between buyer and seller.
- The recording of financial transactions enables a business to
  - monitor its performance
  - provide information which may be required by law
- The **purchases documents** used by a business buying goods include:
  - the *purchase order,* which places the order with the supplier
  - the *invoice*, which lists the goods and tells you what you owe
  - the *credit note*, which is sent to you if you are due a refund
  - the *goods received note*, which records the goods when they arrive
- The **sales documents** used by a business selling goods include the purchase order and invoice mentioned above – they also include:
  - the *order received note*, an internal record of the receipt of the order
  - the *delivery note*, which is sent with the goods
  - the *statement of account,* sent to the buyer summarising what is owed
  - the *remittance advice* which is sent to the seller by the buyer when payment is made
- It is important that purchases and sales documents are completed accurately. If mistakes are made, the consequences can be serious, eg
  - the wrong goods supplied
  - an incorrect amount charged

key terms

Value Added Tax	VAT is a tax on the supply of goods and services, ie a tax on spending; it is charged on invoices by VAT-registered businesses
trade discount	is a discount given to customers who trade regularly with the seller: it is deducted on the invoice
cash discount	is given to the buyer in some instances when payment is made by the buyer within a short period of time, ie well before the credit period expires; it is deducted on the invoice

multiple-choice questions

1 A purchase order is used to

A tell the purchaser how much the goods cost

B place an order with the seller

C pay the seller for the goods

D fix the price on a purchase of goods

2 A remittance advice is

A an advice note telling the buyer what goods were sent

B an advice note telling the seller that the wrong goods were sent

C a document advising the seller of payment

D a document advising the buyer of payment

Questions 3 – 5 relate to the following information:

An invoice with a number of errors has resulted in the following problems:

A the wrong goods sent

B a query on the total amount payable

C the goods sent to the wrong person

D an order sent twice

Which of these problems is likely to have been caused by the following?

3 The wrong unit price used

4 The wrong product code used

5 The wrong customer account number used

6 Decide whether each of these statements is True (T) or False (F)

(i) the goods received note is sent with the goods

(ii) the order received note is sent to the buyer

A (i) T (ii) T

B (i) T (ii) F

C (i) F (ii) T

D (i) F (ii) F

3 Documents for payments and receipts

GNVQ SPECIFICATIONS

Element 6.2

Explain financial transactions and complete supporting documents

performance criteria – a student must:

1 - 3	See Chapter 2 for pcs 1, 2 and 3
4	explain the use of payments documents and complete an example clearly and accurately
5	explain the use of receipts documents and complete an example clearly and accurately
6	explain why it is important to complete documents correctly and give possible consequences of incorrect completion
7	identify and explain security checks for business documents

what this chapter covers

This chapter is very practical in nature: you will examine and complete the documents involved when a business makes payment and when it receives payment. You will also see why documents have to be completed accurately and you will appreciate the need for security checks.

what you will learn from this chapter

- a business can make manual payments involving cash and a petty cash voucher, or a cheque, bank giro credit, debit card or credit card
- a business can make payments by computer transfer between the banks (Bankers Automated Clearing Services – BACS) or between the businesses and the banks (Electronic Data Interchange – EDI)
- a business can receive money in the form of payment by cash, cheque, debit card, or credit card
- when a business receives money it will normally pay it into the bank on a paying-in slip; the bank will regularly issue a bank statement
- when errors are made on documents, the consequences can be serious
- it is important that a business sets up a system of security checks to help avoid errors and unauthorised transactions

payments in cash

pc 6.2.4

the cashless society?

Despite the growth in the use of plastic cards, cash is the most common way of paying for goods and services – newspapers, magazines, sandwiches, cans of drink, bus fares, stationery – the list is very long.

Most cash tills will show on a screen the money amount of the purchase and also the change to be given. The till will also issue a *receipt* for *all* purchases when cash, a cheque, a debit card or a credit card is used. In the example below a customer has bought a pack of coloured paper and some biros from Mitre Stationery. A till receipt has been issued.

a till receipt for a cash transaction

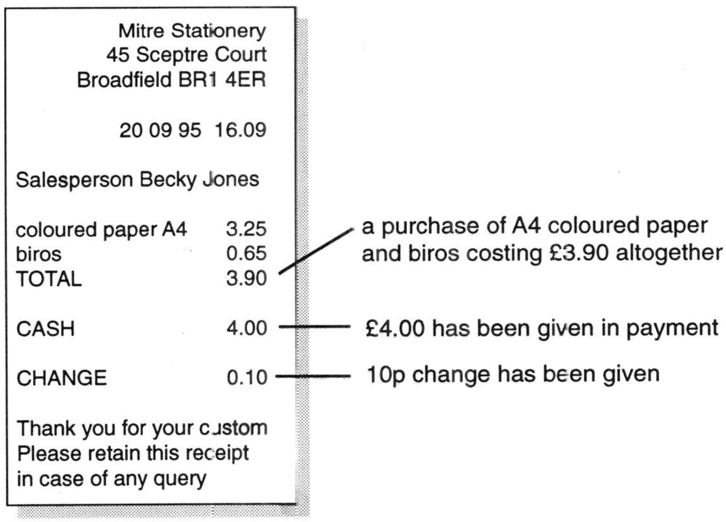

petty cash

pc 6.2.4

what is petty cash?

Sometimes businesses will make payments for small amounts in cash – known as 'petty cash'. Petty cash is a float of cash (notes and coins) kept in a locked cash box in the business under the control of someone in authority – the petty cashier. Clearly this money can only be used for *business purposes,* and not for personal items like employees' sandwiches.

petty cash voucher

In order to get petty cash from the tin, the employee will need to get a slip of paper known as a *petty cash voucher* signed by someone in authority. *To this voucher must be attached the receipt for the payment.* A petty cash voucher is illustrated below.

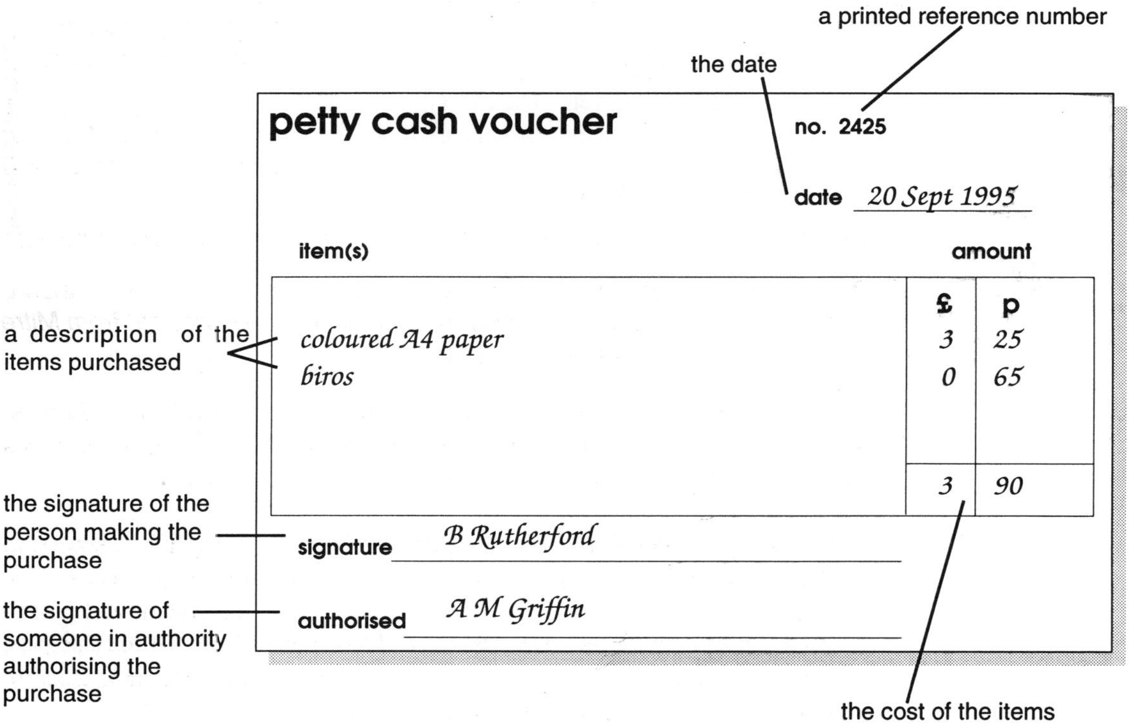

payments by cheque

pc 6.2.4

what is a cheque?

a cheque is a written order to the bank signed by its customer (known as the 'drawer') to pay a specified amount to a specified person (the 'payee')

In other words a cheque is an instruction by the person writing the cheque to their bank to pay a named person a sum of money.

Cheques are commonly used in business by buyers of goods and services settling bills by post. As we saw in the last chapter, the cheque is normally accompanied by a remittance advice detailing what is being paid. Look at the illustration of a cheque on the next page.

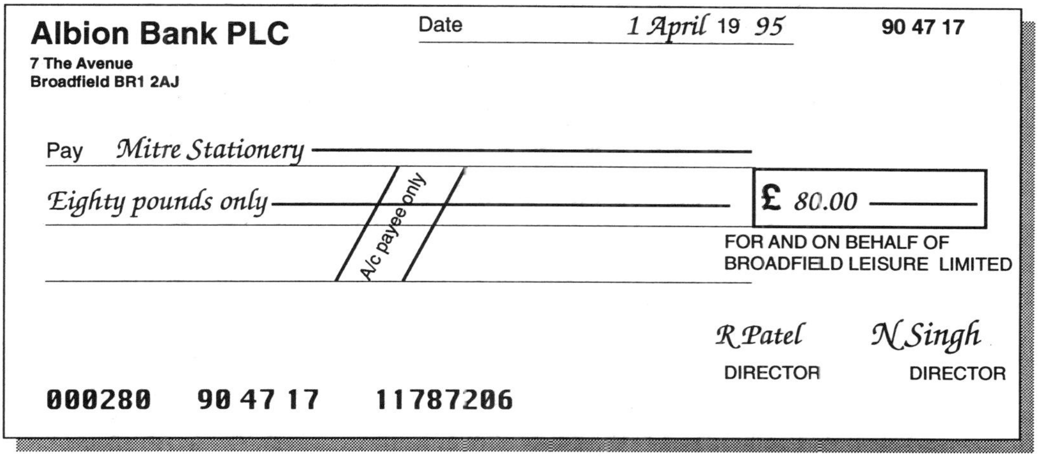

This cheque has been written out by two directors of Broadfield Leisure Limited in settlement of an invoice for £80 for stationery bought from Mitre Stationery. Note the following points:

drawer The business which has issued (written) the cheque is Broadfield Leisure Limited – this company is the *drawer* of the cheque. Most limited company cheques need two or more signatures. Here two directors have signed.

payee The business receiving the money, Mitre Stationery, will pay the cheque into the bank, and the money will go onto the bank account on the same day. The cheque will be processed in the three day bank clearing system and it will finish up at the Albion Bank in Broadfield (see the address on the cheque), where, if there is enough money on Broadfield Leisure Limited's bank account, and the cheque has no errors on it, it will be 'paid'.

amount The amount is written in both words and figures. The amount in words and figures *must* be the same. If there is a difference, the cheque might not be 'paid' by the bank. Note here that there are lines drawn after the amount – this stops the payee from 'fiddling' by altering and increasing the amount!

date The cheque must have a valid date. This means that the cheque cannot have a future date (be 'postdated'). Cheques go out of date after six months.

bank card? No bank card is used to back the cheque because the cheque is being sent through the post – bank cards can only be used for 'over the counter' transactions. Also, many businesses do not have bank cards.

crossing The two parallel lines and the words "A/c payee only" are a *crossing* – they mean that the cheque can only be paid into the bank account of Mitre Stationery (the payee), and not into any other account.

STUDENT ACTIVITY 3.1
performance criterion 6.2.4

completing cheques

tasks

You are to complete the following cheques fully and accurately and add the necessary signatures. Use today's date and sign your own name if you think you need to.

1 R Singh is paying Pronto Wholesalers £4346.78 in settlement of a recent statement for goods supplied to his shop. The cheque only needs one signature. R Singh is authorised to sign.

Western Bank PLC Date 19 **80 47 17**
9 The Avenue
Broadfield BR1 2AJ

Pay

A/c payee only

£

R SINGH STORES

083837 80 47 17 38478374

2 Mary White, Finance Officer of Wybold College is writing and signing a cheque paying Mitre Stationery for stationery supplies costing £1,250.50. The cheque needs two signatures, one of which can be Mary White's.

Albion Bank PLC Date 19 **90 47 17**
7 The Avenue
Broadfield BR1 2AJ

Pay

A/c payee only

£

WYBOLD COLLEGE

075165 90 47 17 11719516

making payment by plastic card

pc 6.2.4

Businesss can also make payment using *plastic cards*. There are two basic types: the *debit card* and the *credit card*.

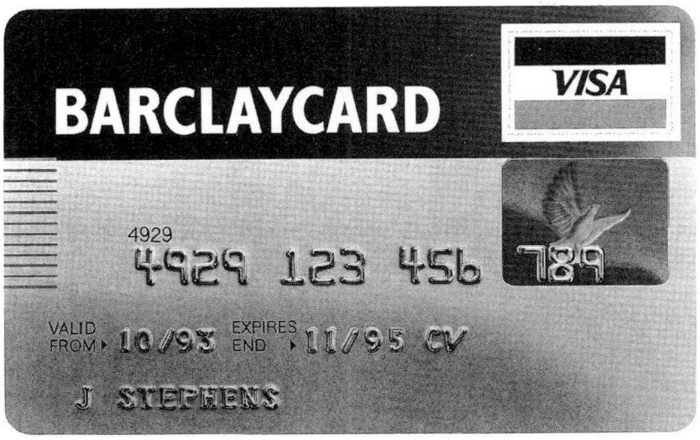

Barclays Connect – a debit card

Barclaycard – a credit card

debit card

A debit card – shown above left – is a plastic card issued by a bank or a building society to personal and business customers. It enables the customer to make payment for goods and services *without having to write out a cheque.* Common examples of debit cards include 'Switch' and 'Connect' cards. When a debit card is used in a shop, the shop receives its money either

- by electronic link through the cash till to its bank account (a process known as EFTPOS – Electronic Funds Transfer at Point Of Sale), *or*
- by the shop using a manual imprinter to produce a paper *voucher* which is then paid into the shop's bank account on a *paying-in slip*

A debit card is also commonly used to guarantee ('back') cheques issued over the counter (but not for limited company customers).

credit card

Credit cards enable the user to purchase goods over the counter, through the post and by telephone. Payment is made *at a later date* when a monthly statement listing all the purchases made is sent to the holder and payment requested. A business *accepting* a credit card payment will again receive its money *either* direct into the bank account through an electronic till (EFTPOS) *or* by paying into the bank sales vouchers processed manually. Many businesses issue credit cards to their employees to enable them to pay for *business* expenses which they incur, eg petrol used by a travelling sales rep. This helps the employee and also the business because the employee's spending can be monitored and controlled!

paying by bank giro credit

pc 6.2.4

If a business wishes to make a payment direct to a bank account it can do so by filling in a blank paper slip known as a *bank giro credit* and paying it in over the bank counter with a cheque for the same amount. The details completed by the business are shown below shaded grey – these are explained in full on page 66 where we look at the paying-in slip.

paying by computer – BACS

pc 6.2.4

from cheques to BACS

The banks and their big customers (eg British Gas) are currently encouraging businesses and private individuals to make payments using an interbank computer transfer system called BACS (Bankers Automated Clearing Services). This system enables payments to be made in two ways:

- it can send payments to other bank accounts ***– direct credits***
- it can take money off bank accounts ***– direct debits***

It is a far cheaper way of processing payments than writing out a cheque or completing a bank giro credit each time you want to send money.

BACS direct credits – bulk payments

Suppose at the end of the month a business has to pay wages to fifty employees with bank accounts and has to settle up with twenty suppliers. Instead of writing out a large number of cheques or bank giro credits, all the customer has to do is to provide the information about the payments on computer file. This is then sent to the BACS processing centre in West London by mail, on disc or tape, *or* direct by telephone line. The information is fed into the BACS computer and three working days later the payment will leave one bank account and be received on the other bank or building society account.

direct debits

When a business collects money from someone else's account through the BACS system, it uses a *direct debit.* The direct debit system is useful for organisations such as insurance companies and credit card companies which receive a large number of payments *where the amounts can vary.* The normal procedure is for the customer who is making the payment to complete and sign a written authority (mandate) prepared by the business collecting the money – eg an insurance company. This form (mandate) is then processed and input onto the computer by the bank which *receives* the money.

In the example below Hermes Products is paying Tradesure Insurance Company for its insurance cover. The form allows Tradesure Insurance's bank to take the money from Hermes Products' bank account. When Hermes Products has completed and signed the form it will be returned to Tradesure Insurance, who will in turn return it to their bank.

DIRECT Debit

Tradesure Insurance Company
PO Box 134, Helliford, HL9 6TY

Originator's Identification No 914 208

Reference (to be completed by Tradesure Insurance) 71962310

PLEASE COMPLETE THE DETAILS AND RETURN THIS FORM TO TRADESURE INSURANCE

Name and address of Bank/Building Society

ROYAL BANK OF WALES
THE PARADE
ABERYSTWYTH
DY1 9TU

to the Bank/Building Society

- I instruct you to pay direct debits from my account at the request of Tradesure Insurance Company
- The amounts are variable and may be debited on various dates
- Tradesure Insurance Company may change the amounts and dates only after giving me notice

account name	account number	sort code
HERMES PRODUCTS LTD	17096235	99-01-72

signature(s)	date
[illegible]	19/7/95

standing orders

A common example of an individual direct *credit* made through the BACS system to someone else is a *standing order*. The business that needs to make regular payments completes a written authority (a mandate),instructing the bank what payments to make, to whom, and when. The bank then sets up the instructions on its computer, and the payments are made automatically by computer link through BACS on the due dates.

Remember that in the BACS system:

- a *direct debit* is set up by the person who *receives* the money
- a *direct credit* (eg standing order) is set up by the person *sending* the money

STUDENT ACTIVITY 3.2
performance criterion 6.2.4

direct debits

DIRECT Debit

task

This task involves an investigation into the use of direct debits. You are to collect examples of direct debit forms. Sources include the 'utilities' such as gas, electricity and water companies; credit card application forms; Council Tax payment requests. You will also find examples in textbooks, although it is preferable to obtain a real example, a 'primary' source.

Examine the forms and answer the following questions.

(a) What do the forms say about the amounts paid?

(b) What do the forms say about the dates on which payments should be made?

(c) If a business fills in a direct debit form, where should it be sent?

(d) Explain briefly how a direct debit differs from a standing order.

Problem! an additional investigation

Your business has signed a direct debit form to Tradesure Insurance Company. The form does not specify an amount. You then find on your business bank statement that £1,500 has been deducted in the first month rather than the £150 agreed with Tradesure Insurance. Does your business have any protection or any 'come back'?

Electronic Data Interchange (EDI)

pc 6.2.4

You will have seen that the BACS system enables payments to be made by link-ups between *bank computers*. Systems now exist whereby business documents such as purchase orders and invoices are generated on computer file and the data sent between the computers of the *buyer and the seller.* This can then be followed up by a payment instruction on the due date.

This system, known as *Electronic Data Interchange (EDI)*, is extensively used in the UK, particularly by large retailing organisations which need to renew stock frequently on a Just-in-Time basis.

what is EDI ?

EDI is a system which transfers commercial and administrative instructions between computers using agreed formats for the messages. The two parties involved agree a standard format for the electronic messages which take the place of purchase orders, delivery instructions, invoices, credit notes and statements. The international standard transfer system is *UN/EDIFACT,* although there are other standards, such as *TRADACOMS* used by retailers.

EDI transfers

The transfer is normally sent from one computer to another via a third party known as a VAN (value added network). A value added network operates like an electronic post office: you deposit your information electronically in your 'post box' and the value added network transfers it to the 'postbox' of your trading partner.

The benefits of EDI include: reduced handling costs, reduced postage costs, reduced paper storage costs, fewer errors (there is less re-keying of existing computer data) and faster payment.

EDI payments

In the normal course of paper-based trading (ie using paper invoices and other business documents), settlement is usually made by cheque which is posted to the supplier or by BACS (an inter-bank computer transfer system). The banks now are developing systems whereby the buyer can use the EDI system for authorising the bank to make payment to the supplier's bank. NatWest's BankLine Interchange, for example, can be used for making payments to individual suppliers or to a number of suppliers. As the buyer's computer system already has details of each trade transaction – the parties involved and the amounts – it is a simple matter to add the banking details of the supplier, so that settlement can be made by BACS.

receipts documents

pc 6.2.5

So far in this chapter we have looked at the ways in which a business can make payment for goods and services. We have examined the documents involved and in many instances learnt how to complete them.

We now 'turn the tables' and examine the process from the point of view of the business *receiving* the money and then paying it into the bank. We will examine and complete a number of different documents:

- the handwritten receipt
- the cheque (from the point of view of a business *receiving* one)
- the paying-in slip
- the bank statement

the handwritten receipt

When a business sells goods or services on a 'cash' (immediate settlement) basis, the buyer will need a *document* to provide evidence that money has been spent on those particular goods or services. It may be a travelling salesman buying petrol, or an office manager buying stationery from a shop. If there is no documentary evidence, the business (or the tax inspectors) may wonder where the money has gone – has the salesman used the money to take his wife out? Has the office manager bought himself a new briefcase? If the seller issues a formal handwritten *receipt*, there is no doubt about the transaction. Look at the example shown below.

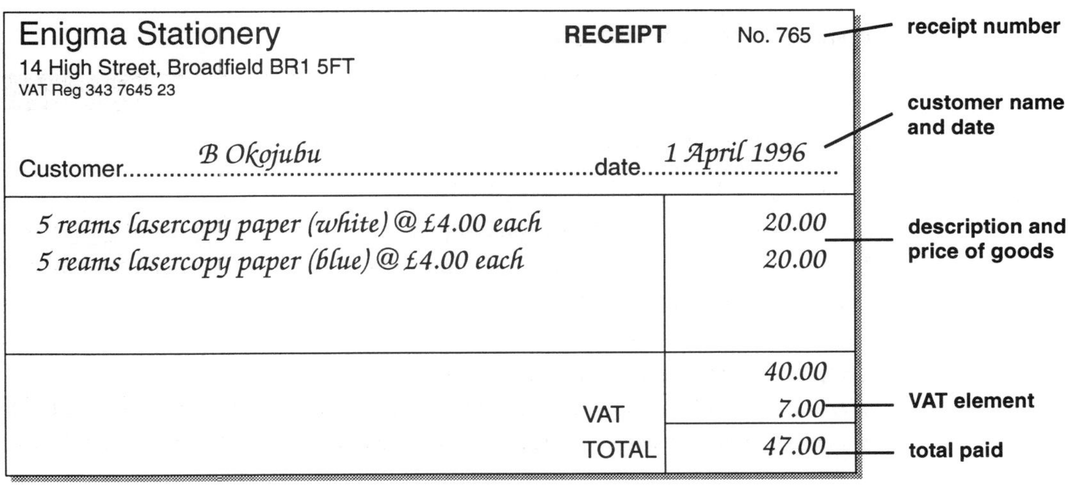

Enigma Stationery — RECEIPT — No. 765
14 High Street, Broadfield BR1 5FT
VAT Reg 343 7645 23

Customer: B Okojubu — date: 1 April 1996

5 reams lasercopy paper (white) @ £4.00 each	20.00
5 reams lasercopy paper (blue) @ £4.00 each	20.00
	40.00
VAT	7.00
TOTAL	47.00

STUDENT ACTIVITY 3.3
performance criterion 6.2.4

completing receipts

task 1

Collect a variety of receipts – either blank ones or copies of completed receipts. Sources include local businesses (eg petrol stations) and stationers (who sell blank receipts in pads). Examine and compare them in class.

task 2

Design and draw up your own receipt. Use a computer package if you can. Invent your own business name and address for a lighting supplies firm. Remember to include a VAT registration number – you should assume that the business charges VAT.

task 3

Make (or print out) three copies of your receipt and enter the following sales transactions:

(a) 2 flexilamps @ £13.99, plus 2 candlelight bulbs @85p each sold to George Meredith

(b) 1 standard lamp @ £149.95, plus one 100 watt bulb @ 99p, sold to Alex Bell

(c) 2 Georgian lamps @ £35.99 sold to Miss S Fox

Use today's date and add VAT at the current rate to the prices given.

receiving cheques

pc 6.2.5 & 6

A business can receive cheques in a variety of ways:

- a shop can receive cheques *over the counter*
- a business can receive cheques *through the post* in settlement of invoices

In both cases, the business receiving the cheque will have to *check* it carefully before paying it into the bank.

why bother to check the cheque?

If there is anything wrong with the cheque and it is paid into the bank, it may be returned *unpaid* four or five days later by the bank whose name appears on the cheque. In other words if there is anything wrong with the cheque, the money will go onto the business bank account *and then be taken off again three or four days later* and the cheque will be posted back to the business for it to sort out!

what should you check?

We will use the example of a business receiving cheques through the post. The details that should be checked are:

signature?	the cheque must be signed by the customer – it is completely invalid if it is not
name of business?	the name of the business receiving the cheque must be written after the word 'pay' and must be spelt correctly
the date?	the date must be written in the appropriate place at the top of the cheque – note that a cheque more than six months old is invalid
words and figures?	the amount in words and the amount in figures must agree – for example 'fifty pounds' and '£50' – if the cheque is to be paid
any corrections?	if the person writing out the cheque has made a mistake and corrected it, the correction should be signed or initialled by the person signing the cheque (the 'drawer')
missing details?	contrary to common belief, if any detail is missed off a cheque (eg date, amount in words) this can be filled in by the business receiving the cheque; the important exception to this is the signature!

what to do if there is a mistake on the cheque

If there is a problem with a cheque and it cannot be sorted out on the spot (eg a missing date written in), the cheque will have to be returned to the customer with a polite request for the mistake to be put right (and signed or initialled) or for a new cheque to be issued. Sellers should beware because it is not unknown for a buyer who is short of money to issue a cheque and 'forget' to sign it in the knowledge that it will have to be sent back again!

problems with unpaid – 'bounced' – cheques

One problem the seller will not be able to spot is if the buyer has not got any money in the bank. If this is the case and the seller pays the cheque into the bank, the cheque will probably be 'bounced'. This means that the cheque will be sent back by the bank where the buyer has his/her account with the words "Refer to Drawer" written in red across the top of the cheque. This can be loosely translated as "there are no funds in the customer's bank account – contact the customer yourself for the money!" This is bad news for the seller: unless he or she can get cash from the buyer or the return of the goods, the transaction is probably a 'bad debt' – the money will be lost.

STUDENT ACTIVITY 3.4

performance criteria 6.2.4 & 5

problems with cheques

task

You work in the Accounts Department of Osborne Electronics Ltd. Part of your job is to check the payments received in the post. On 1 April you receive a number of problem cheques.

You are to:

- identify the problem in each case
- state what you would do to put things right (as far as you can)

(a) a cheque is received with the date missing

(b) a cheque is received dated 1 September of the previous year

(c) a cheque is received dated 1 November of the previous year

(d) a cheque is received with the drawer's signature missing

(e) a cheque is received where the words say "fifty pounds only" and the figures say "£50.50"

(f) you notice that the name of your business is spelt "Usbourne Electronics"; a colleague says "Why don't you change it and sign it? It will be OK."

(g) you receive a letter from your bank enclosing a cheque for £5,000 paid in five days previously; the cheque has "Refer to drawer" written on it

To relate this Activity to current business practice your Tutor could invite someone who works in a bank to come and talk about problem cheques and other 'bank' topics raised in this chapter.

the paying-in slip

pc 6.2.5

A business uses a paper paying-in slip to pay money into its bank account. The paying-in slip is also known as a 'bank giro credit' or 'credit transfer'. *Personal customers* normally have paying-in slips at the back of their chequebooks. *Business customers,* however, are normally issued with books – known as 'paying-in books' – full of paying-in slips. A paying-in slip can be used for paying in:

- cash
- cheques
- sales vouchers for debit cards and credit cards (but only where the tills of the business are *not* linked up to the bank's computer)

paying into the business account

Look at the example below which shows Sabre Stationery paying money into its bank account at Albion Bank in Broadfield on 1 April 1995. The money the business is paying in comprises:

cash

- two £20 notes
- one £5 note
- five £1 coins

cheques

- three cheques for £50.00, £30.00 and £20.00

The back of the paying-in slip is illustrated on the next page.

date *1 April 1995*

credit *Sabre Stationery*

£50		
£20	40	00
£10		
£5	5	00
£1	5	00
50p		
20p		
10/5p		
bronze		
Total cash	50	00
Cheques etc *(see over)*	100	00
£	150	00

date *1 April 1995*

cashier's stamp and initials

bank giro credit

90 - 47 - 17

Albion Bank plc

BROADFIELD

credit SABRE STATIONERY

items	fee
3	

paid in by *B Glover*

£50		
£20	40	00
£10		
£5	5	00
£1	5	00
50p		
20p		
10/5p		
bronze		
Total cash	50	00
Cheques etc *(see over)*	100	00
£	150	00

please do not write or mark below this line

634102 90 47 17 14517226 79

details already printed on the paying-in slip

When a paying-in book is provided for a business, some details are already printed on the paying-in slip. These include:

- the name and branch of the bank
- the 'sort code' of the bank branch (a six digit number – 90 47 17 on the credit shown here) – a sort code is the banking equivalent of a post code – each bank branch has a different number
- the name of the account – here Sabre Stationery
- the account number of the business – here it is the eight digit number printed at the bottom of the slip

details completed by the business on the front of the slip

These include:

- a breakdown of the categories of any cash being paid in – note that it is the *amount* which is entered in each case
- the *total* of the cheques being paid in
- a grand total of the cash and the cheques
- the date
- the signature of the person paying the money into the bank
- a record of the money being paid in noted on the counterfoil

details completed by the business on the back of the slip

- a list of the individual cheques – here there are three
- a total of all the cheques – here £100

counterfoil

	50	*00*
	30	*00*
	20	*00*
£	*100*	*00*

cheques

Beamish Limited		*50*	*00*
Pronto Alarms		*30*	*00*
D Cox		*20*	*00*
carried over	£	*100*	*00*

STUDENT ACTIVITY 3.5
performance criterion 6.2.5

paying-in slips

task 1

Collect a variety of paying-in slips from local banks. (Ask at the enquiry counter if there are none on display in the banking hall).

task 2

Complete a suitable paying-in slip for the following items:

CASH	*CHEQUES*
1 x £50 note	*H N Ford £50.00*
5 x £20 notes	*Broadfield College £1,250.50*
7 x £10 notes	*R Hanif £15.50*
25 x £1 coins	*H Smith £20.50*
25 x 50p pieces	
10 x 10p pieces	
£5.25 in bronze	

Make up your own business name and eight digit account number. Use today's date and sign your own name on the paying-in slip.

the bank statement

pc 6.2.5

The bank's record of payments in and out of the bank account will be sent to the business in the form of a bank statement. Look at the example on the next page. You will see the following details on the bank statement:

account details

The top of the statement shows the details of the bank account:

- the name and branch address of the bank
- the name and number of the account

transaction columns

There are columns for:

- the date of the transaction
- payments out of the account
- payments into the account
- the 'balance' – ie the amount left in the account after each transaction

statement of account		ALBION BANK PLC		
account: Sabre Stationery number: 14517226		Broadfield Branch 7 The Avenue Broadfield BR1 2AJ		
date	particulars	withdrawn	paid in	balance
1996				
1 Oct	balance brought forward			1000.00 CR
1 Oct	cheque 182289	100.00		900.00 CR
9 Oct	cheque 182290	150.00		750.00 CR
11 Oct	Direct debit ABC Insurance	50.00		700.00 CR
16 Oct	Paid in		300.00	1000.00 CR
31 Oct	balance carried forward			1000.00 CR

transactions on the bank statement

The bank statement shown above sets out the transactions on the bank account of Sabre Stationery for the month of October 1996. Now look at the following details:

the date The year is shown at the top of the date column, while the date of each transaction is shown by the *day* and the *month.*

particulars

- *cheques* shown here have been written out by Sabre Stationery and passed through the banking system; note that the cheque number is shown
- *direct debits* show the name of the organisation which has collected the money from the bank account
- *paid in* shows that Sabre Stationery has paid in money on a paying-in slip
- *balance brought forward* is not a payment in or out of the account; it means 'this is the money in the account on the first day of this statement'
- *balance carried forward* is not a payment in or out of the account; it means 'this is the money in the account on the last day of this statement' – it is the figure which will be shown ('carried forward') on the first line of the November statement

balance The balance column shows the amount of money in the account after each transaction. 'CR' is short for 'credit' which means that there is money in the account. If the business has an overdraft on the account (if it owed the bank money), the balance figure would be followed by 'DR' ('debit').

STUDENT ACTIVITY 3.6
performance criterion 6.2.5

the bank statement

statement of account

ALBION BANK PLC

Broadfield Branch
7 The Avenue
Broadfield BR1 2AJ

account: Osborne Electronics Ltd
number: 01099124

date	particulars	withdrawn	paid in	balance
1995				
2 Oct	Balance brought forward			625.50 CR
9 Oct	Cheque 352817	179.30		446.20 CR
10 Oct	Paid in		485.04	931.24 CR
17 Oct	Cheque 352818	169.33		761.91 CR
23 Oct	Paid in		62.30	824.21 CR
24 Oct	Paid in		100.00	924.21 CR
26 Oct	Cheque 352819	821.80		102.41 CR
26 Oct	Unpaid cheque	250.00		147.59 DR
30 Oct	Paid in		108.00	39.59 DR
31 Oct	Balance carried forward			39.59 DR

tasks

Study the bank statement shown above and answer the following questions:

1. What do "Balance brought forward" and "Balance carried forward" mean? Why are there no figures in the withdrawn and paid in columns for these items?
2. What are the numbers following the word "cheque"? What will the business check these numbers against?
3. What do "CR" and "DR" mean?
4. What has happened to the bank account in the last week of October? Could the business have foreseen this? What can they do about the situation?

problems with errors

pc 6.2.6

Errors on documents can cause a variety of problems, and very often reflect badly on the level of customer care in a business. We have already seen in the last chapter that errors on invoices can result in the wrong goods being sent, the wrong amount being charged, and so on. Errors in payments and receipts documents also have their unfortunate consequences – for example:

- a cheque made out for the wrong amount may result in a delay in obtaining the goods or services ordered
- wrong dates on BACS instructions – a recent example is that of a bank employee who put the wrong date on the payment of several thousand employees' wages and salaries
- a mistake of addition on a paying-in slip – the business as a result could have difficulty in tallying up its records with the bank statement
- a mistake on the bank statement – again – the business could have difficulty in tallying up its records with the bank statement

The answer to these problems is careful checking of documents within a business (and the bank!). Clearly if a business was careless enough it could end up in a position of acute financial crisis because it just would not know where it stood – it could run short of cash and people to whom it owed money could start bankruptcy proceedings. This is obviously a very worse case – but it does happen occasionally.

security checks

pc 6.2.7

Businesses are vulnerable both to errors and to fraud. They can guard against both by introducing rigorous security checks to prevent one individual either perpetrating a "howler' or a "fiddle". For example:

- all purchase orders and petty cash vouchers need an *authorised signature*
- invoices should only be paid when the business is satisfied by *checking the original order and the goods received note* that the goods have been received in acceptable condition
- *cheques should be signed by the right people* – as we saw earlier a company cheque is normally signed by two or more authorised directors
- *segregation of duties* – making sure that the same person does not do two jobs where there may be opportunity for major error or a temptation to defraud the business, eg the responsibility for receiving goods and paying for goods should be given to different people

EVIDENCE COLLECTION ASSIGNMENT 3

payment documents

Element 6.2, pcs. 4, 6 & 7

introduction

This assignment tests your understanding of the use of payment documents and the importance of correct completion and security checks.

task 1

pc. 6.2.4

Collect examples of the following blank business documents (or design your own if you cannot find an original): petty cash voucher, cheque, bank giro credit, remittance advice. Write short notes on how and when each document is used.

task 2

pc. 6.2.4

Assume you are working in the Accounts Department of Flair Fashions Limited. Your "in-tray" contains a number of payment requests. You are to complete *one* of the four documents in Task 1 for *each* payment. In each case use your own name and assume you can sign or complete the document. If you need further signatures, ask your Tutor. Use today's date. Your banking details are Albion Bank, Broadfield, code 90 47 17, account 12715373.

(a) A note from the Accounts supervisor saying "Please settle with Nicole Leatherware a.s.a.p. Cheque for £4,595 already signed." The cheque is pinned to the note, but there is no other documentation. Make up any details you need for this exercise.

(b) You have to make a "one-off" wages payment of £250.50 to a employee, Rachel Moore, who banks at Lloyds Bank, Peachfield (code 30 56 38). Her bank account number is 28768246. She is off sick at the moment and unfortunately her wage packet has already been made up in cash.

(c) You have to settle an account with Broadfield Supplies Limited. The amount due is £12,456.98.

(d) A note from a colleague Joan Smith saying "Bought more office coffee. Please reimburse. Receipt for £8.75 attached."

task 3

pcs. 6.2.6 & 7

(a) What would be the consequences if you had quoted the wrong amount in all four cases in Task 2? How could you guard against this happening?

(b) What arrangements are normally made in a limited company business for the signing of cheques? How will the bank know about who has to sign limited company cheques? Talk to your local bank.

EVIDENCE COLLECTION ASSIGNMENT 4

receipts documents

Element 6.2, pcs. 5, 6 & 7

introduction

This assignment tests your understanding of the use of receipts documents and the importance of correct completion and security checks.

This assignment, like the previous assignment is based on Flair Fashions Ltd, and comprises a series of day-to-day tasks carried out at the counter and in the Accounts Office.

You may find it useful to interview someone who works in a similar business to help explain the background to the tasks – the checking procedures and security measures, for example.

You will need to obtain a blank receipt and paying-in slip. (You can adapt them from examples used in previous exercises). In all activities, use and sign your own name where you need to, and use today's date.

task 1

pc. 6.2.5

Ms. S Stone calls and buys a PVC apron, using a debit card. She says she wants a formal VAT receipt because she can claim the money back from her employer. The till receipt (which includes but does not show VAT) totals £18.80.

task 2

pcs. 6.2.5 & 7

You have been asked to make up a paying-in slip for paying into the bank on the same day. The cash and cheques for paying in are:

CASH	*CHEQUES*
3 x £50 notes	£34.50 from A Brown
9 x £20 notes	£27.78 from G Smith
6 x £10 notes	£65.50 from J Jones
35 x £1 coins	£45.00 from G Gupta
12 x 50p coins	£21.99 from T Tartini
16 x 10p coins	£45.99 from H Schmidt
8 x 5p coins	
£12.40 in bronze	

State any checking procedures and security measures you are likely to undertake when dealing with this task.

task 3

pc. 6.2.6

You receive a number of cheques during the day, and some of them seem to have errors on them. Examine the cheques shown below and

(a) write down what (if anything) is wrong with them

(b) state what action you would take in each case

(c) state what would happen if you did *not* take any action

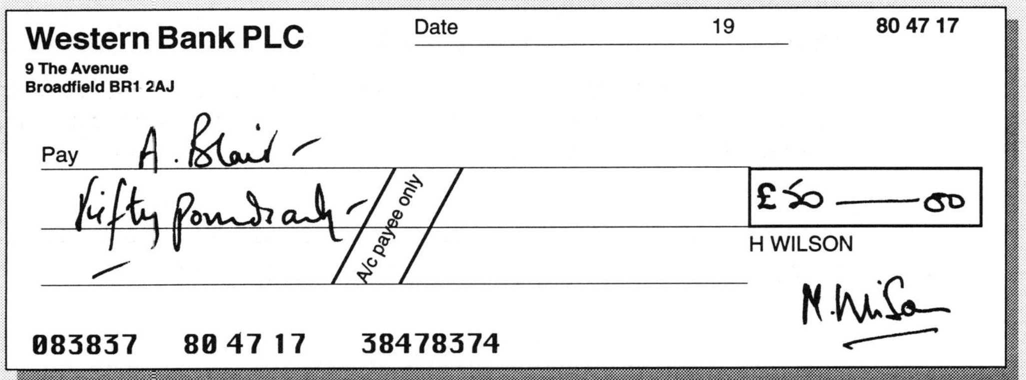

Western Bank PLC
9 The Avenue
Broadfield BR1 2AJ

Date 19

80 47 17

Pay A. Blair –

Fifty pounds only –

A/c payee only

£50—00

H WILSON

H. Wilson

083837 80 47 17 38478374

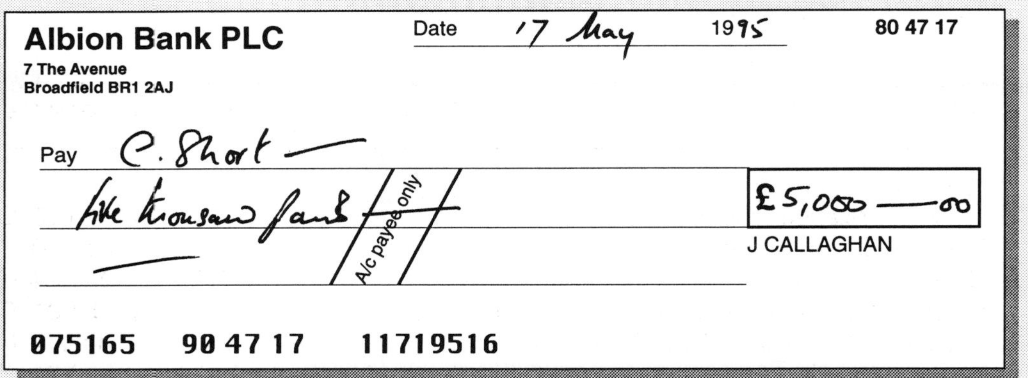

Albion Bank PLC
7 The Avenue
Broadfield BR1 2AJ

Date 17 May 1995

80 47 17

Pay C. Short —

Five thousand pounds —

A/c payee only

£5,000—00

J CALLAGHAN

075165 90 47 17 11719516

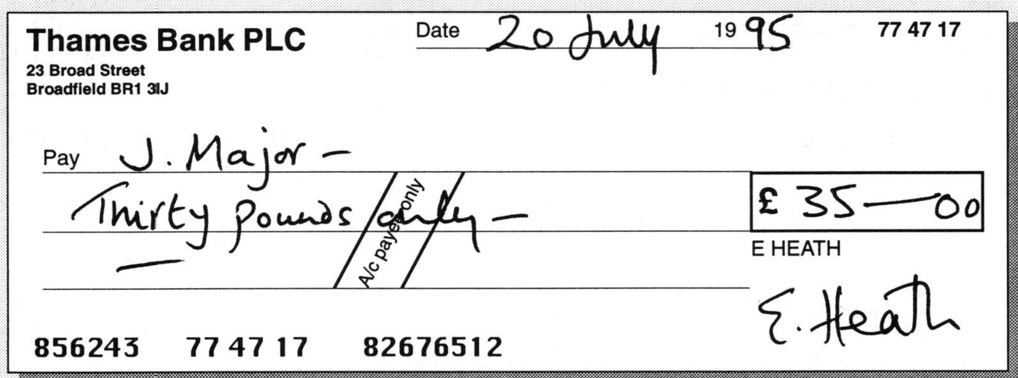

Thames Bank PLC
23 Broad Street
Broadfield BR1 3IJ

Date 20 July 1995

77 47 17

Pay J. Major –

Thirty pounds only –

A/c payee only

£ 35—00

E HEATH

E. Heath

856243 77 47 17 82676512

task 4

pc. 6.2.5

You have been asked by the Supervisor to write some notes for new trainees working in the Accounts Department. What she would like is a series of word-processed A4 sheets. Each sheet will cover a different type of document. They will be headed as follows:

(a) When to use and how to complete a Receipt.

(b) How to fill in a paying-in slip.

(c) How to spot errors on cheques, and what to do about them.

(d) How to recognise entries on a bank statement (the Supervisor asks that new trainees should be able to explain all the entries on the example bank statement shown below).

statement of account

ALBION BANK PLC

Broadfield Branch
7 The Avenue
Broadfield BR1 2AJ

account: Flair Fashions Limited
number: 12715373

date	particulars	withdrawn	paid in	balance
1995				
1 Nov	Balance brought forward			120.00 CR
9 Nov	Cheque 123456	179.30		446.20 CR
10 Nov	Paid in		485.04	931.24 CR
17 Nov	DD Broadfield City Council Rates	169.33		761.91 CR
23 Nov	BACS Fancy Dress Ltd		62.30	824.21 CR
24 Nov	Paid in		100.00	924.21 CR
27 Nov	Cheque 123457	821.80		102.41 CR
27 Nov	Unpaid cheque	250.00		147.59 DR
28 Nov	Bank charges	56.50		39.59 DR
30 Nov	Balance carried forward			39.59 DR

chapter summary and key terms

- A business can make manual payments involving:
  - cash and a petty cash voucher
  - a cheque
  - a bank giro credit
  - a debit card or a credit card
- A business can make payments by computer transfer between the banks using Bankers Automated Clearing Services (BACS).Payments can be:
  - *direct credits*: individual payments (standing orders) or bulk payments
  - *direct debits*: money collected from bank accounts (eg gas bills)
- Businesses are increasingly using Electronic Data Interchange (EDI), a computer communication system between businesses to send orders, invoices and payment instructions.
- A business can receive money in the form of payment by cash, cheque, debit card, or credit card.
- When a business receives money it will normally pay it into the bank on a paying-in slip; the bank will regularly issue a bank statement.
- When errors are made on documents, the consequences can be serious. It is therefore important that a business sets up a system of security checks to help avoid errors and unauthorised transactions.

key terms

petty cash	a secured 'float' of cash kept within the business for small purchases, authorised by a petty cash voucher
cheque	is a written order to the bank signed by its customer (known as the 'drawer') to pay a specified amount to a specified person (the 'payee')
BACS	Bankers Automated Clearing Services is a system of direct computer transfers between the bank accounts of businesses and individuals
EDI	Electronic Data Interchange is a computer communication system between businesses used for sending orders, invoices and payment instructions.
receipt	a document issued by a seller as evidence of a cash (immediate payment) transaction.

multiple-choice questions

1 A petty cash payment is BEST described as a

A cash payment to staff for personal expenses

B payment of notes and coins into the bank account

C cash payment for a small item of business expense

D payment made by a junior member of staff

2 A cheque can be defined as a written order from the

A drawer to the payee

B bank to the payee

C bank to the drawer

D drawer to the bank

Questions 3 – 5 relate to the following information:

A cheque can have the following:

A no date

B no drawer's signature

C the date is three months ago

D the words "Refer to Drawer" written across the top

Which of these can be treated as follows?

3 Pay it into the bank

4 Send it back to the drawer for completion

5 Fill in the missing item

6 Decide whether each of these statements is True (T) or False (F)

(i) a BACS direct debit is used to collect money from bank accounts

(ii) a BACS direct credit is used to pay employees' wages

A (i) T (ii) T

B (i) T (ii) F

C (i) F (ii) T

D (i) F (ii) F

4 The cost of goods and services

GNVQ SPECIFICATIONS
Element 6.3
Calculate the cost of goods or services

performance criteria – a student must

1 explain direct costs and indirect costs of businesses
2 identify correctly a unit of production or unit of service from given data
3 calculate the direct costs of the production or service for a time period
4 calculate indirect costs of the organisation for a time period
5 calculate the total (absorption) cost of a unit of the production or service
6 explain variable and fixed costs in terms of their relationship with production
7 calculate the variable costs of a unit of the production or service from given data
8 calculate the marginal cost of a unit of the production or service

what this chapter covers

In this chapter we see how accounting helps the owner of a business to calculate the cost of a product – whether goods or services. This type of accounting is called cost accounting. We look at the principles involved and see how they are applied, in a Case Study, to the costing of goods and services.

what you will learn from this chapter

- an understanding of the types of costs involved in a product
- the procedures to be followed when calculating the total cost for goods and services
- the importance of distinguishing between fixed and variable costs
- how to calculate marginal cost (the cost of producing an extra item) , and how it is significant to the owner of a business

direct costs and indirect costs

pc 6.3.1

For any product – whether goods or a service – there are always three costs involved:

- materials
- labour
- expenses

These costs can be categorised into those which are *direct costs* and those which are *indirect costs*. The total of these costs makes up the total cost of the product:

direct costs + indirect costs = total cost

direct costs

Direct costs are directly associated with the product of the business, ie they can be identified as being related to the product:

- *direct materials* – the materials used which can be identified with the product, eg wood for making furniture, paper for a photocopier
- *direct labour* – wages paid to those who make the product, eg assembly line workers, photocopier operator
- *direct expenses* – the expenses which can be attributed directly to the product, eg royalties payable to the designer of a product, depreciation – the fall in value(see below) of machinery and equipment used in making the goods or providing the service, power costs (such as electricity and gas)

indirect costs (overheads)

Indirect costs are associated with running the business, ie they cannot be identified as being related to the product:

- *indirect labour* – wages and salaries paid to those who are not directly involved with the product, eg managers, supervisors, maintenance staff
- *indirect expenses* – running expenses of the business, such as administration, telephone, depreciation (see below), power, which cannot be attributed directly to the product

The indirect costs are often described as the overheads of the business, ie

indirect labour + indirect expenses = overheads

depreciation

Depreciation – the fall in value of something – is a cost to the business that can be categorised as a direct cost *or* an indirect cost, depending on how closely it is linked to the product.

Depreciation is the fall in value of productive assets, such as machinery and equipment. Assets wear out, or are replaced because they have become out-of-date, and the aim of the business is to spread the cost of the fall in value over the useful life of the asset. The calculation of depreciation is:

cost of asset ÷ assumed useful life

for example:

- a computer costs £1,000 and is expected to last for five years – the annual depreciation is £200 (£1,000 ÷ 5 years)
- a photocopier costs £10,000 and will be replaced after making one million copies – the depreciation per copy is 0.01p (£10,000 ÷ 1,000,000 copies)

Notice how, in the examples, depreciation can be calculated on a time basis (the computer), or on a units of output basis (the photocopier). It is for the business to decide which method is most appropriate for particular assets. Where depreciation is on a time basis, the cost goes into indirect expenses; where it is on a units of output basis, it is a direct expense.

One particular point that you should note about depreciation is that it is a 'non-cash expense': thus the business does not pay out any money from its bank account for depreciation. Money is paid out when the asset is bought and it is this cost which is spread over the life of the asset. Using the example of the computer (above), a payment of £1,000 is made to buy the asset, and a cost of £200 is entered in each of the profit statements of the business for the next five years, but no further money is paid from the bank account.

unit of production and unit of service

pc 6.3.2

For any business, whether it manufactures a product or provides a service, it is important to identify the appropriate *unit of output* for that business in terms of either *units of production* or *units of service*. For example:

business		
car manufacturer	unit of production	car
football manufacturer	unit of production	football
hairdresser	unit of service	labour hour
garage servicing department	unit of service	labour hour of mechanic
bus company	unit of service	passenger mile
telephone company	unit of service	call unit

These units of production or service are known as *cost units*, to which costs can be charged. Only when a business knows the cost of producing each unit can it make decisions about the price at which the production will be sold. The topic of pricing decisions is covered fully in the next chapter.

Once the units of production or service are identified, the business is then able to calculate how many units can be produced or provided in a given time period, such as a day, week, month, quarter (three months), or year. For example, the garage will work out how many hours of mechanics' time are available each week, or the car manufacturer will work out how many cars it can produce in a year.

STUDENT ACTIVITY 4.1
performance criteria 6.3.1 - 2

costs in business

task

Investigate one business from each of the lists (or agree different products and services with your tutor).

production	*service*
• cake making	• car tuning
• photocopying	• household cleaning service
• dried flower arrangements	• golf lessons
• picture framing	• window cleaning
• jewellery manufacture	• secretarial service
• growing mushrooms	• taxi service

For each business you are to:

(a) identify the direct costs and indirect costs

(b) calculate the number of units of production or service for a particular time period

Support your investigations with a written explanation.

Note: wherever possible you should link your investigations to real businesses. You will be asked to carry out further work with these businesses in the next Student Activity – so it may be possible, at this stage, to build up a working relationship with the businesses.

calculating direct costs

pc 6.3.3

Having established the number of units of production or service for a particular time period, the next task is to calculate the *direct costs* for that time period. As we have seen earlier in this chapter, the direct costs comprise:

- *direct materials* – identifiable with the product
- *direct labour* – the wages paid to those who make the product
- *direct expenses* – attributable to the product

For each of these costs we multiply the unit cost by the number of units of output for the particular time period. For example, if direct materials cost £1 for each unit of the product, and we calculate that 1,000 units will be made in the time period, then the direct cost of materials is £1,000 for that time period.

The amounts of the three direct costs are added together to give the total direct costs of the production or service for the time period:

direct materials + direct labour + direct expenses = direct costs

Note that direct costs are calculated on the basis of the number of units of production or service. This means that direct costs are a variable cost which changes with different levels of output. For example, if the direct cost of a unit of production is £10, then:

- 100 units will have direct costs of £1,000
- 200 units will have direct costs of £2,000
- 0 units will have direct costs of £0

In practice, direct costs may not change precisely as they are shown here but, certainly, we can say that direct costs are variable costs that change directly in response to changes in output. We will look further at variable costs (and also their opposite – fixed costs) later in this chapter.

calculating indirect costs

pc 6.3.4

The *indirect costs*, or *overheads*, of the production or service must be calculated for the particular time period. Indirect costs comprise:

- *indirect labour* – wages and salaries paid to those are are not directly involved with the product
- *indirect expenses* – running expenses of the business

Often indirect costs do not fall neatly into the time period we wish to use when calculating costs. For example, rent might be payable every month; insurance premiums every year; electricity, gas and telephone bills every three months; other expenses, such as office stationery and marketing expenses are incurred over different time periods. In all these circumstances, it is necessary to convert the cost into the time period being used for the units of the production or service. For example, an annual cost can be converted into a weekly cost by dividing, not necessarily by 52, but by the number of working weeks when goods are made or a service provided: this is likely to be between 48 and 50.

allocation of indirect costs

Once the indirect costs have been calculated, we must then ensure that their total cost is included in – or *allocated* to – the units of the production or service for a particular time period. Only by including indirect costs in the total cost of the output can a business recover their cost from the sales made.

The amounts of the two indirect costs are added together to give the total indirect costs of the production or service for the time period:

indirect labour + indirect expenses = indirect costs (overheads)

Note that indirect costs are usually calculated on a time basis and do not vary with different levels of production or service. For example, the rent of the factory premises is unchanged whether 0, 100 or 200 units of the product are made. Thus, for the short-term at least, we treat indirect costs as being fixed costs, ie they do not vary with different levels of output. However, in the long-term, no costs are fixed: for example, if a factory that has been making 200 units a week decides to increase production to 2,000 units a week, then it is likely that it will need to rent another factory – thus the 'fixed' cost of rent is no longer fixed. In practice, indirect costs tend to go up by steps – eg rent of one factory unit, rent of two factory units – hence such costs are often known as 'stepped costs'. By contrast, variable costs change directly with different levels of output. Both of these can be illustrated graphically as follows:

fixed cost -
eg factory rent which changes *in step* as output increases

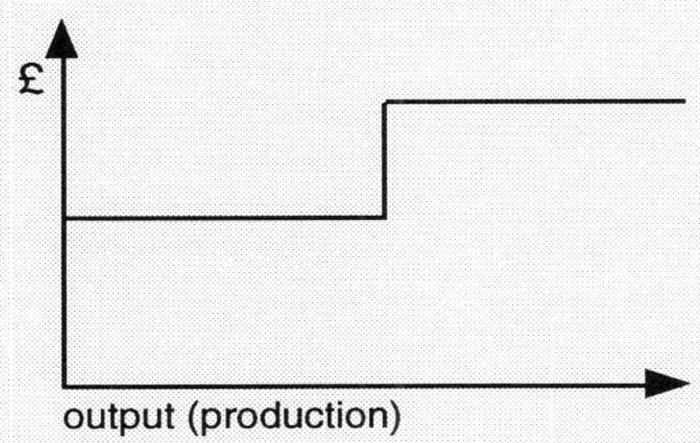

variable cost -
eg direct materials, which changes *proportionally* to different levels of output

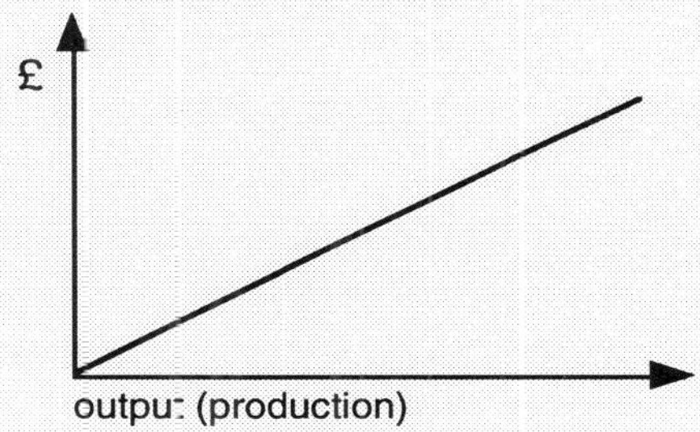

calculating the total cost

pc 6.3.5

Once the direct and indirect costs for a time period are known, the total cost of a unit of production or service can be calculated, as follows:

$$\frac{\text{direct costs + indirect costs}}{\text{units of production}} = \text{total cost of a unit}$$

The total cost is also referred to as the *absorption cost* – because it absorbs, or includes, both the direct (variable) costs and the indirect (fixed) costs. Once total cost is known, the business can use the information to help it make pricing and other decisions – this topic is fully covered in the next chapter.

calculating the cost - a summary

pc 6.3.1 -5

The process of calculating the total (absorption) cost of goods or services has been detailed on the previous pages. To summarise, the process takes the following steps:

- identify the unit of goods or service
- calculate the number of units for a particular time period
- calculate the direct costs for the particular time period
- calculate the indirect costs for the particular time period
- calculate the total (absorption) cost of a unit

This process is illustrated in the diagram below.

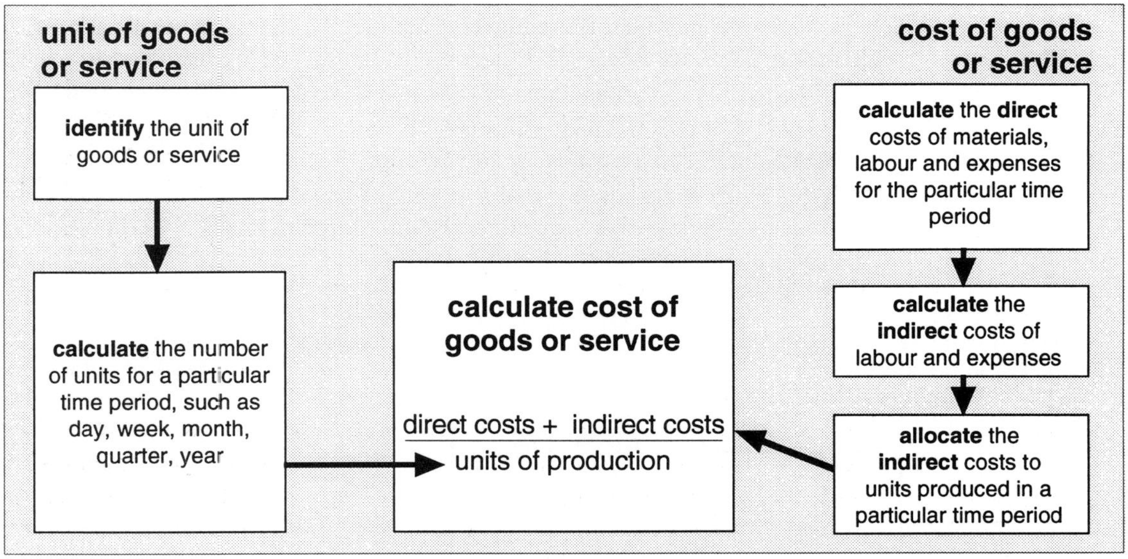

We will now see, by means of a Case Study, how two new businesses – one manufacturing goods, and the other providing a service – calculate the cost of goods or service.

CASE STUDY

pc 6.3.1 -5

Philippa and Sophie – costing of a new business

situation

Twin sisters are planning to set up in business separately:

- *Philippa will make cane baskets for sale to local craft shops*
- *Sophie will offer a computer service providing word processing, desktop publishing and other facilities*

They approach you for assistance in the costing of goods and services.

Philippa's business

Making cane baskets has been a hobby of Philippa's since she went to a basketry evening class. She already sells some of her goods to local shops and, now that she has left college, intends to see if she can turn her hobby into a full-time job. If things go well, she plans, in the longer term, to employ 'home workers' who will make the baskets for her, while she will attend to the marketing and administration of the business. For the moment, she will work from her parents' house but, if business develops, she will need to rent a small craft workshop.

Sophie's business

Sophie has always been interested in computers and, in recent years, has set herself up with a business computer system with software for word processing, database management (mailshots), payroll, and desktop publishing (publicity leaflets). Now that she has left college, she wants to develop a computer bureau so that she can make a living from her hobby. At present the computer system occupies a spare room in her parents' house. She realises that, if business develops, she will need to rent office premises in the town centre.

solution

We will follow Philippa and Sophie's businesses and cost the goods and services provided by them using the steps outlined in the earlier part of this chapter. Note: As both of these are small businesses run by the owner with no employees, the expected cash drawings of the owners have been treated as a cost: thus the cost per unit includes drawings. In larger businesses, the owner would take out cash drawings after calculating net profit.

step 1: identifying the unit of goods and service

How do we go about identifying the unit of goods or service in the businesses planned by Philippa and Sophie?

***Philippa's** business will be to make a product – cane baskets, all of the same size. Therefore the unit is each basket – this is the cost unit. If Philippa were to make other products from cane, each unit of output would be a cost unit.*

***Sophie** will provide a service – as a computer bureau. Her unit of service is best costed on a time basis – eg each hour of computer time is a cost unit.*

The next task is to calculate the number of units of goods and service provided in a time period. We will calculate for the two businesses for each week, although different time periods could be used.

***Philippa** tells us that she will work in the business for 35 hours each week. As she is the only person involved in the business, she will not only make the baskets but will also be involved in marketing and administration. She plans to spend 25 hours each week on making baskets, five hours each on marketing and administration. When making baskets she can complete one each hour. Therefore she will have 25 units of output each week.*

***Sophie** will work 40 hours each week. She will spend 30 hours working for customers, 4 hours on marketing and 6 hours on administration (which will include developing her skills in the use of new software). Therefore she will have 30 units of service each week.*

step 2: calculating direct costs

***Philippa** gives you the expected direct costs of her business each week:*

- *direct materials – cane and bases for the 25 baskets she plans to make each week will cost £40.00*
- *direct labour – Philippa hopes to draw £140.00 each week from the business for a 35-hour week; as she plans that 25 hours will be spent each week on making baskets, the direct labour cost will be*

  $$£140 \times \frac{25}{35} = £100.00$$

- *direct expenses – at present Philippa doesn't anticipate any direct expenses; however, if she makes any special orders she may well need to hire a machine especially for this extra work.*

  The total of direct costs each week is:

  £40.00 (materials) + £100.00 (labour) = ***£140.00***

*For **Sophie**'s business, the expected direct costs each week are:*

- *direct materials – each week she expects to buy for use on customers' work, two boxes of floppy disks, one box of printout paper, and one box of labels, at a total cost of £35.00*
- *direct labour – she plans to draw £150.00 for her 40-hour week; of this time, 30 hours will be spent on customers' work, so her direct labour cost will be* $\pounds150.00 \times \frac{30}{40} = \pounds112.50$
- *direct expenses – her main direct expense will be the purchase of new and up-dated computer software, and depreciation of the hardware, ie computers and printers; in total she estimates these to be £45.00 each week.*

The total of direct costs each week is:

*£35.00 (materials) + £112.50 (labour) + £45.00 (expenses) = **£192.50***

step 3: calculating indirect costs

***Philippa** gives you the expected indirect costs of her business:*

- *indirect labour – as the only person working in the business we have already seen that Philippa will spend 25 hours each week in making baskets, ie direct labour; the other 10 hours spent each week on marketing and administration are indirect labour, the cost of which will be*

  $\pounds140.00 \times \frac{10}{35} = \pounds40.00$ *per week*
- *indirect expenses – for Philippa, these are costs such as office stationery, advertising leaflets, electricity for heating and lighting, telephone, travel expenses, etc, which she has budgeted at £1,100.00 for the first year (if she moves the business from her parents' house to a craft workshop, there will be additional costs of rent paid, business rates, repairs and maintenance).*

*For **Sophie's** business, the expected indirect costs are:*

- *indirect labour – of Sophie's 40-hour working week, she will spend 10 hours on marketing and administration, the cost of which will be*

  $\pounds150.00 \times \frac{10}{40} = \pounds37.50$ *per week*
- *indirect expenses – Sophie expects to have similar types of expenses as Philippa, together with computer disks for her own use, printer ribbons and computer manuals – she budgets the amount of indirect expenses at £1,550.00 for the first year.*

step 4: allocating indirect costs to output

The indirect costs of ***Philippa****'s business (see above) are expected to be:*

- *indirect labour £40.00 per week*
- *indirect expenses £1,100.00 each year*

Philippa *plans to take 2 weeks' holiday each year, so the weekly indirect costs will be:*

• *indirect labour*	= *£40.00*
• *indirect expenses £1,100.00 ÷ 50 weeks*	= *£22.00*
total of indirect costs each week	= *£62.00*

Sophie*'s business is expected to have the following indirect costs (see above):*

- *indirect labour £37.50 per week*
- *indirect expenses £1,550.00 each year*

Sophie *plans to take 4 weeks' holiday each year so, as she will be working for 48 weeks, the weekly indirect costs will be:*

• *indirect labour*	= *£37.50*
• *indirect expenses £1,550.00 ÷ 48 weeks*	= *£32.30*
total of indirect costs each week	= *£69.80*

step 5:
calculating total (absorption) cost of a unit of goods and service

Philippa *intends to make 25 baskets each week. The costs (see above) are:*

• *total of direct costs each week*	= *£140.00*
• *total of indirect costs each week*	= *£ 62.00*
total costs each week	= *£202.00*

The total cost per basket is:

$$\frac{£202.00}{25 \text{ baskets}} = £8.08 \text{ per basket}$$

Sophie *plans to spend 30 hours each week on customers' work. The costs already calculated are:*

• *total of direct costs each week*	= *£192.50*
• *total of indirect costs each week*	= *£ 69.80*
total costs each week	= *£262.30*

The cost per hour of service to customers is:

$$\frac{£262.30}{30 \text{ hours}} = £8.74 \text{ per hour}$$

conclusion

Philippa

As Philippa has included the amount she wishes to draw from the business each week in the costings, this means that she needs to sell baskets for a minimum average price of £8.08 each. Clearly some baskets will be sold to shops who will wish to buy at a trade price, while others will be sold direct to customers – probably at higher prices – who are buying for themselves. However, Philippa needs to recognise that, in order to cover her costs, she must sell all her production of baskets at a minimum average price of £8.08. Note that we have assumed that the baskets made by Philippa are all of the same size: if she decides to make them in a range of sizes, this would have to be allowed for in the costings.

Sophie

Sophie has also included the amount that she wishes to draw from the business in her costings. She must charge a minimum of £8.74 per hour for each hour that she provides a service to her customers.

STUDENT ACTIVITY 4.2

performance criteria 6.3.3 - 5

calculating total cost

task

For the two businesses – one producing goods, the other providing a service – selected in Student Activity.1 earlier in the chapter, you are to calculate the total (absorption) cost of a unit of goods or service. The steps to be followed are:

- calculate the direct costs for the particular time period
- calculate the indirect costs
- allocate indirect costs to units produced in the particular time period
- calculate the unit cost of the goods or service

You should support your calculations with written explanations.

note

Where you have been able to investigate a real business you should, as far as possible, attempt to find out the actual costs incurred. Be tactful here, as many businesses will not wish to disclose costs, because the information will be of interest to rival companies, as well as revealing profit margins. Where actual costs are not forthcoming, reasonable estimates should be made.

variable and fixed costs

pc 6.3.6

At the start of the chapter we saw that there are always three costs which make up the product, whether goods or a service. These costs are:

- materials
- labour
- expenses

We have also seen how some costs vary with different levels of output, while other costs remain fixed. Thus we can classify costs as being either variable costs or fixed costs. The diagram below shows the differences between fixed, and variable costs:

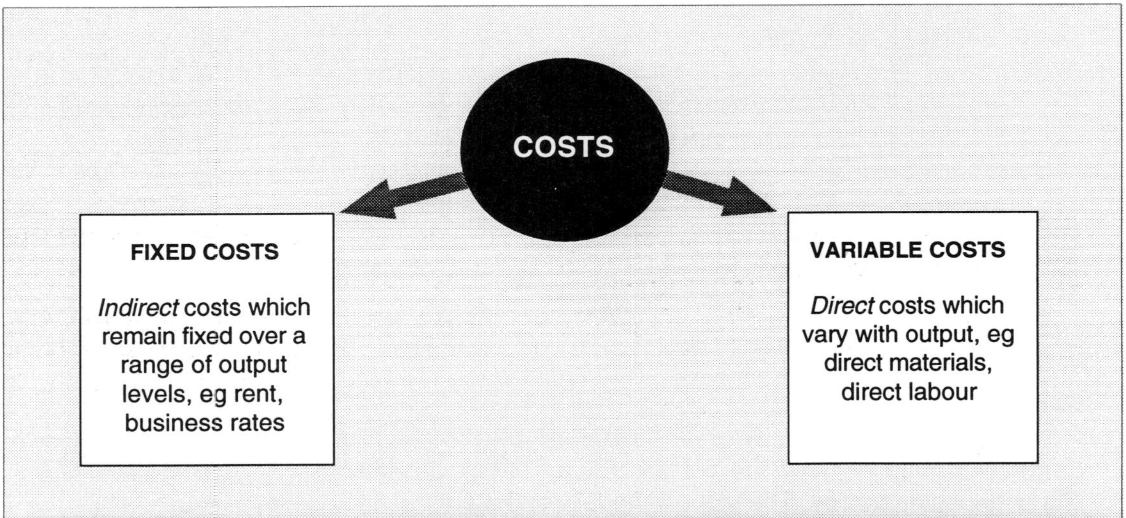

Note: it is assumed here that indirect costs are fixed and direct costs vary directly with the level of production

Do appreciate that the nature of costs, ie whether fixed or variable, can change as the business alters. For example:

- a fixed cost, such as factory rent, is only likely to be fixed at or near current production levels; if output is doubled or trebled, then it is likely that an additional factory will need to be rented
- instead of using a labour-intensive process (with the variable cost of direct labour), it may be possible to automate production by using a machine (with depreciation on the machine being classed as either a direct variable cost or, more often, as an indirect fixed cost)
- a large increase in production may enable materials to be bought more cheaply through bulk-buying, thus the unit cost of direct materials will be reduced

- the goods or service could be produced by using a cheaper grade of labour, so lowering the direct labour cost

We shall be looking at the relationship between fixed and variable costs in more detail in the next chapter when we look at the breakeven chart.

variable costs and marginal cost

pc 6.3.7 -8

As we have seen earlier in this chapter, the variable costs of a product comprise:

- direct materials
- direct labour
- direct expenses

These three costs are added together to give us the total variable cost for each unit of the product (we shall see this being done in the Case Study which follows this section).

The total of the variable costs is important because it is often – but not always – the marginal cost of producing a unit of the product.

Marginal cost is the incremental cost (that is, the additional cost) of producing one extra unit.

For most purposes, marginal cost does not involve fixed costs (such as the rent of a factory); instead it includes the variable costs which increase with the production of a further unit of output. However, sometimes marginal cost will include a fixed cost as shown in the following examples.

examples of marginal cost:

The rent of a factory unit is £5,000 per year. The capacity of a factory unit is to make 20,000 units of product 'Exe' each year. The variable cost of each unit of 'Exe' is £100. Now consider the following:

- The factory is currently making 19,999 units each year. What is the marginal cost of making one more unit? The answer is, of course, the variable cost of £100 per unit.
- The factory is now making 20,000 units each year. What is the marginal cost of making one more unit? The answer here is not just the variable cost of £100 per unit but £5,100, because a new factory unit will have to be rented at a cost of £5,000 (and there are likely to be increases in other costs if a second factory unit is taken on).

The two situations shown here indicate that marginal cost is the incremental (additional) cost of producing one extra unit, ie how much it will cost to make one more.

CASE STUDY

pc 6.3.7 -8

Wyvern Bike Company – variable costs and marginal costs

situation

The Wyvern Bike Company makes 100 bikes a week, and its costs are as follows:

weekly costs for producing 100 bikes

	£
direct materials (£20 per bike)	2,000
direct labour (£25 per bike)	2,500
direct expenses (£5 per bike)	500
fixed overheads	3,000
TOTAL COST	8,000

Note: the factory has the capacity to produce 150 bikes a week, with no increase in fixed overheads.

- *What is the variable cost of producing one bike?*
- *What is the marginal cost of producing one bike?*
- *A friend of the owner wants a bike making next week – this will be extra to normal production. What price will be charged to cover the cost of making this bike?*

solution

The ***variable cost*** *of producing one bike:*

	£
direct materials	20
direct labour	25
direct expenses	5
variable cost per unit	50

The ***marginal cost*** *of producing one bike will be £50, ie the incremental, or additional, costs. (As the factory is not working to full capacity there will be no increase in fixed overheads).*

The friend will be charged ***£50****, ie the variable cost, rather than the absorption cost of £80 per unit (ie £8,000 ÷ 100 bikes).*

STUDENT ACTIVITY 4.3
performance criteria 6.3.6 - 8

fixed and variable costs

situation

John Walker Limited makes high quality training shoes (trainers). Currently production is running at 25,000 pairs of trainers each year. The following cost information is available:

direct materials (per pair)	£15
direct labour (per pair)	£12
direct expenses (per pair)	£1
fixed overheads	£245,000 each year

Note: the factory has the capacity to produce 30,000 pairs of trainers each year, with no increase in fixed overheads.

tasks

1 Calculate the variable cost per unit of production

2 Calculate the absorption cost per unit of production

3 State the price that should be charged to employees who want to buy trainers for their own use – ensure that the company 'covers its costs' from this extra production which will be in addition to normal production. Explain the reason for the price you recommend and indicate the circumstances when a different amount might apply.

EVIDENCE COLLECTION ASSIGNMENT 5

calculating the cost of goods and services

Element 6.3

introduction

Two friends are planning to set up separate businesses: Tony will make wooden garden seats, while Karen will offer a gardening service. They are looking for advice about the cost of their products, and ask you to carry out some calculations for them. For this Assignment you will choose *one* business to assist.

tasks

the facts and figures

From discussion with them you have found out the following cost information:

Tony: garden seat manufacture

- wood and other materials will cost £11.50 per garden seat
- each seat will take four hours to make
- Tony will work in the business for 40 hours each week which will be spent as follows: 28 hours on manufacturing, 5 hours on administration and 7 hours on marketing the finished product; nobody else will be employed at present
- Tony plans to draw £120 per week as wages from the business
- he will take two weeks' holiday each year
- rent of a small factory unit and office will cost £4,160 per year; business rates will cost £1,040 per year
- a specialist machine will need to be purchased at a cost of £600 – it is expected to last for two years (104 weeks, less two weeks' holiday each year = 100 weeks' usage) at the planned level of production
- other running expenses and insurance are expected to be £780 per year

Karen: gardening service

- in the spring, summer and early autumn Karen will offer a grasscutting service for 30 weeks, and, in the late autumn and winter, a digging service, using a mechanical rotovator, will be offered for 20 weeks; she will take two weeks' holiday each year
- a heavy duty petrol lawnmower will be purchased at a cost of £900; it is expected to last for 300 weeks' use
- a rotovator will be purchased at a cost of £600; it is expected to last for 100 weeks' use

- Karen will buy a secondhand van to transport the gardening equipment: the cost of this will be £2,400 – it is expected to last for four years
- van running costs are estimated at £1,040 per year
- both the lawnmower and rotovator will use £1.50 of petrol per hour
- both the lawnmower and rotovator will need an annual service costing £100 each; spare parts are estimated at £80 per year for the lawnmower, and £100 for the rotovator (treat all these costs as indirect expenses)
- Karen will work a 40-hour week which will be spent as follows:

  25 hours working for customers, ie using the mechanical equipment, lawnmower or rotovator, 5 hours travelling to customers, 5 hours on administration and 5 hours on marketing (eg meeting new customers)
- she plans to draw £160 per week as wages from the business
- the van and all gardening equipment will be kept in a lock-up garage which will cost £10 a week for rent and £104 per year for business rates
- other running expenses and insurance are expected to be £1,300 per year

calculations to carry out

Taking one business only – either Tony's or Karen's – you are to undertake the following tasks for that business:

pcs 6.3.1 & 6 **1** Identify the direct and indirect costs. Give an explanation and indicate which costs will vary with production levels, and which will remain fixed.

pc 6.3.2 **2** Identify the unit of goods and service, justifying your choice.

3 Calculate the number of units of the goods and service provided in a week. Explain your workings.

pc 6.3.3 **4** Calculate the direct costs of the goods and service each week. Explain your workings.

pc 6.3.4 **5** Calculate the indirect costs of the goods and service. Explain your workings.

6 Calculate the allocation of indirect costs to weekly output. Explain your workings.

pc 6.3.5 **7** Calculate the total (absorption) cost of a unit of the goods and service. Explain your workings.

pcs 6.3.7 & 8 **8** Describe what is meant by variable cost and marginal cost. Explain how either Tony or Karen will apply the principle of marginal costing when charging a friend for an extra unit of goods and service.

notes

- assume that each business will operate for 50 weeks each year
- no wages will be drawn during the two weeks' holiday taken each year
- rent paid, business rates, and other running expenses (including Karen's van depreciation and running costs) will apply for the whole year, but must be allocated using the 50 weeks that the businesses are operating
- for Karen's business, do not calculate separate unit costs for grasscutting and rotovating – instead, calculate an overall unit cost

chapter summary and key terms

- There are three costs which make up a product: materials, labour and expenses.
- These costs are categorised into either direct costs or indirect costs.
- The unit of production or service needs to be identified, and then the number of units in a particular time period can be calculated.
- The direct and indirect costs of production or service are then calculated for the time period.
- The total (absorption) cost of a unit of the production or service is then calculated.
- Costs can be classified as *fixed*, (such as indirect costs) or *variable*, (such as direct costs).
- A knowledge of the nature of each cost enables calculation of the marginal cost of producing a unit of production.

key terms

direct costs	costs which are directly associated with the product of the business (direct materials + direct labour + direct expenses)
indirect costs	costs which are associated with running the business, and which cannot be identified as being related to the product (indirect labour + indirect expenses)
unit of production	the output of the business expressed in terms of units, eg cars, footballs, labour hour, passenger mile
cost units	units of production to which costs can be charged
total (absorption) cost	$\dfrac{\text{direct costs + indirect costs}}{\text{units of production}}$
fixed costs	indirect costs which do not vary with the level of production of the product or service, eg rent of premises
variable costs	direct costs which vary with the level of production of the product or service, eg materials, labour
marginal cost	the incremental (additional) cost of producing one extra unit

multiple-choice questions

1 Which of the following costs is usually calculated as a direct cost?

A assembly line workers' wages
B supervisor's salary
C rent of the factory
D office stationery

2 Which of the following costs is usually calculated as an indirect cost?

A materials used in the product
B assembly line workers' wages
C maintenance salaries
D royalties payable to the designer of a product

3 The costs of a business can be divided between direct costs and indirect costs. Decide whether each of these statements is True (T) or False (F).

(i) during the August holiday shut-down a manufacturing company will incur both direct and indirect costs

(ii) a service company can incur both direct and indirect costs

Which option best describes the two statements?

A	(i)	T	(ii)	T
B	(i)	T	(ii)	F
C	(i)	F	(ii)	T
D	(i)	F	(ii)	F

Questions 4 – 6 relate to the following information:

A company makes 500 chairs a week at its factory. The costs are

direct materials	£5,000
direct labour	£2,500
direct expenses	£1,000
fixed overheads	£4,000

These costs can be expressed as:

A variable cost per unit
B fixed cost per unit
C total (absorption) cost per unit
D marginal cost per unit

Which of the above would be calculated as:

4 £25.00

5 £17.00

6 £8.00

5 Pricing decisions and breakeven

GNVQ SPECIFICATIONS
Element 6.4
Explain basic pricing decisions and breakeven
performance criteria – a student must

1 identify basic factors which determine price and describe related pricing strategies
2 explain breakeven point
3 draw and label a breakeven chart from given data
4 analyse the breakeven chart
5 explain reasons for using a breakeven chart

what this chapter covers

In the last chapter we looked at how to calculate the cost of a product – either making goods or providing a service. In this chapter see how the selling price to the customer is worked out by looking at a number of pricing strategies. Closely linked to pricing strategies is the need for a business to know the level of sales at which it breaks even, ie the point at which total sales revenue equals total cost.

what you will learn from this chapter

- the main factors that determine the selling price of a product are the need for the business to make a profit, the prices of competing products, and whether or not there is any under-used capacity in the business
- the main pricing strategies are cost-plus pricing, market led pricing, and marginal cost/contribution pricing
- linked to pricing strategies is breakeven, which is the point at which total sales revenue equals total cost
- a breakeven chart expresses in a visual form the relationship between fixed costs, variable costs, and selling price
- a breakeven chart is used to help with business decisions when starting a business, measuring profits or losses at varying levels of production and sales, and examining 'what if?' questions

factors which determine price

pc 6.4.1

A price is the amount of money that is agreed between a buyer and a seller which enables the exchange of a product – goods or a service – to take place.

There are three main factors that a business must consider when deciding the price at which to sell its goods:

- *the need to make a profit* – in the long-term, selling price must be higher than total cost
- *prices of competing products* – the selling price is determined largely by what other suppliers of the product are charging
- *under-used capacity* – selling some of the output at a cut price, eg selling unsold tickets cheaply at a theatre just before the performance

For each of these factors which determine price, there is a related pricing strategy:

- *the need to make a profit* – the pricing strategy is *cost-plus pricing*
- *prices of competing products* – the pricing strategy is *market led pricing*
- *under-used capacity* – the pricing strategy is *marginal cost/contribution pricing*

We will now look at each of these in more detail.

cost-plus pricing

pc 6.4.1

The calculation for cost-plus pricing is:

cost price + profit = selling price

Cost is usually calculated on the basis of total (absorption) cost (see page 84) – which adds all the costs of each cost unit.

Profit can be calculated:

– *either* as a percentage mark-up on cost price (ie the profit, being a percentage of cost price, is added to cost price to give selling price)

– *or* to give a percentage return on capital employed (ie the money invested in the business)

The Case Study which follows illustrates the ways in which a company can use cost-plus pricing to determine the selling price for its products.

CASE STUDY

pc 6.4.1

Leathercraft Limited: cost-plus pricing

situation

Leathercraft Limited makes high-quality 'executive' chairs. Each year, at its factory in Mereford, it makes 2,000 chairs and its costs are as follows:

annual costs of producing 2,000 chairs

	£
direct materials (£100 per chair)	200,000
direct labour (£70 per chair)	140,000
fixed overheads	100,000
TOTAL COST	440,000

The company is currently reviewing its selling prices and is considering cost-plus pricing based on:

- *either a 40 per cent mark-up on cost price (ie profit is 40 per cent of cost price, which is added to cost price to give selling price)*
- *or a 20 per cent return on capital employed*

Leathercraft Limited has capital employed of £1,000,000.

solution – percentage mark-up method

selling price is calculated as:

	£
total costs	440,000
40 per cent mark-up (40% x £440,000)	176,000
selling price	616,000

Using percentage mark-up, the selling price per chair will be:
£616,000 ÷ 2,000 chairs = £308 per chair.

solution – percentage return on capital employed method

Return on capital employed is a performance measure, expressed as a percentage, which compares profit with the capital needed to run the business. It is expressed as:

$$\frac{\text{profit}}{\text{capital employed}} \times \frac{100}{1} = \text{percentage return on capital employed}$$

For Leathercraft Limited the capital employed is £1,000,000. A 20 per cent return on capital employed is the target return set by the company. Thus, the profit required is:

£1,000,000 x 20% = £200,000
ie, capital employed x percentage return = profit

Selling price is calculated as:

	£
total costs	440,000
20 per cent return on capital employed	200,000
selling price	640,000

Using percentage return on capital employed, the selling price per chair will be: £640,000 ÷ 2,000 chairs = £320 per chair.

conclusion

The two methods of cost-plus pricing used in the case study give different selling prices per cost unit:

- *percentage mark-up: £308 per chair*
- *percentage return on capital employed: £320 per chair*

Whilst both methods meet the target requirements of mark-up and return on capital employed, it does not follow that Leathercraft Limited will be able to sell its chairs at either price. It might be that its customers will find a supplier who is able to produce chairs of the same quality but at a cheaper price; in other words, the price Leathercraft will charge is market led (see next page).

STUDENT ACTIVITY 5.1
performance criterion 6.4.1

pricing strategies – cost-plus pricing

Mereford Private Hospital Limited carries out a large number of minor operations for day patients. For next year it plans 2,500 operations based on the following costs:

annual costs for 2,500 minor operations

	£
direct materials (£100 per operation)	250,000
direct labour (£200 per operation)	500,000
fixed overheads	200,000
TOTAL COST	950,000

The hospital is reviewing its pricing policy for minor operations and is considering cost-plus pricing based on:

- either a 25 per cent mark-up on cost price
- or a 20 per cent return on capital employed

The capital employed for the minor operations section of the hospital is £1,000,000.

Calculate the price per minor operation using the two cost-plus pricing methods.

market led pricing

pc 6.4.1

When a business has a product or service for which there is considerable demand and over which it has sole rights, it may be able to set and maintain its own price level (subject to government intervention on the grounds of monopoly pricing).

Most businesses, however, must set their prices in comparison with other suppliers of the same or similar products and services. In the economy of the free market, buyers will tend to buy from the supplier that can produce the product, or supply the service, at least cost. Thus, in an ideal world (but not always in reality), inefficient suppliers will be forced out of the market and, in order to re-establish themselves, will have to look carefully at their costings and/or production techniques.

There are many examples of market led pricing, some of which benefit the buyer:

the price of similar products

Supermarket shelves, as an example, often contain 'rival' brands of the same product, eg tins of baked beans, cans of cola drink. Whilst each manufacturer will always tell you that their product is infinitely superior to that of their rivals, market led pricing means that there is little, if any, difference in price. Whilst supermarket 'own brand' products are usually a little cheaper, the pricing is still market led, ie the price of branded goods, minus a few pence.

the price of seasonal products, eg fresh fruit

By and large the market leads the price: a supplier of strawberries cannot charge significantly more than competitors.

price cutting

In recent years there have been many examples of price cutting started by one retailer and then spreading across the whole industry, ie the price cutting has been market led. Examples include newspapers,and holidays – see the Case Study which follows.

summary

With market led pricing:

- selling prices are determined largely by what others charge for the same product
- where competition exists, the buyer will tend to buy from the cheapest seller

CASE STUDY

pc 6.4.1

holiday 'price wars' – market led pricing

situation

This Case Study looks at examples of market led pricing in the holiday industry.

Until recently, whenever you booked a holiday through a travel agent, the price you paid was that shown in the tour operator's brochure – the only exception being if the holiday was a special offer, such as a 'late availability'. Nowadays most travel agents offer discounts of up to 10 per cent – one company led the way, and the others followed. Take a look at the offers available from travel agents on your local High Street; at the time of writing, some of the deals are:

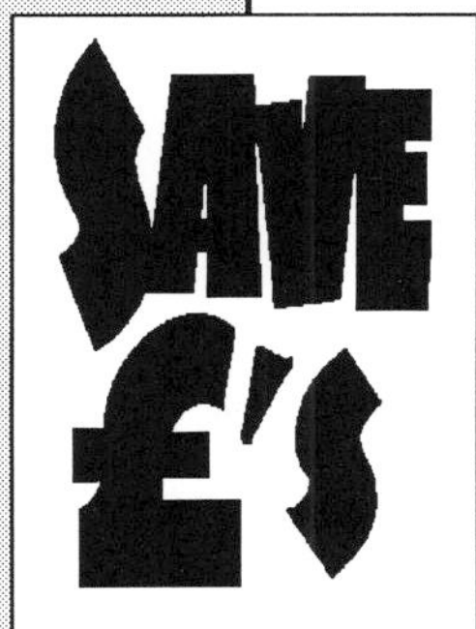

Massive discounts – great summer deals
Going Places

Up to 10 per cent cash discount or free insurance Forward Travel

Summer holiday discounts: 10 per cent off Lunn Poly

Up to 10 per cent off selected holidays
Thomas Cook

It should be pointed out that such offers are not available all of the time and there are usually some restrictions, eg from particular brochures, or a certain minimum holiday price. Offers are usually advertised when the new season's brochures are published so as to encourage early booking; also, if holidays are not selling well, the offers will be made in an attempt to boost trade.

With holiday offers like this, there is usually some 'small print' – for example, the requirement to buy the travel agent's own travel insurance. This usually proves to be more expensive than that available from other insurers but, on balance, there is likely to be a saving on the holiday overall.

conclusion

Market led pricing has reduced the prices of holidays to the customer. Holiday companies have all acted in response to a move by one of the larger companies in the industry. The others have followed in order to be able to maintain market share – their profitability is likely to have been affected but, with lower prices, it is hoped that more people will be tempted to go on holiday.

STUDENT ACTIVITY 5.2
performance criterion 6.4.1

pricing strategies – market led pricing

Carry out an investigation into the selling prices of the following products:

- a white medium sliced loaf of bread
- a can of cola drink
- a litre of unleaded petrol
- a 420g tin of baked beans
- a kilo of fruit or vegetables (depending on the season)

task

You are to investigate:

- The selling price of each of the products from two outlets of a similar size, eg two large supermarkets, two corner shops, two large garages, two market stalls.
- A comparison of the price of similar products sold at the same outlet, eg rival brands of cola drinks; for petrol, find two garages close to each other – preferably selling different brands – and compare the prices for unleaded petrol.

What conclusions do you draw about market led pricing?

marginal cost/contribution pricing

pc 6.4.1

In the long term, every business which seeks to make profits, must cover its costs and make a profit from the selling prices of its product. As we have seen earlier in the chapter, traditionally this involves cost-plus pricing techniques which add a percentage to total (absorption) cost. However, it is common to use marginal cost (or contribution pricing) for 'special sales' so as to take up any under-used capacity. (You will remember from the last chapter that the marginal cost is the incremental – or additional – cost of one extra unit.)

contribution

The principle is that, provided a business is already profitable at its current level of output, any additional sales it can make at a price above marginal cost makes a contribution to fixed costs and profits. Contribution is calculated as:

	unit sales price
minus	unit marginal cost
equals	contribution to fixed costs and profit

For a business that is already profitable, the contribution from extra sales will increase profits; for a business that is currently making a loss, the contribution goes towards the fixed costs and, so, will reduce the amount of the loss. Note that selling price must always be above marginal cost, otherwise the business will make a loss on each unit that it sells.

A very good example of marginal cost/contribution pricing is that of an airline which sells tickets at different price levels, eg first class, business class, standard class, etc. The airline might well be profitable if it can sell 60 per cent of its seats at the normal fare. Profits can be increased by selling the remaining 40 per cent of the seats at lower prices. The marginal (additional) cost of an extra passenger is little more than the cost of the in-flight meal, so there is great potential to increase profits by selling sufficient tickets to fill all the seats on the aircraft.

When using marginal cost pricing, the important point is that additional sales must take up under-used capacity. For example, the airline might sell sixty seats at normal fares on an aircraft with a capacity of 100, but would not wish then to sell a further sixty seats at lower prices: it would have to provide an extra plane in order to satisfy the twenty cheap fares 'bumped' from its original flight – an overall loss would be made. The key to increasing the profit from additional sales is to ensure that a contribution to profit is made from the special sales. The Case Study which follows illustrates this principle.

CASE STUDY

pc 6.4.1

Wyvern Bike Company – contribution pricing

situation

The Wyvern Bike Company makes 100 bikes each week. The bikes sell for £100 each. Wyvern's costs are as follows:

weekly costs for producing 100 bikes

	£
direct materials (£20 per bike)	2,000
direct labour (£25 per bike)	2,500
direct expenses (£5 per bike)	500
fixed overheads	3,000
TOTAL COST	8,000

The management of the company has been approached by a mail order warehouse which wishes to buy:

- *either 50 bikes each week at a price of £60*
- *or 100 bikes each week at a price of £40*

The bikes can be produced in addition to existing production, with no increase in overheads. The special order is not expected to affect the company's existing sales. How would you advise the management?

solution

The total (absorption) cost of producing one bike is £80 (£8,000 ÷ 100 bikes). The mail order warehouse is offering either £60 or £40 per bike. On the face of it, with an absorption cost of £80, both orders should be rejected. However, as there will be no increase in the company's fixed overheads, we can use the marginal cost pricing system to help with decision making. The marginal cost per bike is £50 (direct materials £20 per bike, direct labour £25 per bike, direct expenses £5 per bike), and so any contribution, ie selling price less marginal cost, will flow straight into increased profits:

50 bikes at £60 each

Although below absorption cost, the offer price of £60 is above the marginal cost of £50 and increases profit by the amount of the £10 extra contribution, ie (£60 – £50) x 50 bikes = £500 extra profit.

100 bikes at £40 each

This offer price is below absorption cost of £80 and marginal cost of £50; therefore there will be a fall in profit if this order is undertaken of (£40 – £50) x 100 bikes = £1,000 reduced profit.

weekly profit statements

	Existing production of 100 units	*Existing production + 50 units @ £60 each*	*Existing production + 100 units @ £40 each*
	£	£	£
Sales revenue (per week):			
100 bikes at £100 each	10,000	10,000	10,000
50 bikes at £60 each	–	3,000	–
100 bikes at £40 each	–	–	4,000
	10,000	13,000	14,000
Less production costs:			
direct materials (£20 per bike)	2,000	3,000	4,000
direct labour (£25 per bike)	2,500	3,750	5,000
direct expenses(£5 per bike)	500	750	1,000
fixed overheads	3,000	3,000	3,000
PROFIT	2,000	2,500	1,000

The conclusion is that the first order from the mail order warehouse should be undertaken, and the second declined. The general rule is that, once the overheads have been recovered, provided additional units can be sold at a price above marginal cost, then profits will increase.

STUDENT ACTIVITY 5.3
performance criterion 6.4.1

pricing strategies – contribution pricing

Wyvern Airways is a local airline which flies to short-haul destinations within the UK and Europe. The costs of flight WA 005 to Paris, which uses a 100 seater aircraft are as follows:

direct materials	£12.50 per passenger
direct labour	£10.00 per passenger
direct expenses	£2.50 per passenger
fixed overheads	£3,500 per flight

For next week's flight, sixty seats have been sold at a standard-class fare of £100 each.

tasks

1 You are to calculate:

- the total (absorption) cost per seat on this flight with sixty seats sold
- the marginal cost per seat
- the profit or loss if no further tickets are sold for this flight

2 The marketing manager thinks it unlikely that any further standard-class fares will be sold. There are two possibilities that she must consider:

- to release the surplus seats to a firm that sells cheap flights: the airline will receive £45 for each seat sold and, from past experience, the marketing manager expects thirty seats to be sold
- to sell all forty spare seats to a local newspaper, which will offer them as prizes for a 'spot-the-ball' competition: the newspaper will pay £35 per seat

You are to advise the marketing manager whether either of these possibilities should be considered; explain your reasoning, and illustrate your answer with profit statements.

breakeven

pcs 6.4.2 - 3

what is breakeven?

Breakeven is the point at which total sales revenue equals total cost.

In other words breakeven is the point at which the business makes neither a profit nor a loss.

importance of breakeven

For a business, breakeven is a critical point: the business needs to know if a product will generate profit, ie by selling at above breakeven point. Breakeven is also an important part of the Business Plan: a lender will want to know that it will get its money back.

the breakeven chart

We shall be producing a breakeven chart, which will show in a visual form when (or if) a product breaks even. In order to do this we need to know:

- selling price per unit
- product costs
  - variable costs (such as direct materials and direct labour) per unit
  - fixed overhead costs
- limitations, such as the maximum production capacity, or size of the market

what the breakeven chart shows

The breakeven chart shows us:

- the point at which the business breaks even
- the profit or loss of the business over a range of output levels
- the relationship between total cost and sales over a range of output levels
- the relationship between fixed costs and variable costs

Breakeven charts are not used solely by manufacturers: all businesses can use the concept. For example, a shop will wish to know the sales it has to make each week to meet costs; a sports centre will wish to know the ticket sales that have to be made to meet costs.

Now read the Case Study to see how a breakeven chart is prepared.

CASE STUDY

pcs 6.4.2 - 3

Fluffy Toys Limited – breakeven

situation

Fluffy Toys Limited manufactures soft toys, and is able to sell all that can be produced. The maximum factory capacity is 700 toys each month. The variable costs (direct materials and direct labour) for producing each toy are £10 and the selling price is £20 each. The fixed costs of running the business are £5,000 per month. How many toys need to be produced and sold each month for the business to cover its costs, ie to breakeven?

solution

This problem can be solved by means of a breakeven chart which shows in a visual form the relationship between costs and sales, and the amount of profit or loss over a range of output levels. The breakeven chart uses money amounts as the common denominator between fixed costs, variable costs, and sales revenue. The chart appears at the top of the next page.

From the chart we can read off the breakeven point both in terms of units of production, 500 units on the 'x' axis, and in sales value, £10,000 on the 'y' axis.

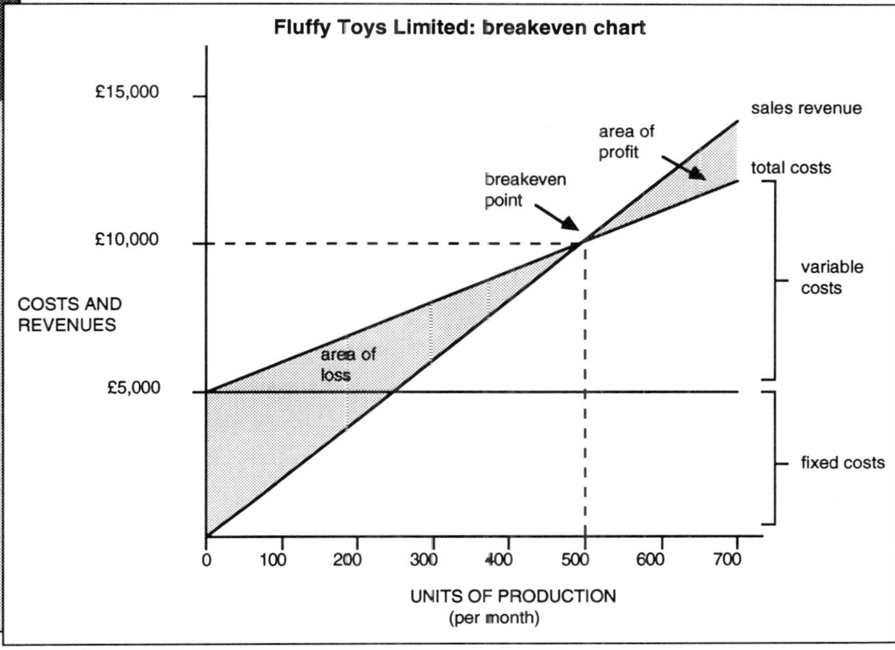

how to draw a breakeven chart

- For best results use graph paper.
- With a breakeven chart, it is usual for the vertical axis (the 'y' axis) to show money amounts; the horizontal axis ('x') shows units of production/sales.
- In a breakeven chart all lines are straight. This means that only two points need be plotted for each line; for example, with sales, choose a number that is fairly near to the maximum expected, multiply by selling price per unit, and this is the point to be marked on the chart. As the sales line always passes through zero, you now have two points along which to draw a straight line for sales revenue.
- The fixed costs are unchanged at all levels of production, in this case they are £5,000. Thus the fixed costs are shown by a horizontal straight line.
- The variable costs commence, on the 'y' axis, from the fixed costs amount, not from 'zero'. This is because the cost of producing zero units is the fixed costs. (A common error is to start the variable costs from the zero point instead of the fixed costs line.)
- The fixed costs and the variable costs form a total costs line.
- The point at which the total costs and sales revenue lines cross is the breakeven point.
- When drawing a breakeven chart it is often difficult to know what total value to show on each axis, ie how many units, and/or how much in costs and revenues? As a guide, look for a maximum production or sales level that will not be exceeded: this will give the 'x' axis. Multiply the maximum sales by the unit selling price to give the maximum sales revenue for the 'y' axis.
- Label the chart fully, as shown above.

analysing the breakeven chart

pc 6.4.4

Using the breakeven chart, we can analyse the business in terms of:

- units of production
- value of sales
- profit or loss at given levels of production and sales
- margin of safety

We will now examine each of these, referring back to the Case Study.

units of production

From the breakeven chart we can read off the 'x' axis the breakeven point in terms of units of production – draw a vertical line from the breakeven point down to the 'x' axis (which shows units of production). In the Case Study, breakeven point is at 500 units of production each month.

value of sales

The breakeven chart also shows the breakeven point in terms of sales value – draw a horizontal line from the breakeven point across to the 'y' axis (which shows money amounts). In the Case Study, the value of monthly sales to breakeven is £10,000: we can double-check this amount by multiplying units of production (500 units) by selling price (£20 per unit).

profit or loss at given levels of production and sales

In analysing a breakeven chart, it is all too easy to concentrate solely on the breakeven point. However, the chart tells us much more than this: it also shows the profit or loss at any level of production/sales contained within the graph. All we have to do is to measure the gap between sales revenue and total costs at a chosen number of units, and read the money amounts off the 'y' axis. For example, at an operating point of 700 units, the profit 'gap' is £2,000 (the difference between sales revenue of £14,000 and total costs of £12,000) – this may be difficult to see on the chart shown on the previous page, but if you were to re-draw it using graph paper, the figures would be clear.

margin of safety

This is the number of units of production by which the selected operating point (eg the planned production or sales level) exceeds the breakeven point. It is calculated as:

	selected operating point (eg planned production or sales level)
minus	breakeven production
equals	margin of safety in units

The margin of safety for Fluffy Toys Limited is labelled on the following breakeven chart, assuming that the selected operating point is a production level of 700 units.

Fluffy Toys Limited: breakeven chart

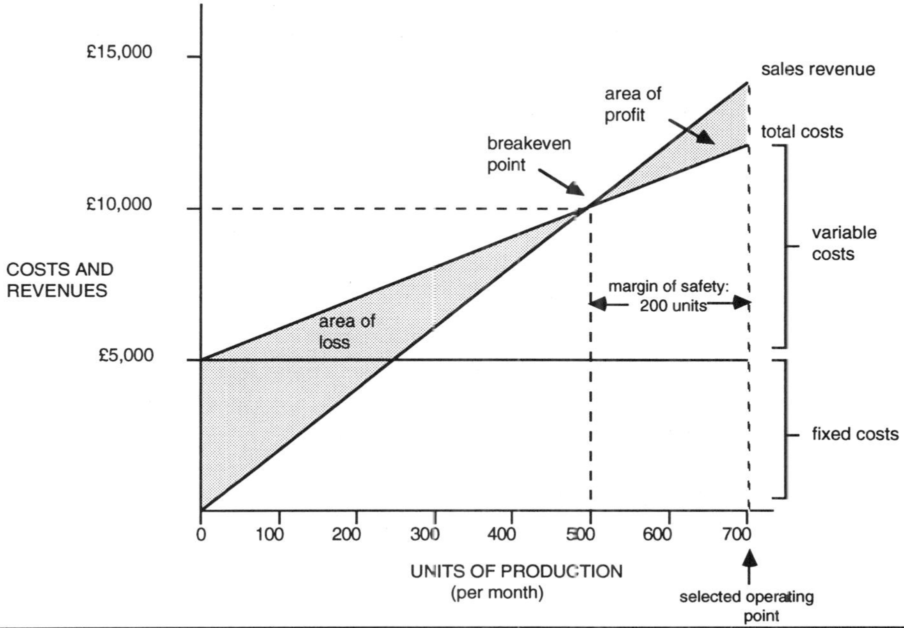

The breakeven chart shows that, at a selected operating point, the margin of safety is 200 units, (ie 700 units, minus 500 units at breakeven). Note that margin of safety can also be expressed in terms of sales value, eg 200 units at a selling price of £20 each equals a margin of safety of £4,000 of sales.

In interpreting margin of safety for Fluffy Toys Limited, we can say that production can fall by 200 units, or sales can fall by £4,000, before the business reaches breakeven point and ceases to make a profit.

limitations of breakeven analysis

pc 6.4.4

The problem of breakeven analysis is that it assumes that the relationship between sales revenue, variable costs and fixed costs, remains the same at all levels of production. This is a rather simplistic view because, for example, in order to increase sales, a business will often need to offer bulk discounts, so reducing the sales revenue per unit at higher levels. The limitations of breakeven analysis can be summarised as follows:

- The assumption is made that all production is sold. There is no point in preparing the cost data, calculating the breakeven point, and estimating the profits to be made if the product will not sell in sufficient quantities.

- Fixed costs do not remain fixed at all levels of production: for example, a decision to double production is likely to increase the fixed costs – an increase in factory rent, for example. Fixed costs are often described as 'stepped costs', because they increase by a large amount all at once and, when plotted on a chart, they take the form of a step, for example:

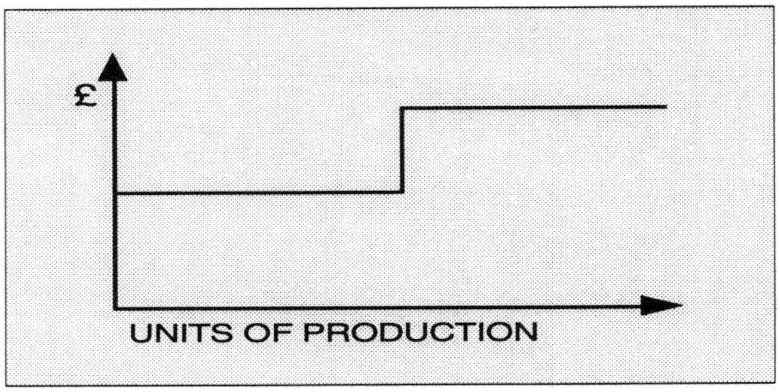

- The profit or loss shown by the chart is probably only true for figures close to current production levels – the further away from current figures, the less accurate will be the profit or loss shown.

reasons for using a breakeven chart

pc 6.4.5

when starting a business

The breakeven point is important in order to see the level of sales that the new business needs in order to cover costs, or make a particular level of profit. The feasibility of achieving the level can then be considered by the owner of the business, and other parties such as the bank manager. A breakeven chart is often included in the Business Plan.

to measure profits and losses

Within the limitations of breakeven analysis (see above), profits and losses can be estimated at varying levels of production and sales. (Remember that this can be done only where the new production is close to current levels and where there is no major change to the structure of costs – ie it is not possible to extrapolate.)

to examine 'what if?' questions

Questions such as 'what if sales fall by 10 per cent?' and 'what if rent increases by 20 per cent?' can be answered – in part at least – by a breakeven chart. The effect on the profitability of the business can be seen, subject to the limitations noted earlier. A question such as 'what if sales increase by 300 per cent' can only be answered by examining the effect on the nature of the fixed and variable costs and then re-calculating the breakeven point.

STUDENT ACTIVITY 5.4
performance criteria 6.4.2 - 5

using breakeven charts

The Last Company is famous for its hill-walking boots. The following cost information is available:

selling price (per pair of boots)	£60
variable costs (per pair)	£40
fixed overheads	£200,000 per year

The company has the factory capacity to manufacture 15,000 pairs of boots each year.

1 Draw and label a breakeven chart (if available to you, use a graphics program on a computer to present the chart).

2 Analyse the breakeven chart by stating:

- the number of pairs of boots that must be sold in order to breakeven
- the value of sales that must be made to breakeven
- the profit or loss if the company decides to make (a) 8,000, (b) 13,000, or (c) 15,000 pairs of boots this year
- the margin of safety, expressed in terms of pairs of boots, if the company plans to make 13,000 pairs of boots this year (show the margin of safety on the breakeven chart)

Note: you are to explain the reasoning and significance for each of the figures stated.

additional activities

3 John Jelks runs a craft workshop which makes reproduction antique clocks. At present production is limited by the capacity of the workshop to 50 clocks each week. The following information is available:

Wholesale selling price per clock	£20
Direct materials per clock	£4
Direct labour per clock	£5
Weekly fixed expenses:	
• rent and rates	£100
• fuel and power	£20
• other costs	£34

(a) Find the weekly break-even point by drawing and labelling a graph.

(b) What would be your profit if you produced 20 clocks a week? 50 clocks a week?

4 A person in business says to you, "Breakeven charts? They are a load of rubbish! In my business we sell just as much as we can – you can forget breakeven!" Write a polite response to the businessperson, explaining the reasons for using breakeven charts.

EVIDENCE COLLECTION ASSIGNMENT 6

pricing decisions and breakeven

Element 6.4

introduction

This assignment tests your understanding of

- pricing and pricing strategies
- the preparation and analysis of breakeven charts

tasks

pc 6.4.1

1 Prepare a short report which:

- explains the basic factors that influence the pricing of goods or services
- takes one particular good or service of your choice, and describes the related pricing strategy for that product

pcs 6.4.2 - 4

2 Graham Wick manufactures cricket bats, and has the following monthly costs:

costs:	selling price (per bat)	£35
	variable costs (per bat)	£20
	fixed overheads	£12,000

The business has the factory capacity to make 1,200 bats each month.

You are to:

- Draw and label a breakeven chart (if available, use a graphics program on a computer to present the chart)
- Analyse the breakeven chart by stating:
  - the number of cricket bats that must be sold in order to breakeven
  - the value of sales that must be made to breakeven
  - the profit or loss if (a) 600 bats, and (b) 1,200 bats are made and sold each month
  - the margin of safety, expressed in terms of cricket bats, if production is currently 1,000 bats per month (show the margin of safety on the breakeven chart)

Note: you are to explain the reasoning and significance for each of the figures stated

pc 6.4.5

3 Choose one of the following situations and explain how a breakeven chart can be used to help with business decisions:

- starting a business
- measuring profits or losses
- examining 'what if?' scenarios

chapter summary and key terms

- The main factors that determine the selling price of a product are: the need to make a profit, the prices of competing products and the availability of any under-used capacity

- The main pricing strategies, which relate to the above factors are:
  - cost-plus pricing (need to make a profit)
  - market led pricing (prices of competing products)
  - marginal cost/contribution pricing (under-used capacity)

- A breakeven chart shows:
  - the point at which the business breaks even
  - the profit or loss over a range of output levels
  - the relationship between total cost and sales over a range of output levels
  - the relationship between fixed costs and variable costs

- From the breakeven chart, we can analyse the business in terms of units of production, the value of sales, the profit or loss at given levels of production and sales, the margin of safety.

key terms

price	the amount of money that is agreed between a buyer and a seller which enables the exchange of a product to take place
cost-plus pricing	cost price *plus* profit = selling price (note that profit can be calculated as either a percentage mark-up on cost price, or to give a percentage return on capital employed)
market led pricing	selling prices are largely determined by what others charge for the same product
contribution	unit sales price *minus* unit marginal cost = contribution per unit towards fixed costs and profit
marginal cost/contribution	where a product is sold at a price which is above marginal cost, but below absorption cost; it is used for pricing 'special sales' which take up under-used capacity
breakeven	where total sales revenue equals total cost
margin of safety	the amount of production by which the selected operating point exceeds the breakeven point; (expressed either in units or as a sales value)

multiple-choice questions

1 Cost-plus pricing is used to calculate:

A the absorption cost

B the contribution

C the marginal cost

D the selling price

2 Decide whether each of these statements is True (T) or False (F).

(i) selling at a price above marginal cost can be done to utilise under-used capacity

(ii) cost-plus pricing is used when the selling price is set close to that charged by competitors

A	(i)	T	(ii)	T
B	(i)	T	(ii)	F
C	(i)	F	(ii)	T
D	(i)	F	(ii)	F

3 Which of the following is not used in a breakeven chart?

A fixed costs

B capital employed

C sales revenue

D variable costs

Questions 4–6 relate to the following information:

A breakeven point 150 units; sales 125 units

B breakeven point 300 units; sales 400 units

C breakeven point 500 units; sales 500 units

Which of the above applies to the following?

4 A business which makes a profit

5 A business which breaks even

6 A business which makes a loss

SECTION 2

GNVQ UNIT 7
FINANCIAL FORECASTING AND MONITORING

introduction to content

This section explains how a business sets out its actual and expected financial performance in the form of financial statements. These are either forecasts (looking ahead) or final accounts (looking back over the year). This section also shows how performance can be assessed by various interested parties by analysing the financial statements. The first chapter looks at business accounting systems (where the figures come from), the second examines financial statements (how the figures are presented). Chapters then follow on sources of finance for business, financial forecasting and the monitoring of business performance.

It should be stressed that although you are investigating accounting systems, you do not have to carry out book-keeping procedures. Where possible you should investigate computer accounting systems. The main aim of the Unit is to train you to interpret and analyse financial data.

assignments

As in the last Unit, the Assignments here are self-contained and provide you with the figures you need. They are:

6 Business accounting systems

GNVQ SPECIFICATIONS
Element 7.3
Produce and explain profit and loss statements and balance sheets
performance criteria – a student must

1 explain a basic accounting system suitable for a small business
2 identify and explain accounting periods
3 extract a trial balance from given accounting records

Note: performance criteria 4 to 6 of this Element, covering the preparation and purposes of financial statements, are dealt with in the next chapter.

what this chapter covers

This chapter looks at the accounting systems used by small businesses to record financial transactions. We shall see the structure of the accounting system, and the place of financial statements, which are prepared at regular intervals. Finally we will see how a trial balance is prepared from the records in order to check the arithmetical accuracy of the accounting system.

what you will learn from this chapter

- an understanding of the type of accounting system used by a small business – based on both handwritten and computer methods
- the way in which a business uses accounting periods in order to review its progress, and the reasons for producing accounting information more frequently than once a year
- how to prepare a trial balance from the accounting records as a method of checking the arithmetical accuracy of the accounting records

the accounting system

pc 7.3.1

The accounting system for a business is the process of recording information from documents (such as invoices and receipts) into the accounting records, checking that the information has been recorded correctly, and then presenting the information in a way which enables the owners and managers of the business to review progress. It can be summarised as follows:

documents
processing of documents relating to purchases, sales, payments and receipts

↓

accounting records
recording financial transactions in the accounting system using the double-entry book-keeping system

↓

trial balance
the extraction of figures from all the double-entry accounts to check their arithmetical accuracy in the form of a list, known as the trial balance

↓

financial statements
production from the double-entry accounts of:
- profit and loss statement
- balance sheet

collectively known as the 'final accounts'

Most businesses use an accounting system based on the *double-entry book-keeping system*, whereby each financial transaction is recorded in the ledgers *twice*. Some small businesses will use a *single-entry system*, whereby each transaction is entered *once* only in a cash book, which records receipts and payments of money.

Accounting records are usually kept in one of two forms:

- handwritten records
- computer records

written accounting records

This is the traditional form of keeping 'the books', particularly for the smaller business. The main record is the ledger which, many years ago, would be a large leather-bound volume, neatly ruled, into which the book-keeper would enter each business transaction in immaculate handwriting into individual accounts. In modern times, the handwritten ledger is still used, and stationery shops sell ledgers and other accounting books, designed especially for the smaller business.

computer accounting records

Nowadays, computers have come down in price so much that they can be afforded by most businesses. With computer accounting programs, such as Sage™, business transactions are input into the computer and stored on disk. The major advantage of computer accounting is that it is a very accurate method of recording business transactions; the disadvantage is that it may be cumbersome and time-consuming to set up, particularly for the smaller business. Interestingly, the word 'ledger' has survived into the computer age but, instead of being a bound volume, it is represented by data files held on a computer disk.

While the GNVQ Advanced course does not require you to study book-keeping (the mechanics of the accounting system), it does require you to understand what is involved, where the figures come from and what they mean. We will now go on to examine how it fits into the acounting system.

double-entry book-keeping

Double-entry book-keeping involves making two entries in the accounts for each transaction: for instance, if you sell some goods and receive a cheque, you will make an entry in the *sales account* to record the sale, and an entry in the *bank account* to record the receipt of a cheque.

If you are operating a manual accounting system you will make the two entries by hand, if you are operating a computer accounting system you will make one entry on the keyboard, but indicate to the machine where the other entry is to be made, by means of a numerical code.

accounts

The sources for the entries you make are the financial documents. The ledger into which you make the entries is normally a bound book (in a non-computerised system) divided into separate accounts, eg a separate account for sales, purchases, each type of business expense, each customer, each supplier, and so on. Each account is given a specific name, and a number for reference purposes.

In a computer system, the accounts are held as data files on a disk, and each account becomes a computer record with its own reference number.

the different ledgers

Because of the large number of accounts involved, 'the ledger' is divided into a number of *different* ledgers:

- ***sales ledger*** – records of sales made to customers, and payments received at a later date, ie each record shows the amount owed by a particular customer (debtor)
- ***purchases ledger*** – records of purchases from suppliers, and payments made at a later date, ie each record shows the amount owed to a particular supplier (creditor)
- ***cash book*** – a record of cash and bank transactions (a cash book is the main accounting record for the single-entry system mentioned earlier)
- ***general (or nominal) ledger*** – a record of all other transactions of the business, such as assets (things owned), expenses (the overheads of the business, eg wages, rent paid), drawings (the amount taken out of the business by the owner), loans to the business (eg by a bank), and the owner's capital (the amount invested in the business by the owner)

The same division of the ledger is seen in computer accounting programs.

trial balance

Double-entry book-keeping, because it involves making two entries for each transaction, is open to error. What if the book-keeper writes £45 in one account and £54 in another? The trial balance – explained in more detail later in this chapter – effectively checks the entries made over a given period of time and will pick up most errors. The trial balance sets out the *balances* of all the double-entry accounts, ie the totals of the accounts for a certain period. As well as being an arithmetic check, it is used to help in the preparation of *financial statements* – the *final accounts* of the business.

financial statements/final accounts

The final accounts of a business comprise the profit and loss statement and the balance sheet.

what the profit and loss statement shows

revenue	*minus*	expenses	*equals*	profit

The profit and loss statement of a business shows the revenue, or income, a business has received over a given period for goods sold or services provided. It also sets out the expenses incurred – the cost of producing the product, and the overheads (eg wages, administration, rent, and so on). The difference between revenue and expenses is the profit of the business. If expenses are greater than revenue, then a loss has been made. The profit (or loss) belongs to the owner(s) of the business. The figures for sales, purchases, and expenses are taken from the double-entry system. The format of a profit and loss statement (often called a profit and loss account) is explained in detail in the next chapter.

what the balance sheet shows

assets what a business owns	*minus*	liabilities what a business owes	*equals*	capital how a business has been financed

The balance sheet of a business gives a 'snapshot' of the business at a particular date – eg the end of the accounting period of the business. It is prepared from the accounting records and shows:

assets what the business owns – eg premises, vehicles, computers, stock of goods for resale, debtors (money owed by customers), money in the bank

liabilities what the business owes – eg bank loans, creditors (money owed to suppliers)

capital where the money to finance the business has come from – eg the owner(s), including from profits made by the business

The format of a balance sheet is explained in detail in the next chapter.

STUDENT ACTIVITY 6.1
performance criterion 7.3.1

explaining accounting systems

task

You are taking part in a presentation to a group of people who are considering setting up in business on their own. Your part of the presentation involves explaining the accounting system to them and, in particular, the type of accounting records they should keep, both manual and computer-based.

(a) Investigate a basic accounting system suitable for a small business in terms of the documents encountered, the accounting records kept, the use of the trial balance, what the financial statements show.

(b) Prepare briefing notes (on a word processor) suitable as a handout for a talk. Do not go into too much detail, but try to make your layout as clear as possible, using bold headings and bullet points.

(c) Prepare a visual aid, such as an overhead projector slide, to illustrate the presentation.

accounting periods

pc 7.3.2

As we have seen earlier in this chapter, the accounting system records day-to-day transactions, and then uses the information, at regular intervals, to prepare the financial statements of profit and loss statement and balance sheet.

The two statements are linked in that a profit and loss statement covers a time period, while a balance sheet shows the state of the business on the last day of the time period, for example:

- profit and loss statement for the year ended 31 December 1995
- balance sheet as at 31 December 1995

The particular time period covered by the profit and loss statement is known as the *accounting period*. Generally, for each individual business, accounting periods cover the same length of time, for example the year-ended 31 December 1995, year-ended 31 December 1996, and so on. As you will see with this example, the last day of one accounting period is immediately followed by the first day of the next accounting period. While accounting periods can cover any length of time, the most common are monthly, quarterly (three monthly), half-yearly, and annually.

monthly and quarterly accounting periods

Many businesses monitor their progress on a monthly and/or quarterly basis. Thus, at the end of each month, or quarter, they will produce a profit and loss account and balance sheet. These statements are then used within the business to assess the level of activity and profitability in the accounting period, and the state of the company – in terms of assets and liabilities – at the end of the period. Such monthly and quarterly financial statements are often used in conjunction with a budgeting system, where targets are set for key activities of the business – eg sales, purchases, expenses – often up to twelve months ahead: the budget figures are then compared with what actually happened and, if necessary, corrective action can be taken for the next accounting period. Note that the monthly or quarterly accounts will be included in total figures for the business' financial year: see annual accounting periods, below.

With computer accounting programs, it is a simple task to print out the profit and loss statement and balance sheet at the end of each month or quarter.

half-yearly accounting periods

Most large public limited companies send information to their shareholders and financial analysts in the form of half-yearly results. These give some information on the company's progress during the first half of the financial year; however, the amount of detail supplied is considerably less than that contained in the formal 'annual report and accounts' – also, the information has not been verified by the auditors (outside accountants who check the figures on behalf of the shareholders).

annual accounting periods

Virtually every business – from sole traders through to the largest multi-national corporations, and government – produces annual accounts. There is, historically, no particular reason for choosing once a year to report results, except that it represents a reasonable time period over which to monitor progress.

There is no requirement for final accounts to end on a particular day in each year, although 31 December is a popular financial year-end for limited companies. Many sole traders and partnerships choose the year-end date of 31 March because the tax year ends on 5 April. The financial year-end does not have to fit with the end of a month. The accounts of Sainsbury's, the supermarket chain, for example, cover the accounting period to 11 March 1995.

The annual financial statements of limited companies are sent to the shareholders and a copy has to be filed with Companies House (where it is available for inspection). Most large companies will also send out a copy of their accounts to anybody who requests one. You should note that some public limited companies also issue an annual summary financial statement which gives less information than the full annual accounts.

STUDENT ACTIVITY 6.2
performance criterion 7.3.2

explaining accounting periods

task

Find out the length of the accounting period and the financial year-end date for:

- two limited companies
- one sole trader
- one partnership

Give the names of the businesses and the dates used.

Prepare on a word processor a short written summary addressed to a group of people about to set up in business. It should explain the more common accounting periods and the reasons for their use. Recommend some year-end dates (including a date for a sole trader).

the trial balance

pc 7.3.3

A trial balance is a list of balances on all accounts in an accounting system.

The trial balance of a sole trader, for example, includes the amounts:

- owing to creditors (people to whom the business owes money)
- owing by debtors (people who owe the business money)
- sales
- purchases
- money – both in the form of cash and the bank balance
- expenses
- drawings (amounts taken out of the business by the owner for his/her own use)
- fixed assets (long-term items owned by the business, such as premises and machinery)
- owner's capital (the amount invested by the owner in the business)
- loans (to the business by banks and other lenders)
- stock (of goods held for resale, eg by a shop, at the start of the financial year)

A trial balance lists the *balance of each account* in order to check the arithmetical accuracy of the accounting system.

balances of accounts

The trial balance uses the *balance* from each account in the accounting system; by the balance of the account we mean the *total* of the account to date. Many types of accounts show the balance after each transaction:

- a bank statement, or building society statement and passbook are examples with which you will be familiar
- a statement of account sent by a business to its customers

You should note certain accounts in a double-entry accounting system usually have debit balances, while others usually have credit balances.

debit balances

These represent assets, and expenses; they include:

- cash account
- purchases account
- fixed asset accounts, eg premises, machinery
- expenses accounts

- drawings account (which records the amount of money taken out of the business by the owner for his/her own use)
- debtors' accounts (for the purposes of a trial balance, the balances of individual debtors' accounts are totalled, and the total is entered in the trial balance as 'debtors')
- stock (of goods held for resale)

credit balances

These represent liabilities, and revenue (income); they include:

- sales account
- capital account (which records the amount invested in the business by the owner)
- loans (to the business by banks and other lenders)
- creditors' accounts (a total is entered in the trial balance, rather than the individual balances of each account)

Note: bank account can be either debit or credit – it will be debit when the business has money in the bank (an asset), and credit when it is overdrawn (a liability).

example of a sole trader's trial balance

Trial balance of Jane Smith as at 31 December 1995

	Debit	*Credit*
Name of account	£	£
Stock at 1 January 1995	12,500	
Purchases	105,000	
Sales		155,000
Administration	6,200	
Wages	20,500	
Rent paid	3,750	
Telephone	500	
Interest paid	4,500	
Travel expenses	550	
Premises	100,000	
Machinery	20,000	
Debtors	15,500	
Bank	450	
Cash	50	
Capital		75,000
Drawings	7,000	
Loan from bank		50,000
Creditors		16,500
	296,500	296,500

notes on the trial balance

- The debit and credit columns have been totalled and are the same amount. Thus the trial balance proves that the accounts are arithmetically correct, ie debit balances equal credit balances. (A trial balance does not prove the *complete* accuracy of the accounting records.)
- The heading for a trial balance gives the name of the business whose accounts have been listed and the date to which it relates.
- A trial balance is prepared at regular intervals – often at the end of each month. The reason for this is that, if an error is found, there will be, at most, one month's book-keeping entries to check back.
- The figure for debtors has been shown as a total amount, £15,500, rather than showing the individual amounts owing by each debtor. This is quite usual and is done in order to cut down on the number of balances listed in the trial balance. The figure for creditors is shown in a similar way.

extracting a trial balance

With a computer accounting program it is easy to print out a trial balance: just go to the menu that deals with the trial balance and select 'print'.

For a handwritten accounting system, the procedure to extract (prepare) a trial balance is as follows:

- Obtain from the book-keeper a list of the balances of all the accounts in the ledger.
- Head up a page, or a computer spreadsheet, with "Trial balance of (name of business) as at (date to which the trial balance relates)".
- On the page or computer spreadsheet, prepare two money columns on the right-hand side: mark the first column 'debit', and the second 'credit'.
- Taking each account in turn, enter the name of the account on the left-hand side and enter its balance in either the debit or credit column.
- When all the accounts have been listed, total – or set the spreadsheet up so that it totals – both the debit and credit columns. They should come to the same amount, ie the total of debit balances equals the total of credit balances.
- The resultant trial balance should look similar to that shown on the previous page.

The trial balance proves the arithmetical accuracy of the accounting data; however, it does not prove complete accuracy – for example, an item could have been recorded on the correct side, ie debit or credit, but in the wrong account. Errors like this normally surface in time: for instance, a customer (debtor) may be charged for goods sold to someone else; the customer will soon let the business know!

if the trial balance doesn't balance ...

If the trial balance fails to balance, ie the two totals are different, there is an error (or errors):

- either in the addition of the trial balance
- and/or in the double-entry book-keeping

It will be the job of the book-keeper or accounts clerk to find the error (or errors).

single column trial balance

The trial balance, as we have seen, lists the balances of accounts in two columns: debit and credit. An alternative method of listing account balances is in the form of a single column trial balance. Here, all the balances are listed in one column, with debit balances being added, and credit balances being shown in brackets and deducted. Proof that the trial balance 'balances' is given by the fact that the 'total' is zero; this gives rise to the name zero sum trial balance. It should be noted that the two column trial balance is the more common format, and is generally favoured by practising accountants. The following example of a single column trial balance uses the same figures extracted for the conventional trial balance seen earlier:

Trial balance of Jane Smith as at 31 December 1995

Name of account	£
Stock at 1 January 1995	12,500
Purchases	105,000
Sales	(155,000)
Administration	6,200
Wages	20,500
Rent	3,750
Telephone	500
Interest paid	4,500
Travel expenses	550
Premises	100,000
Machinery	20,000
Debtors	15,500
Bank	450
Cash	50
Capital	(75,000)
Drawings	7,000
Loan from bank	(50,000)
Creditors	(16,500)
	zero

notes:

- Debit balances are added.
- Credit balances are shown in brackets and deducted.
- The trial balance 'balances' when the 'total' is zero.

importance of the trial balance

A business will extract a trial balance on a regular basis in order to:

- check the arithmetical accuracy of the book-keeping
- enable the preparation of the financial statements: profit and loss statement and balance sheet

Now carry out the Student Activity which follows in order to give you practice in extracting a trial balance.

STUDENT ACTIVITY 6.3
performance criterion 7.3.3

extracting a trial balance

The book-keeper of Lorna Fox has extracted the following list of balances as at 31 March 1995:

	£
Stock at 1 April 1994	8,500
Purchases	96,250
Sales	146,390
Administration	10,240
Wages	28,980
Rent paid	1,340
Telephone	1,680
Interest paid	2,350
Travel expenses	1,045
Premises	125,000
Machinery	40,000
Debtors	10,390
Bank overdraft	1,050
Cash	150
Creditors	12,495
Loan from bank	20,000
Drawings	9,450
Capital	155,440

tasks

(Note: a spreadsheet could be used for tasks 1 and 2).

1. Produce a trial balance with columns for *debit and credit* balances.
2. Produce a *single* column trial balance.
3. Take any three debit balances and any three credit balances and explain to someone who does not understand accounting records why they are listed as such, and what this means to the business.

chapter summary and key terms

- The basic accounting system of a small business can be manual or computer-based; it involves a sequence of processing documents, using accounting records, extracting a trial balance and the production of financial statements: profit and loss statement and balance sheet.

- Whilst accounting records are kept up-to-date on a day-to-day basis, accounting periods of time are used for production of financial statements and monitoring the business. Common accounting periods are monthly, quarterly, half-yearly, and annually.

- A trial balance lists the balances of every account and is extracted at regular intervals in order to check the arithmetical accuracy of the accounting records. A trial balance can be presented with columns for debit and credit balances, or in single column form with debit balances added and credit balances deducted. Both forms of trial balance show that the sum of debit balances and credit balances is zero (because total debits = total credits)

- The trial balance is also used to enable the preparation of the financial statements: profit and loss statement, and balance sheet.

key terms

double-entry book-keeping	the method by which accounting records are kept – it involves making two entries in the accounts for each financial transaction
ledger	the accounting records as whole, often divided into four sections: sales ledger, purchases ledger, cash book, general (or nominal) ledger
accounts	individual records of transactions contained within the ledger, eg an account in the name of each debtor, creditor
financial statements	the final accounts: profit and loss statement, and balance sheet
accounting period	time period covered by financial statements – monthly, quarterly, half-yearly, annually
trial balance	a list of balances on all accounts in an accounting system; a trial balance can be presented in double column or single column form

multiple-choice questions

1 In an accounting system which of the following represents the most logical sequence of events?

A financial statements, trial balance, accounting records, documents

B accounting records, documents, trial balance, financial statements

C documents, accounting records, trial balance, financial statements

D documents, accounting records, financial statements, trial balance

2 Decide whether each of these statements is True (T) or False (F).

(i) in a trial balance the bank account could be in either the debit or credit column

(ii) the single-entry system records each financial transaction in the ledgers twice

A	(i)	T	(ii)	T
B	(i)	T	(ii)	F
C	(i)	F	(ii)	T
D	(i)	F	(ii)	F

3 In a trial balance which of the following accounts normally has a debit balance?

A loan

B bank overdraft

C sales

D purchases

4 In a trial balance which of the following accounts normally has a credit balance?

A drawings

B capital

C cash

D premises

The following ledgers relate to questions 5 and 6

A purchases ledger

B nominal ledger

C cash book

D sales ledger

5 In which of the above will debtors accounts be recorded?

6 In which of the above will the bank account be recorded?

7 Financial statements

GNVQ SPECIFICATIONS

Element 7.3

Produce and explain profit and loss statements and balance sheets

performance criteria – a student must

4 identify each account on the trial balance correctly in relation to profit and loss or balance sheet items

5 produce and explain profit and loss and balance sheet in vertical form from the trial balance figures

6 explain the purposes of balance sheets and profit and loss statements

Note: performance criteria 1 to 3 of this Element have been covered in the previous chapter.

what this chapter covers

This chapter links with the previous one by starting off with the trial balance. We will use the figures shown on the trial balance to enable us to prepare the financial statements of a business: profit and loss statement, and balance sheet. We shall also see why these statements are prepared, and the purposes for which they are used.

what you will learn from this chapter

- how to relate each figure shown on the trial balance to either profit and loss statement or balance sheet
- a definition of a profit and loss statement, together with its structure and layout
- a definition of a balance sheet, together with its structure and layout
- how to prepare financial statements from a trial balance
- the purposes of the financial statements, including their part in enabling owners and managers to monitor performance, and their role in raising finance for the business

the trial balance and its link with final accounts

pc 7.3.4

As we have seen in the previous chapter, the trial balance is prepared from a list of the balances on all accounts in the ledger. We have looked already at how the trial balance proves the arithmetical accuracy of the accounting data. We will now see how the trial balance provides the data for the preparation of financial statements: profit and loss statement and balance sheet.

Shown below is the trial balance seen in the last chapter.

Trial balance of Jane Smith as at 31 December 1995

	Debit	*Credit*
Name of account	£	£
Stock at 1 January 1995	12,500	
Purchases	105,000	
Sales		155,000
Administration	6,200	
Wages	20,500	
Rent paid	3,750	
Telephone	500	
Interest paid	4,500	
Travel expenses	550	
Premises	100,000	
Machinery	20,000	
Debtors	15,500	
Bank	450	
Cash	50	
Capital		75,000
Drawings	7,000	
Loan from bank		50,000
Creditors		16,500
	296,500	296,500

Note: stock at 31 December 1995 was valued at £10,500

In order to prepare the financial statements of a business using a trial balance, we need to identify the assets and liabilities, and the expenses and revenue amounts. These are shown in the trial balance as either *debit* or *credit* balances.

debit balances

These comprise *assets* of the business (items owned), and *expenses* representing the total of purchases made and the cost of overheads for the year. Thus the debit money column indicates that this business has made purchases of goods at a cost of £105,000 during the year, while wages is an overhead, a cost to the business of £20,500. The balances for premises, machinery, stock, debtors, cash and bank indicate, in money terms, an asset of the business. The debtors' figure includes the individual balances of all the firm's debtors, ie those customers who owe money to the firm.

credit balances

These comprise *liabilities* of the business (items owed), and revenue (income) amounts, including the total of sales made. For example, the sales figure shows the total amount of goods that has been sold by the business during the year. The figures for owner's capital, loan from the bank and the creditors shows the amount of the liability at the trial balance date. The creditors figure includes all the individual balances of the business' creditors, ie those suppliers to whom the business owes money.

treatment of stock

Stock means the materials and items which the business holds which it intends to sell. Stock obviously has a money value for the business.The question is, how is it recorded in the accounting records? You will see that the trial balance debit column includes an item for the stock value at the *start* of the year, while the end-of-year valuation is noted *after* the trial balance. For the purposes of financial statements, the stock of goods is valued by the business (and often verified by the auditor) *at the end of each financial year.* The year-end stock value is noted *at the end of the trial balance* because it does not, at this stage, form part of the accounting records – it is just stock that has been counted and valued. The valuation is entered into the accounting system when the final accounts are prepared.

the trial balance and final accounts

We can now indicate against each figure from the trial balance, in a column to the right, which financial statement it will appear in:

- expenses and revenue appear in the profit and loss statement (abbreviated to 'P&L')
- assets and liabilities appear in the balance sheet (abbreviated to 'BS')

If this routine is carried out with the trial balance of Jane Smith, it will then appear as follows:

Trial balance of Jane Smith as at 31 December 1995

Name of account	*Debit* £	*Credit* £	
Stock at 1 January 1995	12,500		P&L
Purchases	105,000		P&L
Sales		155,000	P&L
Administration	6,200		P&L
Wages	20,500		P&L
Rent paid	3,750		P&L
Telephone	500		P&L
Interest paid	4,500		P&L
Travel expenses	550		P&L
Premises	100,000		BS
Machinery	20,000		BS
Debtors	15,500		BS
Bank	450		BS
Cash	50		BS
Capital		75,000	BS
Drawings	7,000		BS
Loan from bank		50,000	BS
Creditors		16,500	BS
	296,500	296,500	

Stock at 31 December 1995 was valued at £10,500 P&L *and* BS

Note: P&L = profit and loss account; BS = balance sheet

a note on the stock figures

It is only the stock *at the end of the year* (the closing stock) that is shown as an asset in the balance sheet.

As you will see in the next section, we use the value of the stock at the start of the year (the opening stock) from the trial balance, and the closing stock to help us calculate a figure called *cost of sales*, which is used in the profit and loss statement.

Thus the closing stock at the end of a year appears *twice* in the financial statements – firstly in the profit and loss account, and secondly in the balance sheet.

STUDENT ACTIVITY 7.1
performance criterion 7.3.4

linking the trial balance to financial statements

The following trial balance has been extracted from the accounting records of Nick Johnson at 31 December 1995:

Trial balance of Nick Johnson as at 31 December 1995

Name of account	*Debit* £	*Credit* £
Stock at 1 January 1995	25,000	
Purchases	210,000	
Sales		310,000
Administration	12,400	
Wages	47,000	
Rent paid	1,500	
Telephone	1,000	
Interest paid	9,000	
Travel expenses	1,100	
Premises	200,000	
Machinery	40,000	
Debtors	31,000	
Bank	900	
Cash	100	
Capital		150,000
Drawings	14,000	
Loan from bank		100,000
Creditors		33,000
	593,000	593,000

note: Stock at 31 December 1995 was valued at £21,000

task

Mark against each figure from the trial balance (and also closing stock) the financial statement – profit and loss statement, balance sheet – in which it will appear.

Note: we shall by using this information in the next Student Activity to construct the final accounts of Nick Johnson.

profit and loss statement

pc 7.3.5

A profit and loss statement is a financial statement which summarises the revenue and expenses of a business for an accounting period and shows the overall profit or loss.

The profit and loss statement (or, to give it a slightly more formal title, the 'profit and loss account') uses information from the accounting records as shown by the trial balance:

- the sales (or turnover) of the business
- the purchases made by the business
- the overheads of running the business, such as administration, wages, rent paid, telephone, interest paid, travel expenses

The amount of sales is the *revenue* of the business, while the amounts of purchases and overheads are the *expenses* of the business.

layout of a profit and loss statement

In broad terms, the profit and loss account consists of a calculation

REVENUE LESS EXPENSES = PROFIT OR LOSS

If revenue is greater than expenses, then the business has made a profit; if expenses are greater than revenue, then a loss has been made.

Profit and loss statement
of Jane Smith for the year ended 31 December 1995

	£	£
Sales		155,000
Opening stock (1 January 1995)	12,500	
Purchases	105,000	
	117,500	
Less Closing stock (31 December 1995)	10,500	
Cost of Sales		107,000
Gross profit		48,000
Less overheads:		
Administration	6,200	
Wages	20,500	
Rent paid	3,750	
Telephone	500	
Interest paid	4,500	
Travel expenses	550	
		36,000
Net profit		12,000

notes to the profit and loss statement on the previous page

- The statement is presented in a *vertical* format, ie it runs down the page. Two columns are used for money amounts: the right-hand column contains sub-totals and totals, while the left-hand column is used for listing individual amounts, eg of overheads, which are then totalled and carried to the right-hand column.
- *Cost of Sales* represents the cost to the business of the goods which *have been sold* in this financial year. Cost of sales is:

opening stock	(stock bought previously)
+ purchases	(purchased during the year)
– closing stock	(stock left unsold at the end of the year)
= cost of sales	(cost of what has actually been sold)

- The amounts for sales and purchases include only items in which the business trades – eg a shoe shop buying shoes from the manufacturer includes the amount in its purchases figure; when the shoes are sold the amount is recorded as sales. By contrast, items bought for use in the business, such as a new till for the shop, are not included with purchases but are shown as assets on the other final account, the balance sheet.
- As this is a trading business which buys and sells goods, the statement shows two levels of profit: *gross* profit and *net* profit. (Note that a service sector business, such as a secretarial agency, or an accountancy firm, will show only a net profit or loss, because it does not buy and sell goods but provides a service).
- Gross profit is calculated as:

  sales – cost of sales = gross profit

  If cost of sales is greater than sales, the business has made a *gross loss.*
- Net profit is calculated as:

  gross profit – overheads = net profit

  If overheads are more than gross profit, the business has made a *net loss.*
- The overheads are the running costs of the business, for example administration, wages, rent paid, telephone, interest paid, travel expenses.
- The *net profit* is the amount the business earned for the owner(s) during the year, and is subject to taxation. The owner(s) can draw some or all of the net profit for personal use – the accounting term for this is *drawings.* However, it might be that part of the profit will be left in the business in order to help build up the business for the future.
- The example profit and loss statement shown here is for a sole trader, ie one person in business. For other business units, such as partnerships and limited companies, the profit and loss statement will show how the net profit is shared amongst the owners of the business – an agreed share of profits to each partner, dividends to shareholders.

balance sheet

pc 7.3.5

A balance sheet is a financial statement which shows the assets, liabilities and capital of a business at a particular date.

As we saw in the last chapter, balance sheets are different from profit and loss statements which show profits for a time period such as a year; by contrast balance sheets show the state of the business at one moment in time – things could be somewhat different tomorrow; in fact a balance sheet is often described as a 'snapshot' of a business at one moment in time.

The balance sheet lists:

- the *assets* (amounts owned by the business), such as premises, vehicles, stock for resale, debtors (amounts owed by customers), cash, bank (if not an overdraft)
- the *liabilities* (amounts owed by the business), such as creditors (amounts owed by the business to suppliers), bank overdraft and loans
- the *capital*, the amount of the owner's finance put into the business

The money amounts of the assets, liabilities, and capital are taken from the accounting records of the business.

layout of the balance sheet

the balance sheet shows the value of the assets used by the business to make profits and how they have been financed. This concept may be expressed as follows:

ASSETS MINUS LIABILITIES = CAPITAL

Thus the balance sheet shows the asset strength of the business, in contrast to the profit and loss statement, which shows the profits from the trading activities.

A more detailed example of a balance sheet, using the figures from Jane Smith's trial balance (page 135) is shown on the next page. Note that it is presented in a vertical format, and assets and liabilities are listed under the headings of fixed assets, current assets, current liabilities, long-term liabilities, and capital: these terms are explained in detail after the balance sheet.

Balance sheet of Jane Smith as at 31 December 1995

	£	£
Fixed assets		
Premises		100,000
Machinery		20,000
		120,000
Current assets		
Stock	10,500	
Debtors	15,500	
Bank	450	
Cash	50	
	26,500	
Less Current liabilities		
Creditors	16,500	
Working capital		10,000
		130,000
Less Long-term liabilities		
Loan from bank		50,000
NET ASSETS		80,000
FINANCED BY		
Capital		
Opening capital		75,000
Add net profit		12,000
		87,000
Less drawings		7,000
		80,000

We will now explain each of the main headings, starting from the top of the balance sheet:

fixed assets

These comprise the long-term items *owned* by a business which are not bought with the intention of selling off in the near future, eg premises, machinery, motor vehicles, office equipment, fixtures and fittings, etc. When a business buys new fixed assets, such expenditure is called *capital expenditure* (in contrast to *revenue expenditure* which is the cost of the business' overheads shown in the profit and loss statement).

current assets

These comprise short-term assets which change regularly, eg stocks of goods for resale, debtors (amounts owed to the business by customers), bank balances and cash. These items will alter as the business trades, eg stocks will be sold, or more will be bought; debtors will make payment to the business, or sales on credit will be made; the cash and bank balances will alter with the flow of money paid into the bank account, or as withdrawals are made.

By tradition, fixed and current assets are listed starting with the most permanent, ie premises, and working through to the most liquid, ie nearest to cash: either cash itself, or the balance at the bank.

current liabilities

These are liabilities (items owed) which are due for repayment *within twelve months* of the date of the balance sheet, eg creditors (amounts owed by the business to suppliers), and bank overdraft (which is technically repayable on demand, unlike a bank loan which is negotiated for a particular time period).

working capital

This is the excess of current assets over current liabilities, ie *current assets minus current liabilities = working capital.* Without adequate working capital, a business will find it difficult to continue to operate.

long-term liabilities

These liabilities are where repayment is due in *more than one year* from the date of the balance sheet; they are often described as 'bank loan', 'long-term loan', or 'mortgage'.

net assets

This section shows the net amount of assets used by the business, ie fixed and current assets, less current and long-term liabilities. The net assets are financed by the owner(s) of the business, in the form of capital. The total of the net assets therefore equals the total of the 'financed by' section – the balance sheet 'balances'.

capital

Capital is the owner's investment, and is a liability of a business, ie it is *what the business owes the owner.* It is important to realise that the assets and liabilities of a business are treated separately from the personal assets and liabilities of the owner of the business. For example, if a group of people decided to set up in business they would each agree to put in a certain amount of capital to start the business. As individuals they regard their capital as an investment, ie an asset which may, at some time, be repaid to them. From the point of view of the business, the capital is a liability, because it is owed to the owner or owners. In practice, it is unlikely to be repaid as it is the permanent capital of the business.

To the owner's capital is added *net profit for the year*, while drawings, the amount withdrawn by the owner during the year, are deducted, ie:

	owner's capital	(from the trial balance)
plus	net profit for the year	(from the profit & loss statement)
minus	owner's drawings for the year	(from the trial balance)
equals	closing capital	

This calculation leaves a closing capital at the balance sheet date which balances (agrees) with the net assets figure – the balance sheet *balances*. (Please note that drawings must not be included amongst the overheads in the profit and loss account).

In *partnership* balance sheets (see later in the chapter) the same details, ie capital, net profit, and drawings, are shown for each partner, together with other items which relate specifically to the way in which the partners have agreed to share profits and losses.

In limited company balance sheets (see later in the chapter), details of the share capital issued by the company are shown, together with retained profits for the year, ie profit after payment of dividends to the shareholders.

production of financial statements

pc 7.3.5

In the last few pages we have looked at the layout of the profit and loss statement and the balance sheet. We now need to see how these financial statements are produced, using the trial balance as the starting point.

Against each figure from the trial balance we indicate whether it will appear in the profit and loss statement ('P&L') or the balance sheet ('BS'). Please refer back to the trial balance of Jane Smith on page 135 to see how this has been done: note that the stock at the end of the year (which appears as a note to the trial balance) is marked to appear in both 'P&L' and 'BS'.

profit and loss account

The figures from the trial balance that have been marked 'P&L' are now entered onto the profit and loss statement – see the example for Jane Smith on page 137. The procedure is as follows:

- enter the sales figures in the right-hand money column
- now calculate the cost of sales in the left-hand money column, taking care to add the opening stock and to deduct the closing stock; work out the total (for Jane Smith, it is £107,000), and carry it into the right-hand column
- deduct cost of sales from sales to give the figure for gross profit
- in the left-hand money column list the overheads of the business, work out the total (for Jane Smith, it is £36,000), and carry it into the right-hand column
- deduct the total of overheads from gross profit to give the figure for net profit

As we have seen earlier, the right-hand money column contains sub-totals and totals, while the left-hand column is used for listing individual amounts.

balance sheet

For the balance sheet, all figures are entered in the right-hand money column, unless we want to calculate some intermediate figures – see the example of Jane Smith's balance sheet on page 140. Using the items from the trial balance marked 'BS', work as follows:

- list the fixed assets and sub-total
- list the current assets in the left-hand money column and sub-total in the same column (for Jane Smith, the figure is £26,500)
- write down the current liabilities and, if there is more than one, sub-total in the left-hand money column
- deduct current liabilities from current assets to give the working capital figure (£10,000 for Jane Smith) and carry it into the right-hand column
- in the right-hand money column, add together the sub-total of fixed assets and working capital (to give £130,000 for Jane Smith); from this figure deduct long-term liabilities (if any), to give a final 'net assets' figure (£80,000 for Jane Smith)

Now complete the balance sheet by filling in the figures for the 'financed by' section:

- opening capital is from the trial balance
- net profit is the figure from the profit and loss statement; it is added to opening capital and sub-totalled (£87,000 for Jane Smith)
- deduct the figure for owner's drawings to give the total of the 'financed by' section, which balances with 'net assets' (£80,000 for Jane Smith)

Spend a little time reading through and understanding the example of Jane Smith's business, and then move on to the Student Activity which follows.

STUDENT ACTIVITY 7.2
performance criterion 7.3.5

production of financial statements

task 1

Please refer back to Student Activity 7.1. You have already marked up the items from the trial balance of Nick Johnson according to whether they will appear in the profit and loss statement or balance sheet. Now prepare the financial statements (profit and loss statement and balance sheet) of Nick Johnson's business for the year-ended 31 December 1995.

task 2

The trial balance of Alan Harris, who runs a bookshop, has been extracted at the end of his financial year on 30 June 1995, as follows:

Name of account	*Debit* £	*Credit* £
Stock at 1 July 1994	13,250	
Capital		70,000
Premises	65,000	
Motor vehicle	5,250	
Purchases	55,000	
Sales		85,500
Administration	850	
Wages	9,220	
Rent paid	1,200	
Telephone	680	
Interest paid	120	
Travel expenses	330	
Debtors	1,350	
Creditors		7,550
Bank	2,100	
Cash	600	
Drawings	8,100	
	163,050	163,050

note: Stock at 30 June 1995 was valued at £18,100

(a) Using the trial balance, you are to prepare the financial statements (profit and loss statement and balance sheet) of Alan Harris' business for the year ended 30 June 1995.

(b) You are to provide an explanation to Alan of what each financial statement represents, and to write a note on each of the following terms:

- cost of sales
- net profit
- fixed assets
- current liabilities
- capital
- drawings

a note on depreciation of fixed assets

pc 7.3.5

In your investigations into final accounts (financial statements) of businesses you may come across references to 'depreciation', either among the overheads in the profit and loss statement or in the fixed asset section of the balance sheet. Your course does not require you to study depreciation in depth, but you do need to know what the term means when it appears in the final accounts.

Depreciation is the estimate of the amount of the loss in value of fixed assets over a specified time period.

Fixed assets, for example machinery and vehicles, reduce in value – or depreciate – as time goes by, largely as a result of wear and tear. For example if you buy a new car on Thursday you will not be able to sell it for the same price the following Thursday; it will have dropped in value – depreciated – by a substantial amount in that time,

recording depreciation in financial statements

To provide a more accurate view of the financial state of a business, depreciation of fixed assets is recorded in the financial statements as follows:

- include the amount of depreciation for the year as an overhead in profit and loss account; the effect of this is to *reduce* the net profit
- the value of fixed assets shown in the balance sheet is *reduced* to reflect the amount that they have depreciated *since the assets were bought*

The reason for making these adjustments for depreciation is because the business has had the use of the fixed assets during the year: the estimated fall in value of the assets is recorded in profit and loss statement, which now shows a more accurate profit figure while, in the balance sheet, fixed assets are reduced in value to indicate their approximate 'true' value.

an example of depreciation in financial statements

Jane Smith tells you that she wishes you to show £2,000 for depreciation of machinery in her financial statements for 1995. As a result she will include an overhead for 'provision for depreciation for machinery' of £2,000 in her profit and loss statement. In the balance sheet the £2,000 will reduce the value of the machinery as shown below:

Balance sheet of Jane Smith as at 31 December 1995

	£	£	£
Fixed Assets	Cost	Depreciation to date	Net
Premises	100,000	–	100,000
Machinery	20,000	2,000	18,000
	120,000	2,000	118,000

balance sheet of a partnership

pc 7.3.5

So far, in our study of financial statements, we have concentrated on sole traders, ie one person in business on their own. With a partnership – a business owned by two or more partners – the partners must agree such issues as to how much each will contribute to the capital of the company; in what proportion they will share profits and losses (not necessarily equally – it could be in line with their capital); whether any partner is to be paid a partnership salary (perhaps to allow for working in the business full-time, while the partners are part-time).

The balance sheet of a partnership with two partners is shown below:

SMITH AND JONES, IN PARTNERSHIP
BALANCE SHEET AS AT 31 DECEMBER 1995

£	£	£	
Fixed assets	*Cost*	*Dep'n to date*	*Net*
Machinery	84,000	12,600	71,400
Motor vehicles	20,000	7,200	12,800
	104,000	19,800	84,200
Current assets			
Stock		12,600	
Debtors		8,640	
Bank		29,760	
		51,000	
Less Current liabilities			
Creditors		7,230	
Working capital			43,770
NET ASSETS			127,970
FINANCED BY			
Capital accounts			
Smith		80,000	
Jones		45,000	
			125,000
Current accounts	**SMITH**	**JONES**	
Opening balance	1,250	350	
Add: salary	5,000	-	
share of profit	14,000	8,500	
	20,250	8,850	
Less drawings	15,720	10,410	
	4,530	(1,560)	2,970
			127,970

notes on the partnership balance sheet

- Most sections of the balance sheet – fixed assets, current assets, current liabilities, long-term liabilities (not shown above) – are presented in exactly the same way as for a sole trader.
- The 'financed by' section shows, for each partner, a *capital account* and a *current account*:

  – ***capital account*** is normally a fixed investment in the business, the amount each partner contributes being agreed between them; it only alters if a permanent increase or decrease in capital takes place

  – ***current account*** is a fluctuating investment in the business to which the partner's share of profits and salary (if any) are credited, and in which drawings are shown

balance sheet of a limited company

pc 7.3.5

A limited company balance sheet follows the same layout as that of a sole trader and a partnership. Limited companies have to prepare financial statements at the end of each financial year: these must be checked by outside auditors, and a copy filed at Companies House (where it is available for public inspection) and sent to every shareholder. On the next page is the balance sheet of The Body Shop International PLC. Note the following points:

- The balance sheet follows the same layout that we have seen previously.
- Figures are given for both the current year (1994) and the previous year (1993) – this enables comparisons to be made.
- Much additional information is provided by means of notes (not reproduced here).
- Figures are given for both 'the company' and 'the group'. The *company* is The Body Shop International PLC, ie the main (or parent) company, the *group* is both the company and a number of subsidiary companies which it controls. The group accounts show an overall picture of the business.
- *Creditors: amounts falling due within one year* is the *current liabilities* section – the separate amounts are disclosed in a note (not reproduced here) which forms part of the accounts.
- *Creditors: amounts falling due after more than one year* is the *long-term liabilities* section.
- Capital and reserves is the 'financed by' section, and includes *called up share capital* and *share premium account,* which is the shareholders' investment in the company. *Profit and loss account* is the amount of profit earned and retained by the company. This profit will not be in the form of cash, however, but will be money reinvested in business assets.

Balance Sheets

As at 28 February 1994

	Note	Group 1994 £m	Group 1993 £m	Company 1994 £m	Company 1993 £m
Fixed assets					
Intangible assets	11	**3.7**	5.2	**3.7**	5.2
Tangible assets	12	**67.9**	64.8	**49.2**	50.0
Investments	13	–	–	**12.7**	9.7
		71.6	70.0	**65.6**	64.9
Current assets					
Stocks	14	**34.6**	35.3	**18.0**	20.6
Debtors	15	**37.2**	33.6	**38.8**	28.8
Cash at bank and in hand		**24.9**	14.0	**22.0**	9.2
		96.7	82.9	**78.8**	58.6
Creditors: amounts falling due within one year	16	**35.6**	31.2	**32.0**	26.8
Net current assets		**61.1**	51.7	**46.8**	31.8
Total assets less current liabilities		**132.7**	121.7	**112.4**	96.7
Creditors: amounts falling due after more than one year	17	**(32.4)**	(35.2)	**(1.9)**	(3.4)
Provisions for liabilities and charges					
Deferred tax	18	**(3.4)**	(3.8)	**(4.2)**	(3.5)
Minority interests		–	(0.5)	–	–
		96.9	82.2	**106.3**	89.8
Capital and reserves					
Called up share capital	19	**9.4**	9.4	**9.4**	9.4
Share premium account	20	**35.7**	33.5	**35.7**	33.5
Profit and loss account	20	**51.8**	39.3	**61.2**	46.9
		96.9	82.2	**106.3**	89.8

These financial statements were approved by the board on 10 May 1994 and signed on its behalf by:

TG Roddick
Director

The notes on pages 31 to 49 form part of these financial statements.

purposes of financial statements

pc 7.3.6

the purposes

There are, as we will see, various types of users of financial statements. Each user reads the statements for different reasons. The main purposes are to:

- inform the owners and managers of the business
- monitor the performance of the business
- secure and maintain finance for the business
- fulfil statutory obligations
- assess taxation liability

the users

The number of people interested in the financial statements will vary with the type and size of business. For example:

- small business: owner(s), bank manager, Inland Revenue (the tax authorities)
- large business: shareholders, bank and other lenders, Inland Revenue, employees, financial analysts

We will now look in detail at the purposes of financial statements.

inform the owners and managers of the business

The profit and loss statement informs the owners and managers of the amount of sales, overheads, and net profit made during the year, while the balance sheet shows the make-up of the assets, liabilities, and capital. In particular, the amount of profit (or loss) made during the accounting period indicates the level of drawings (sole traders and partnerships), or dividends (limited companies), that can be made.

The relationship between the various amounts shown on the balance sheet will also be considered. For example, owners and managers will look at:

- the value of the organisation's fixed assets
- the amount of long-term liabilities in relation to capital (generally, the total amount of loans to the business should be less than the capital)
- the figures for current asset and current liability items (is there too much stock? too many debtors? too many creditors? or even too much money in the bank?)

monitor the performance of the business

Here the user of the financial statements will be seeking to compare:

- current performance with that of the previous accounting period
- current performance with budgets and forecasts prepared for the period

- current and past performance with that of similar businesses, so as to make an inter-firm comparison

A first review will be to look at the money amounts of items; a more detailed review will involve the calculation of *accounting ratios* to assess business performance. For example in the profit and loss statement, the amounts of sales, total overheads, and net profit will be of interest. In particular, the net profit to sales, expressed as a percentage, is a key indicator. From the balance sheet, the user will be assessing the strength of the business, in terms of assets, when compared with the previous year's figures. We will look more fully at the analysis of financial statements using *accounting ratios* in Chapter 10 which starts on page 202.

secure and maintain finance for the business

A lender, such as a bank, will usually want to see the last three years' financial statements (where available) before agreeing to provide finance. Here the lender will be looking to see that profits have been made. Although the past is not always a guide to what will happen in the future, it does give an indication of the abilities of the people who own the business. Before agreeing finance, the bank will consider a number of questions about the business – enquiring about profitability and particularly the value and type of the assets shown by the balance sheet.

is the business profitable?

For a business that has already secured finance, the lender will wish to see each year's profit and loss statement and balance sheet as they become available, and may also ask for information on a monthly or quarterly basis. The lender is looking at, amongst other things, whether the business continues to be profitable and whether the money cycle is continuing to operate effectively.

what is the value of the assets?

A lender, such as a bank, will also be concerned about the strength of the assets. Most lenders take some form of security from a borrower and, for businesses, this usually means a mortgage (or charge) over assets and, in particular, the buildings. Potential lenders will assess the value of the assets from the balance sheet and decide the best security to take, while existing lenders will look to see if the value of their security has increased.

how much is the business borrowing?

The amount of loans in relation to the capital of the owner(s) – the *'gearing'* – will also be considered. As a general rule, the loans should be much less than the capital, otherwise the lender will ask the question 'whose business is it – yours or ours?' The amounts of loans in relation to capital are compared by means of the gearing ratio; a high gearing ratio shows that loans are high in relation to capital.

statutory obligations

By statutory obligations, we mean the duties imposed upon businesses by law. One of the statutory obligations of a limited company is to produce accounts which are prepared in accordance with the terms of the Companies Acts 1985 and 1989. The shareholders are sent a copy of the accounts, and a set must also be filed at Companies House, where it is accessible to members of the public. In this way, users can obtain the information that they need from the accounts. By contrast, there is no statutory obligation for sole traders and partnerships to produce accounts although, in practice, most will do so. However, these accounts are not available to the public.

assess taxation liability – income tax and corporation tax

Sole traders and partners are liable for *income tax* as individuals. Thus, when a sole trader business makes a profit, the person running the business must show the profit on his or her tax return, along with any other income; similarly, partners must show their share of the profits of the partnership. As noted above, while there is no statutory obligation for sole traders and partnerships to produce accounts, most will do so in order to assess taxation liabilities. Accordingly, it makes good sense for such businesses to use the services of an accountant, who will be able to prepare the accounts and deal with the Inland Revenue on behalf of the owners.

Limited companies are different from sole traders and partnerships in that they are legal bodies in their own right. As such they account directly to the Inland Revenue for the tax due on their profits; this tax is called *corporation tax*. It is calculated on the profit before any distribution of profits (in the form of dividends) is made to the shareholders.

STUDENT ACTIVITY 7.3
performance criterion 7.3.6

the purpose of financial statements

task

The financial statements for the first two years of trading for Wyvern Stationery are shown on the next page. The business, owned by Peter Simpson, sells office and student stationery from a rented shop close to the local college.

Study the accounts and answer the questions.

questions

1 Who are the people interested in reading these financial statements? Explain the purposes for which they will use the accounts.

2 What are the particular points from the statements that Peter Simpson will note from the profit and loss statement. Include a calculation of the net profit percentage for each year, and give a brief comment. Note: the net profit percentage may be calculated as follows:

$$\frac{\text{net profit}}{\text{sales}} \times \frac{100}{1} = \text{net profit percentage}$$

3 List the main changes that have occurred between the two balance sheet dates. Do you think the business has expanded or declined? What is the evidence for your decision?

4 What are the particular points from the statements that Peter Simpson's bank manager will note? Peter's business has an overdraft facility of £3,000, and a bank loan of £2,000.

Peter Simpson, trading as Wyvern Stationery
Profit and loss statements for the year ended 31 December

		last year		*this year*
	£	£	£	£
Sales		27,500		48,200
Less Cost of Sales		18,300		35,186
Gross profit		9,200		13,014
Less overheads:				
Administration	1,550		1,980	
Wages	520		2,050	
Rent paid	1,000		1,250	
Telephone	330		410	
Interest paid	240		520	
Travel expenses	150		200	
		3,790		6,410
Net profit		5,410		6,604

Peter Simpson, trading as Wyvern Stationery
Balance sheets as at 31 December

		last year		*this year*
	£	£	£	£
Fixed assets				
Shop fittings		2,000		2,500
Equipment		1,500		2,250
		3,500		4,750
Current assets				
Stock	3,240		7,230	
Debtors	870		1,925	
Bank	1,820		–	
Cash	85		130	
	6,015		9,285	
Less Current liabilities				
Creditors	2,610		4,730	
Bank	–		2,955	
	2,610		7,685	
Working capital		3,405		1,600
		6,905		6,350
Less Long-term liabilities				
Loan from bank		2,000		1,800
NET ASSETS		4,905		4,550
FINANCED BY				
Capital				
Opening capital		6,000		4,905
Add net profit		5,410		6,604
		11,410		11,509
Less drawings		6,505		6,959
		4,905		4,550

EVIDENCE COLLECTION ASSIGNMENT 7

financial statements

Element 7.3

introduction

This assignment requires you investigate accounting systems and financial statements. It also requires you to construct a profit and loss statement and a balance sheet from figures on a trial balance.

tasks

pcs 7.3.1 -2

1 Write a brief summary of how an accounting system works

(a) when a manual system is used

(b) when a computer system is used

Use diagrams to explain the system. Make mention of the different accounting periods used.

Outline the advantages and disadvantages of using a computer-based accounting system in a sole trader business.

Note: if you can, try and find a business which has recently changed from a manual method to a computer-based system to help you compile your evidence.

2 Your friend, Jane Simpson, runs a small business as a contract caterer. She prepares food for a number of regular business customers, and also takes on the catering for weddings and other functions. The business operates from a rented business unit on a factory estate. Jane does most of the work herself but employs part-time assistants when things get busy. She also employs a part-time book-keeper to look after the double-entry accounts, but Jane feels that she would like to know more about finance and accounting.

The book-keeper has given Jane a list of balances of accounts at the end of the financial year on 30 September 1995:

	£
Stock at 1 October 1994	550
Purchases	14,950
Sales	33,900
Administration	2,400
Wages	3,500
Rent paid	2,250
Telephone	490
Interest paid	995
Travel expenses	685
Equipment	750
Motor vehicle	7,500
Debtors	2,540
Bank overdraft	790
Cash	25
Capital	3,500
Drawings	6,850
Loan from bank	3,250
Creditors	2,045

Note: tasks (a) and (c) should be prepared, if possible, using a computer spreadsheet.

pc 7.3.3

(a) Extract a trial balance (in either double-column or single-column form) from the list of balances as at 30 September 1995.

pc 7.3.4

(b) Mark against each figure from the trial balance the financial statement in which it will appear.

pc 7.3.5

(c) Using the trial balance, prepare a profit and loss statement and a balance sheet for the accounting period to 30 September 1995. Note that Jane has valued the closing stock on 30 September 1995 at £745.

pc 7.3.6

(d) Explain to Jane the purpose of the financial statements that you have prepared and to whom they will be of interest. The business has a bank overdraft facility of £1,000 and a bank loan of £3,250.

chapter summary and key terms

- The financial statements of a business comprise the profit and loss statement and balance sheet.

- The profit and loss statement shows the profit or loss for the accounting period. For a trading business, such as a shop, which buys and sells goods, the profit and loss statement shows two levels of profit: gross profit and net profit (or net loss). For a service sector business, such as a secretarial agency, only a net profit (or net loss) is shown.

- The balance sheet shows the assets, liabilities and capital at a particular date; it is a 'snapshot' of the business at the end of the accounting period.

- The main purposes of preparing financial statements are to:
  - inform the owners and managers of the business
  - monitor the performance of the business
  - secure and maintain finance for the business
  - fulfil statutory obligations
  - assess taxation liability

key terms

profit and loss statement	a summary of the revenue and expenses of a business for an accounting period, which shows the overall profit or loss
gross profit	sales minus cost of sales
cost of sales	opening stock plus purchases minus closing stock
net profit	gross profit minus overheads (or expenses)
overheads	the running costs of the business, such as administration, wages, rent paid, telephone, interest paid, travel expenses
balance sheet	the assets, liabilities and capital of a business at a particular date
assets	amounts owned by or owed to the business, either fixed assets or current assets
liabilities	amounts owed by the business, either current liabilities or long-term liabilities
capital	the amount of the owners' finance invested in the business
drawings	the amount withdrawn from a sole trader or partnership business by the owner(s)
dividends	the amount paid to the shareholders of a limited company as their share of the profits

multiple-choice questions

1 A business has prepared its year-end financial statements for the accounting period to 31 December 1995.

Decide which of these headings is True (T) or False (F).

(i) Profit and loss statement as at 31 December 1995

(ii) Balance sheet for the year ended 31 December 1995

Which option best describes the two headings?

A	(i)	T	(ii)	T
B	(i)	T	(ii)	F
C	(i)	F	(ii)	T
D	(i)	F	(ii)	F

2 Net profit equals

A the amount of the owner's capital

B gross profit add overheads

C gross profit minus the owner's capital

D gross profit minus overheads

3 The balance sheet comprises:

A assets, plus liabilities, equals capital

B assets, minus liabilities, equals capital

C assets, minus liabilities, minus current liabilities, equals capital

D assets, plus capital, equals liabilities

4 Which is a current asset?

A premises

B stock

C capital

D bank overdraft

5 The capital of Peter Talbot, a sole trader, is £44,000 at the beginning of the financial year and £52,000 at the end. Peter has withdrawn £12,000 during the year. The net profit for the year is:

A £20,000

B £12,000

C £44,000

D £8,000

8 Financing of business

GNVQ SPECIFICATIONS

Element 7.1

Explain sources of finance and financial requirements of business organisations

performance criteria – a student must

1. explain the financing requirements of a business
2. explain assets and working capital
3. explain common methods of finance appropriate to the financing requirements
4. explain usual sources of finance appropriate for different methods of finance
5. explain characteristics of common methods of finance
6. explain usual sources of finance for different types of business organisations

what this chapter covers

In this chapter we see how different types of business organisation raise money to finance their current operations and their expansion plans. We look at the different types of financial need – a new factory, more stock, for example – and look at the types of finance raised.

what you will learn from this chapter

- a wide variety of business organisations need to raise finance: sole traders, partnerships, limited companies and non-profit-making organisations
- sources of finance include both internal sources such as the capital the owners put in and the profit which the businesses make, and external sources such as bank overdrafts, loans, share issues and grants
- asset finance is raised for specific business assets – a new factory, new machinery, computers, for example
- working capital finance is raised for the day-to-day cash requirements of a business – buying stock and materials, paying creditors
- the finance needs of a business are an integral part of the business plan which you will be compiling as part of Unit 8 "Business Planning"

financial needs of different businesses

pc 7.1.6

You have already studied the types of business organisation, and in the last chapter will have looked at the balance sheets of a sole trader, a partnership and a limited company, and seen how they are financed by *capital* from the owner, together with external *liabilities* such as bank loans.

Before looking at the different types of finance in detail we will summarise the ways in which different types of business raise money. Study the table below and make sure in your mind of the distinction between *internal* and *external* sources of finance.

sources of finance for different businesses

	internal sources	*external sources*
sole trader	own savings help from the family business profits	bank overdrafts, loans, hire purchase, leasing, grants
partnership	own savings other partners' savings business profits	bank overdrafts, loans, hire purchase, leasing, grants
private limited company	private shareholders' funds business profits	bank overdrafts, loans, hire purchase, leasing, factoring, grants venture capital firms
public limited company	share capital business profits	bank overdrafts, loans, hire purchase, leasing factoring, grants venture capital firms, public share issues
non-profit-making organisation	fund-raising efforts	donations sponsorship grants National Lottery

investigating business finance

pcs. 7.1.1– 6

When investigating business finance you will find a certain amount of material in textbooks, but there is the danger that the information may be out-of-date. Before tackling the Student Activities in this chapter you are recommended to make contact, preferably as a class group, with a business adviser in your locality. For example you could approach an accountant, a bank lending officer, or an adviser from the local Chamber of Commerce or Business Link office. The adviser could look at the Activities you are doing and provide guidance and advice. There is no substitute for a primary source of information in an area such as this.

STUDENT ACTIVITY 8.1

performance criterion 7.1.1 - 6

sources of finance

task

Examine the table on the previous page and answer the questions set out below. You will need to consult resources such as textbooks and business advisers to provide you with all the information you will need.

1 Which form of business is a new enterprise most likely to take?

2 What are the shortcomings of this form of business when it comes to raising finance?

3 Which form of business offers the most opportunity for raising finance? Why is this form of business less common?

4 How can a person starting up in business ensure that his/her personal wealth will not be at risk if the business fails?

5 Investigate recent examples of public share issues. How much finance was raised in each case?

6 What would you think of a business owner who said "My policy is to take as much of the profit out of the business as I can. I work hard for the business, so why shouldn't I?"

7 How well do non-profit making organisations benefit from the National Lottery? Do you think they get enough?

resources planning

pcs. 7.1.2 & 3

fixed assets

You will remember from your study of the balance sheet of a business in the last chapter that fixed assets are:

long-term items owned by a business

If for example, you consider a manufacturing business, its fixed assets may include items such as:

- land and buildings including the factory, the storage facilities, the car park and access roads
- production machinery
- vehicles – delivery vehicles and cars owned by the sales staff and directors
- office equipment – computers, photocopiers, switchboards, telephones, faxes
- fixtures and fittings – storage facilities, furniture, heating and lighting equipment

The list can be very long. Whether you are starting a business for real, or taking part in a Young Enterprise or mini-business scheme, you will have to sit down with your management and make a resources 'shopping list' and then come to the decision as to what resources are essential, and whether you can afford them. One alternative to purchasing which we will consider later is leasing, an arrangement whereby you effectively 'rent' an item of equipment, eg a photocopier or a car. You do not own the asset, but have long-term use of it in return for a regular payment to the leasing company which owns it.

working capital

You will also need to plan for short-term resources for which you will need cash. If, for example, you are a manufacturing business, you will need to

- buy stocks of raw materials which you will process into a finished product
- finance semi-finished products (known as work-in-progress) and stocks of finished products
- pay wages
- pay running expenses as they fall due: business rates, electricity, gas, water, insurance, advertising

If you fail to plan for these – and do not use a cash flow forecast – you are in danger of running out of cash: you will encounter 'cash flow problems', a situation which in the worst case can lead to bankruptcy.

It is essential therefore to plan for sufficient working capital. What is working capital?

Working capital is the amount of money or potential money you have in the short-term, either in the form of cash or bank balances, money owed, or in stock which can be sold, less all the bills you have to meet in the short-term and any bank overdraft.

Working capital is essentially a cash or near-cash 'float' from which you pay bills falling due in the near future. In accounting terms the formula for calculating working capital is

working capital **equals** *current assets* **less** *current liabilities*

Look at the extract from a balance sheet shown below.

	£	£
Current assets		
Stocks – raw materials, work-in-progress and finished goods	20,000	
Debtors – money owed you in the short-term	29,000	
Cash – money held by the business	1,000	
		50,000
Less current liabilities		
Creditors – money you owe to suppliers and for other bills	22,000	
Bank overdraft – money you owe to the bank	3,000	
		25,000
Working capital		25,000

In this example, the total of current assets is £50,000. After the current liabilities of £25,000 have been deducted, working capital of £25,000 is left, a sufficient 'cushion' of short-term finance which is available should the business need it. If, for example, the business increased its purchases of stock and the creditors figure went up by £10,000, the business will have resources available to pay off the creditors.

All businesses therefore need a certain minimum amount of working capital, and the amount required will vary from business to business, depending on the nature of the business (for example, a shop is likely to need less working capital than an engineering business), and on the size of the business.

identifying financing requirements

pc 7.1.3

Although it is easy for a business to state that it needs finance, it is less easy to establish:

- how much finance?
- where will it come from?

how much external finance ?

Finance is normally needed for starting a business, buying a business, or expanding a business. We have already seen that finance can be *internal* (from the owner), or *external* (eg from a bank). The question is often asked "How much will a bank lend?" A provider of external finance – such as a bank – will need reassuring about the owner's commitment to the business, and will not normally want to lend more than the owner is contributing. The lender will ask the business that wants to borrow:

What percentage of the total finance needed by the business are you putting in yourself?

If you are putting in less than 50%, is it possible for you to raise more from your private sources?

If the business is a new one, the provider of finance will rarely lend more than half of the start-up cost, unless it will be repaid quickly. If the owner puts in less than 50%, a lender may quite rightly ask the question: "whose business is it?" If the finance is needed for expanding an existing business, the lender will not normally want to see outside borrowing (including the new borrowing) exceed the capital of the owner(s).

the business plan

It is normal, if you are applying to an outside body for finance – a bank for example – to prepare a written plan, normally referred to as a business plan. This is explained in full in Chapter 11. The business plan sets out your product, expertise, market, your pricing policy and, most important of all, your financial requirements – ie how much you want to borrow. The cash flow forecast is used by the business to forecast expected 'cash in' and expected 'cash out' on a monthly basis. If there is a cash shortfall, particularly in the early months of operations when substantial costs are incurred, then this difference is the amount of external finance required by the business.

matching the finance to the assets

Lenders will normally want to match the period of any lending to the expected life of the asset financed. There are three generally accepted timescales for finance, although you may find definitions which will vary from these:

short-term	1 to 2 years	short-term requirements, ie current assets
medium-term	3 to 10 years	purchase of fixed assets, eg machinery
long-term	11 to 25 years	purchase of land and premises

As you will see, the longer the life of the asset purchased, the longer the loan that will be made available. A lender will obviously be unwilling to lend money over 25 years to finance an ice cream salesman for his summer stocks, but may provide funds over that period to enable a company to purchase a factory unit.

borrowing from the bank

pcs. 7.1.4 & 5

types and sources of finance

We will now consider the various types and sources of finance. It should be noted that some of the sources listed here only provide finance to limited companies: this will be made clear in the text.

The *banks* are the largest providers of finance to all types of businesses. Forms of lending vary from bank to bank, and you should investigate the various schemes available and when they have to be repaid. A bank will be able to arrange, by itself, or through specialised companies which it owns:

- overdrafts
- short and medium-term loans ('business loans')
- commercial mortgages
- leasing for equipment purchase
- factoring services
- venture capital

Before looking at each of these forms of financing, it is important to appreciate how interest rates are set, and also what security is required for lending.

interest rates

The cost of borrowing usually involves two separate expenses:

- an *arrangement fee* – charged when the finance is arranged, and in some cases when it is renewed
- *interest* – a specific charge calculated as a percentage of the amount borrowed

Banks generally set their interest rates at a set percentage (which varies according to the risk element in the lending) above the prevailing Base Rate. Base Rate is an advertised fixed rate, set and varied periodically by the major banks, who use it as a base for working out interest rates for borrowers. No-one ever borrows at Base Rate. Base Rate is varied in line with interest rates in the economy. Interest is normally charged to the bank account of the borrower on a monthly or quarterly basis.

security for lending

Lending to businesses is seen by the financial institutions as being risky, because statistically businesses become bankrupt more often than do personal borrowers. Whereas a bank may lend £2,000 to a private individual for a new kitchen and not require any security cover, business borrowers will nearly always be asked to provide some security. Security can be in the form of:

- a *mortgage* – a legal document which the borrower signs stating in effect that, if the finance is not repaid, the lender can sell whatever is being 'mortgaged'. The items mortgaged can include the house of the borrower (the most common form of security) or investments with a market value, such as stocks and shares and insurance policies

- a *guarantee* – a legal document signed by an individual (the 'guarantor') stating that, if the borrower fails to repay when asked to, then the guarantor will pay up; limited companies are often guaranteed by their directors in this way

Security for business borrowing is normally in the form of:

sole trader	a mortgage over the home or any marketable investments
partnership	a mortgage over the homes or any marketable investments belonging to the partners
limited company	a mortgage over the assets of the company (this document is known as a 'debenture' or a 'fixed and floating charge') and/or the guarantees of the directors

bank fixed asset finance

pcs. 7.1.4 & 5

business loan

This is a fixed medium-term loan, typically for between 3 and 10 years, to cover the purchase of capital items such as machinery or equipment. Interest is normally 2% to 3% over base rate, and repayments are by instalments. Sometimes repayment of principal (the full amount borrowed) can be postponed during the first two years of the loan (a 'repayment holiday') when only interest payments are made.

commercial mortgage

If you are buying premises for your business you can arrange to borrow long-term by means of a commercial mortgage, typically up to 80% of the value of the property, repayable over a period of up to 25 years. Your premises will be taken as security for the loan: if the business fails, the premises will be sold to repay the bank.

bank working capital finance

pcs. 7.1.4 & 5

overdraft

An overdraft is short-term borrowing on bank current account. It is relatively cheap: the banks charge typically 4% to 6% over Base Rate for a new business, 2.5% to 5% over Base Rate for an existing business. Interest is normally charged quarterly, but you only pay interest on what you actually borrow. A 'limit' up to which you can borrow will be granted by the bank, and reviewed annually, when it can be increased, decreased or renewed at the same level. A renewal fee is payable for this service.

An overdraft is the most common form of finance for working capital. It provides the finance when a business needs to pay creditors or meet other short-term bills. It is not a 'bottomless pit' however, and if a bank becomes nervous about the ability of a business to repay, it can ask for the overdraft to be repaid on demand. This can have a catastrophic effect on the cash position of a business, as we saw in the Case Study of John Spender (see pages 18 to 19)

finance arranged through bank-owned companies

pcs. 7.1.4 & 5

fixed asset finance

Finance Houses, which are specialist companies owned in the main by the major banks, offer alternative ways of obtaining fixed assets:

hire purchase

An HP agreement from a finance house enables a business to acquire an asset on the payment of a deposit and to pay back the cost plus interest over a set period, at the end of which ownership of the asset passes to the borrower. Hire purchase is often used to finance vehicles and machinery.

leasing

Leasing arrangements are also provided by finance houses. With a leasing agreement, the business has use of assets bought by the finance house, and the business pays a regular 'rental' payment, normally over a lease period of two to seven years. Ownership of the goods never passes to the business. A common form of lease is a pay back lease or finance lease in which the business will pay back the cost of the item plus finance costs over the period of the lease. Clearly a lease is not a loan, but it can substantially reduce a business' financial requirements when it needs to make a capital purchase. Computer equipment and fleets of company cars are often leased.

working capital finance from bank-owned companies

factoring

Many banks also provide factoring services through specialist factoring companies. A business may have valuable financial resources tied up because its customers owe it money and have not yet paid. A factoring company will effectively 'buy' these debts by providing a number of services:

- it will lend up to 80% of outstanding customer debts
- it will deal with all the paperwork of collecting customer debts
- it can in some instances insure against non-payment of debts

Factoring frees money due to the business and allows the business to use it in its general operations and expansion plans. It is therefore a valuable source of short-term finance.

finance for limited companies: venture capital

pcs. 7.1.4 & 5

Many banks own *merchant banks*, specialist banks which offer advice and financial assistance to limited companies. This financial assistance takes the form of loans and venture capital which provides finance for fixed assets and for working capital. Ownership of a limited company is in the form of shares, known as equity capital, held by the investors. Merchant banks may view such companies as ripe for investment and will inject money either in the form of loans or by the purchase of shares, or both. In return, they may expect an element of control over the company and will possibly insist on having a director on the board of the company. A merchant bank considering investing in a limited company will look for a business with a good profit record, strong management and a viable product range.

The funds introduced by the merchant bank could be used for:

- financing an expansion or launching a new product
- acquisition of another company
- the management of the company 'buying out' control of the company
- financing the employees 'buying out' control of the company
- providing working capital

Other financial institutions active in the venture capital market include venture capital companies, non-banking commercial organisations which attract money from private investors and re-invest in limited companies. Their financial assistance includes loans and investment in share capital. They often require a substantial element of control over the borrowing company.

financing from creditors

pcs. 7.1.4 & 5

Many businesses rely on their creditors as a form of *short-term* financing. If a business needs short-term funds and finds that there is not sufficient money in the bank or within the overdraft limit, it can delay payments to creditors, or obtain longer credit periods. The business effectively obtains an interest-free loan at the expense of its creditors.

It is the small business which often suffers at the hands of the larger business because of this practice:

- if large suppliers are not paid on time by small businesses, credit can be cut off entirely
- if the small business supplies a large business (usually a retail chain), the large business can more or less hold the small business to ransom by delaying payments (over six months in some cases) and threatening to stop buying if the small business does not accept long credit terms

As a consequence many small supplier businesses end up by helping to finance the large retailers.

STUDENT ACTIVITY 8.2
performance criteria 7.1.2 – 5

types of finance

task

Visit your local bank to investigate the different forms of finance available to businesses. You may find it necessary to make an appointment to speak to a bank adviser in a 'business branch' – many banks nowadays provide their services to business in branches specialising in business advice.
Following your research, answer the following questions:

1 What is the difference between fixed asset finance and working capital finance?

2 What bank schemes are available for these two types of financial requirement? Support your answer with illustrations of specific bank schemes and examples of the type of assets they finance.

3 Which type of finance does a factoring service provide? How does it work in practice?

financial assistance from the Government

pcs. 7.1.4 & 5

regional aid

The Department of Trade and Industry (DTI) has divided the UK into different types of area. The type of area in which a business operates or plans to operate will dictate the level of regional aid that will be made available (look at the map on the next page). Regional aid includes grants, subsidies and training. The types of area include:

Assisted Areas (shaded areas on the map)

- *development areas (the darkest areas):* these areas are those which have the greatest unemployment and greatest deprivation
- *intermediate areas (lighter areas on the map):* these are less deprived than the development areas, and are often to be found on the fringes of development areas
- *urban programme areas:* specific inner city areas which are in need of direct and indirect government support

Non-assisted Areas (white areas on the map)

The rest of the country, where a limited amount of assistance is available.

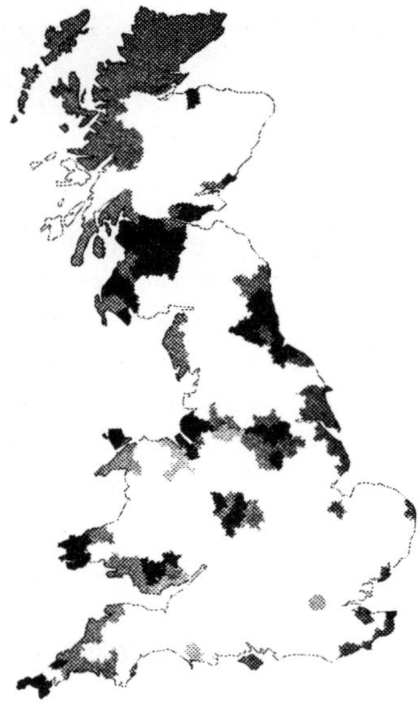

Department of Trade and Industry 'assisted areas'

The Rural Development Commission

The Rural Development Commission provides businesses in rural areas with free advice and technical support. In development areas (see above) loans and grants are available.

The Department of Employment: Loan Guarantee Scheme

The government offers a guarantee for 85% of a bank medium-term loan (2 to 7 years) up to £250,000. This security enables banks and other financial institutions to lend money for projects which would be too risky by normal criteria. The scheme has been very successful, and has enabled many businesses to expand, Waterstones Bookshops in its early days, is a good example.

Training and Enterprise Councils (TECs) – Start-up Schemes

The Business Start-up Scheme, (also known as the The Enterprise Allowance Scheme) is run by the local TECs (Training and Enterprise Councils) and provides financial assistance and training to selected previously unemployed people wanting to set up a new business. The schemes are tailor-made by each local TEC and vary from area to area. An applicant would normally be able to contribute £1,000 to the business and would receive a living wage for a year and business training arranged by the TEC.

Now we will look at a Case Study of how a sole trader raises finance for a new venture, in this case a landscape gardening business.

CASE STUDY

pcs. 7.1.1 - 6

Capability Landscapes – financing a business

Situation 1 – raising the finance

James Brown is a qualified landscape gardener who has been working for a large firm of gardening contractors for five years. His aim has been to gain experience of the trade so that he can eventually set up on his own as an independent landscape gardener. He has chosen the name 'Capability Landscapes' for his business. James intends to work from home, so he will not need premises. He will however need a pickup truck and equipment, including a lawnmower and cultivator. He has saved hard and has accumulated £5,000 in a building society account. In addition, his uncle has promised to lend him £5,000 over five years to help him get established. His uncle has also promised to guarantee any borrowing from the bank. The month is December 1995.

The question is, how much is it all going to cost, and will James need to borrow?

James is not experienced in financial matters, so he contacts his local Business Promotion Centre which puts him in touch with an accountant who specialises in helping small businesses.

Solution

The accountant asks him to set out on paper what items he will need for the business, and how much they are likely to cost – these items will be his assets. His accountant asks him to distinguish between items which he will need permanently in the business – ***fixed assets*** *– and items which he will on a day-to-day basis –* ***current assets****. James produces the following figures:*

Capability Landscapes – assets as at December 1995

	£	£
fixed assets required		
pickup truck, secondhand	8,000	
lawnmower and cultivator	900	
gardening tools	350	
total of fixed assets		9,250
current assets required		
initial stock of plants and seed	1,500	
fertilisers	150	
cash in hand	100	
total of current assets		1,750
TOTAL ASSETS REQUIRED		11,000

how much external finance is needed?

The accountant points out that James requires external finance of £1,000: he needs £11,000 of assets and has only £10,000 available – £5,000 in the building society and a £5,000 loan from his uncle. The accountant recommends that James approaches his bank for an overdraft of £1,000, which can be guaranteed by his uncle. He says that an overdraft is the best solution because it is short-term (for financing working capital) and it is also the cheapest form of borrowing.

The accountant promises to draw up this proposal in a formal business plan for submission to the bank. The plan will include the projected balance sheet set out below. This shows clearly what assets are required and how they are to be financed.

BALANCE SHEET OF JAMES BROWN TRADING AS CAPABILITY LANDSCAPES (PROJECTED AS AT 31 DECEMBER 1995)

	£	£
Fixed assets		
Vehicle		8,000
Equipment		900
Gardening tools		350
		9,250
Current assets		
Gardening stock	1,500	
Fertilisers	150	
Cash	100	
	1,750	
Less Current liabilities		
Bank overdraft	1,000	
Working Capital		750
		10,000
Less Long-term liabilities		
Long-term loan from uncle		5,000
NET ASSETS		5,000
FINANCED BY		
Capital		
Owner's capital		5,000

the interview with the bank

James and his accountant are interviewed by the bank small business adviser who has been sent a copy of the business plan in advance. He readily agrees to James' request for finance. An overdraft limit of £1,000 is set up on the business bank account.

3 years later – the problems of success!

James Brown has been trading successfully for three years. His business has expanded rapidly and his annual income is now £350,000. His balance sheet as at the end of the third year is illustrated below. It shows that he has now built up a capital (his investment plus profits for the three years) of £63,200. His bank overdraft has been increased to £10,000 to cover his day-to-day trading requirements, he has bought another truck and some equipment and tools, and has paid off his uncle's loan.

BALANCE SHEET OF JAMES BROWN TRADING AS CAPABILITY LANDSCAPES (AS AT DECEMBER 1998)

	£	£
Fixed assets		
Vehicles		15,000
Equipment		2,500
Gardening tools		500
		18,000
Current assets		
Gardening stock and chemicals	5,000	
Debtors	50,000	
Cash	200	
	55,200	
Less Current liabilities		
Bank overdraft	10,000	
Working capital		45,200
NET ASSETS		63,200
FINANCED BY		
Capital		
Owner's capital		5,000
Profits accumulated		58,200
		63,200

the problems

He employs ten people, rents a small workshop and yard and has to hire his equipment from a local machine hire firm. He wants to expand and reorganise his business. He again approaches his accountant who helps him to analyse his needs:

premises	*he wants to buy a workshop and yard for £75,000*
equipment	*he wants to acquire more machinery at a cost of £50,000*
debt chasing	*he is finding it increasingly difficult to collect money he is owed by his customers – his debtors owe him a total of £50,000*

His basic problem is not having the cash to be able to invest – it is all tied up in amounts due to him from debtors. He is also rather ambitious in his spending plans: he wants to buy premises for £75,000 and equipment for £50,000 – a total of £125,000 and approximately twice his own capital of £63,200. No lender would be willing to lend more than James Brown's own capital of £63,200. The bank is already lending £10,000 on overdraft.

solution

His accountant and bank small business adviser suggest:

factoring	*the bank's factoring company will manage his debtors, lending him 80% of the £50,000 owing, thus releasing £40,000 which he can use in the business straightaway*
commercial mortgage	*the bank will lend him £40,000 for his new premises against a mortgage of the property; he will contribute the remaining £35,000*
leasing	*the bank's leasing company will buy the equipment he needs and lease it to him for a monthly rental*

how much will it cost?

James will need to ensure that his business can afford these financial costs.

factoring *– an annual charge of 2% of the annual total of debts collected plus interest on amounts borrowed, say at Base Rate + 4%*

commercial mortgage *– interest at Base Rate + 3% plus any repayments, plus an arrangement fee of 1.25% and a extra security fee*

leasing *– monthly rental payments to cover the financial cost of the lease, say twice the capital value of the assets (2 x £50,000) spread over 5 years*

EVIDENCE COLLECTION ASSIGNMENT 8

sources of business finance

Element 7.1

introduction

This assignment tests your understanding of

- the difference between fixed asset finance and working capital finance
- the different sources of finance

tasks

pc 7.1.1 – 6

You work in the lending department of the National Bank plc, 124 High Street, Stourminster, ST1 2JF and receive a number of enquiries during the week from customers wanting finance. What form of finance would you recommend in the situations set out below? Write a letter to each customer explaining:

- the type of finance appropriate to the situation
- the likely repayment period and security requirements

When writing the letters use your own name, the title of Lending Officer, and today's date.

1 Tony Page of 47 Rydale Villas, Stourminster, WR4 5TY, a sole trader builder, is expanding his business. He has got all that he wants in the way of vehicles and equipment, but he needs more money – £25,000 he reckons – to buy building materials and to deal with day-to-day trading requirements. He owns his own house, worth £85,000.

2 Beattie Gold of "Glendale", Mill Street, Stourminster, WR4 5TH, runs a successful and profitable catering business as a sole trader. She owns a bakery and shop in town; they are worth £125,000. She wants to expand by installing more ovens and modernising the bakery; the cost will be £25,000.

3 Barbourne Software Supplies Limited is a mail-order computer software supplier operating from a small warehouse which it owns (Unit 1B Severnside Industrial Estate, Stourminster, WR2 5TF). The business is expanding rapidly and the company wants to purchase an adjacent warehouse (Unit 1A) which has recently become vacant following a bankruptcy. The price of the unit is £175,000. The name of the managing director is Bill Wates.

chapter summary and key terms

- A wide variety of business organisations need to raise finance. They include sole traders, partnerships, limited companies and non-profit-making organisations.
- Sources of finance include internal sources such as the capital the owners put in and the profit which the businesses make, and external sources such as bank overdrafts, loans, share issues and grants.
- Assets include items such as land, buildings, production machinery and office machines.
- Asset finance is raised for specific business assets – a new factory, new machinery – and can be raised from the owners, investors, banks, finance companies and by way of Government grants.
- Working capital is the difference in money terms between current assets and current liabilties; it represents the day-to-day requirements of a business and is used for buying items such as raw materials and stock.
- Working capital finance is raised from the owner, through bank overdrafts and from money owed (but not yet paid) to creditors.

key terms

fixed assets	items bought for permanent use in the business
working capital	current assets less current liabilities (what you have got less what you owe in the short term)
internal finance	finance provided by the owner(s) and profits made
external finance	finance from outside lenders and providers
overdraft	borrowing by a business on its current account – for working capital
leasing	an asset bought by a finance house and 'rented' to the business – eg a car, a computer
hire purchase	an asset bought by a finance house and paid for by the business in instalments – eg machinery
factoring	the buying and management by an outside company of the book debts (amounts owing) of a business
venture capital	an investment by an outside company in the share capital of a limited company – a form of financing

multiple-choice questions

1 Working capital can be defined as

A fixed assets less current assets

B current assets less current liablilities

C fixed assets less share capital

D fixed assets less current liabilities

2 Working capital finance methods include

A overdraft, owner's funds, factoring

B overdraft, owner's funds, commercial mortgage

C owner's funds, commercial mortgage, factoring

D venture capital, hire purchase, overdraft

Questions 3 – 5 relate to the following information:

A business can raise finance in a number of ways:

A by factoring

B by leasing

C through venture capital investment

D arranging an overdraft

Which of the above applies to the following?

3 An investment in the share capital of the business.

4 Financing an asset which does not belong to the business.

5 Lending money against the invoices issued by a business.

6 Decide whether each of these statements is True (T) or False (F)

(i) The DTI "Assisted Areas" are confined to deprived urban areas.

(ii) The Rural Development Commission's main aim is to help people setting up business in country areas.

A	(i) T	(ii) T
B	(i) T	(ii) F
C	(i) F	(ii) T
D	(i) F	(ii) F

9 Financial forecasting

GNVQ SPECIFICATIONS

Element 7.2

Produce and explain forecasts and a cash flow for a small business

performance criteria – a student must:

1 explain the purposes and components of forecasts
2 produce a capital budget and trading forecast for a twelve-month period for a small business
3 explain capital budget headings and trading forecast headings
4 explain the purpose of a cash flow as a component of a forecast to a business seeking finance
5 explain the significance of timing in a cash flow forecast
6 explain cash in-flow and cash out-flow headings
7 collect data for each heading to support informed forecasts
8 produce feasible forecasts of cash in-flow and cash out-flow for one twelve-month period
9 produce monthly and cumulative net balances for a twelve-month period
10 explain the consequences of incorrect forecasting

what this chapter covers

In this chapter we see why a business needs to plan ahead and forecast its likely need for fixed assets, its sales and expenses, and the flow of money in and out of its bank account.

what you will learn from this chapter

- the purpose of forecasting – to support the business plan, to suggest different courses of action, to set targets and to monitor performance
- the capital budget plans for the purchase of fixed assets such as premises, machinery and vehicles
- the trading forecast projects sales income and expense items such as raw materials, wages, water rates, telephone bills and other running costs
- the cash flow forecast projects the amount of money in the bank account month-by-month; it brings together the capital budget and the trading forecast and highlights the importance of the timing of payments

the planning process

pc 7.2.1

the need to plan

Businesses need to plan. Whether the business is a small business – a sole trader, for example – or a large public limited company, the owner or management will need to take informed decisions about products to sell, markets to develop and the resources that will be needed in the way of finance, manpower, premises and equipment. Business planning is like physical exercise to the human body – it keeps all systems working efficiently, gets rid of unnecessary flab and induces a healthy glow! Without a planning process a business will drift aimlessly.

Much of this chapter relates to GNVQ Unit 8 "Business Planning" and you will see that the Business Plan which you will be writing (or maybe are already writing) is the culmination of the planning process – a formal written document presented to a lender such as a bank, containing the forecasts which we will be looking at later in this chapter.

the planning process

The planning process can be seen as having four distinct stages:

1. Setting objectives– making decisions about how the business could develop
2. Collecting information – establishing what resources the business has, and what resources the business will need
3. Formulating an overall plan on the basis of this information
4. Monitoring progress once the plan has been put into operation

You will see that planning is an *ongoing process*. The fourth stage – monitoring progress – is critical, If the plan is not working, something will have to be done. If the situation is not monitored, the business could run into serious trouble. For example if a soap powder is found to make holes in clothes (as happened with a well-known brand!) it will have to be withdrawn.

forecasting and planning

In this chapter we will be concentrating on the *third stage* of the planning process – planning ahead on the basis of information given and providing a yardstick by which performance can be monitored.

the purpose of forecasting

pc 7.2.1

what is a forecast?

A forecast – also known as a budget – is a financial plan for a set time period (often 12 months)

Forecasts can be:

- for *income* – eg the *sales budget*– the expected sales income for the year
- for *expenditure* – eg the *capital budget* – spending on fixed (capital) assets for the year
- for *income and expenditure*, for example:
  - the *trading forecast* which projects sales income and expenses such as purchases of materials and wages
  - the *cash flow forecast* which projects money received and money spent as it passes through the bank account, telling the business how much money there is likely to be in the bank account during the year

what format?

There is no set format for a forecast. A forecast can be a simple statement containing amounts and dates – for example a list of fixed assets to be bought during a year. It can also be set out in spreadsheet format in columns and rows broken down into smaller time periods (often monthly or four weekly), as in the example below.

extract from a sales forecast for 1996

	Jan	Feb	Mar	Apr	May	Jun	Total
	£	£	£	£	£	£	£
product A	1,000	1,000	1,000	1,000	1,000	1,000	6,000
product B	1,500	1,500	1,500	1,500	1,500	1,500	9,000
product C	2,500	2,500	2,500	2,500	2,500	2,500	15,000
etc . . .							

Sometimes forecasts can have columns for the actual figures to be entered against the projected figures as the year progresses. The example above is a six-month extract from a simple sales forecast which shows sales income for a variety of products. During the year the management will be able to compare these figures with the actual figures to give them an idea of the performance of the business. Note that the layout shown here does not include columns for the insertion of the 'actual' figures.

why forecast?

Making a forecast is a useful discipline for a number of reasons:

looking ahead

It is a useful exercise for businesses to look ahead and set specific objectives. This process is easier for larger businesses which have the resources to enable managers to have time to plan. The problem with planning and forecasting by a busy small business is that the owner is likely to place the planning process right at the bottom of the "pile of things to be done by yesterday." As a result the planning process in many small businesses can be very basic, and in some cases non-existent.

assessing alternatives

The planning and forecasting process will force a business to assess alternative courses of action, for example:

"Do I open a new shop in the out-of-town shopping centre or do I develop a mail order department?"

"Do I manufacture this new toy, or can I import it cheaply from China?"

supporting the business plan

Forecasts are a central part of any Business Plan. The business has to convince the prospective lender who is shown the plan that the business idea is feasible, is affordable and will be profitable if the product sells. The most important forecast in any business plan is the *cash flow forecast* which shows how the operation of the business will affect the bank account and will indicate how much needs to be borrowed.

setting targets and monitoring performance

As you can see from the sales forecast on the previous page, specific *targets* have been set for sales of individual products. As the year progresses, the business will *monitor* the sales figures and see how well targets are being met. It should be stressed that forecast targets *can be changed* during the year. If product A is a flop and Product B is selling more than expected, the forecast can be redrafted accordingly. You will gather from this that computer spreadsheets are very useful for setting up budgets, as they can recalculate automatically if any figures are changed.

the capital budget

pc 7.2.2

A capital budget is a statement specifying the fixed (capital) assets a business plans to purchase in a given time period.

When a business makes its plans for the year it will have to decide whether it needs to purchase any *capital (fixed) assets*. Capital assets are items bought for *permanent use* in the business. For a large company they might include a new factory or a new production line; for the small business they might include a new delivery van or computer system. Whatever the scale of the business, the purchase will require money, either in the form of cash from the business or in the form of finance from a lender. The capital budget therefore sets out the following information:

- *specifications* of the asset to be purchased
- the *amount* it is going to cost
- the expected *date* of purchase

The amount(s) and date(s) can then be input into the cash flow forecast (the projected amounts of money coming in and out of the business) so that the likely effect on the cash position of the business can be seen. It is possible, for instance, that the business cannot afford to pay for the asset in cash, in which case it could look for outside finance or consider hire purchase or leasing . The capital budget for a small business may be as simple as the table set out below. Note that the individual *types* of asset listed in the left-hand column – premises, vehicles, machinery and equipment – are known as *budget heads* (categories of expenditure).

Capital budget for 1996

budget head	*asset purchased*	*date*	*amount (£)*
Premises	Warehouse extension	June	120,000
Vehicles	Delivery Van	Oct	18,000
Machinery and equipment	Computer system	Nov	7,500
Total amount			145,500

You should note that forecasts are *linked together*: the capital budget will depend on there being enough money in the business (shown in the cash flow forecast), and this in turn depends on there being sufficient sales (shown in the *trading forecast*, explained in the next section).

the trading forecast

pc 7.2.2

A trading forecast is a statement setting out the forecast sales and expenses for the year.

No business can budget for buying capital assets or will be in a position to draw up a cash flow forecast until it has forecast its likely income and expenses for the year. This is carried out in a financial plan known as a *trading forecast*, also called the *profit and loss forecast*. At its most basic level, the trading forecast is a statement which *projects* a year-end profit and loss statement. Look at the simple example of the trading forecast of a manufacturing business shown below.

Small manufacturing business –Trading Forecast for 1996

	£	£
Sales income		500,000
less expenses		
Purchases of raw materials	250,000	
Wages	100,000	
Water rates	500	
Telephone	1,000	
Other running costs	50,000	
		401,500
Profit for the year		98,500

Note that these figures are *projections* based on:

- what the business expects to sell
- what the business expects the raw materials will cost
- the wages due for the projected level of production
- expenses due for the year

The expenses due have been simplified in this trading forecast. 'Other running costs' would include items such as advertising, office expenses, insurance, heating and lighting bills, business rates and interest paid on borrowed money. Note that none of the figures shown in the trading forecast includes VAT.

where do the figures come from?

In a small business it is likely that all the necessary figures will be in the hands of the owner, and so drawing up the trading forecast will be a simple affair, and will lead on to the cash flow forecast.

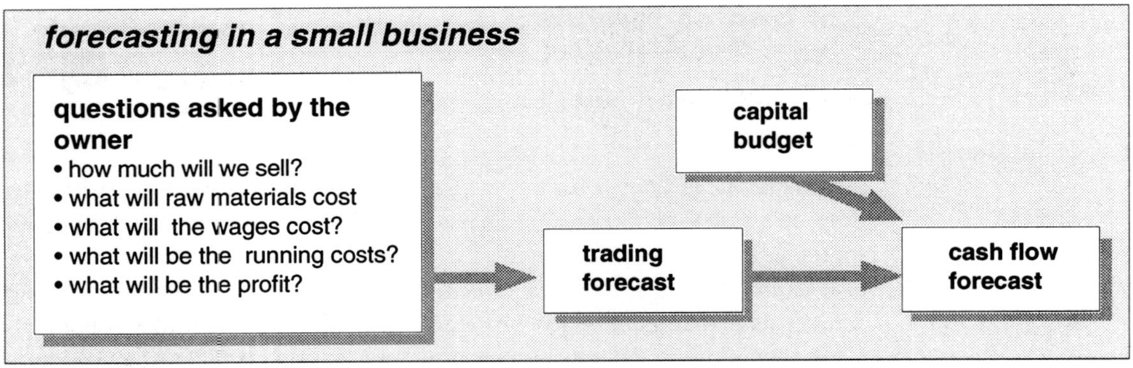

forecasting in the larger business

In a larger business the situation is more complex: the figures will be derived from a series of forecasts from individual departments, eg the sales budget, the purchases budget, the production budget, the overheads budget. These figures are then combined with the capital budget requirements in the cash flow forecast. This in turn contributes to the master budget which contains a profit & loss forecast and a forecast balance sheet .

Now compare the diagram below with the small business diagram above. You will see that the *principles* of budgeting remain the same; it is just that the *process* is more simple in the small business.

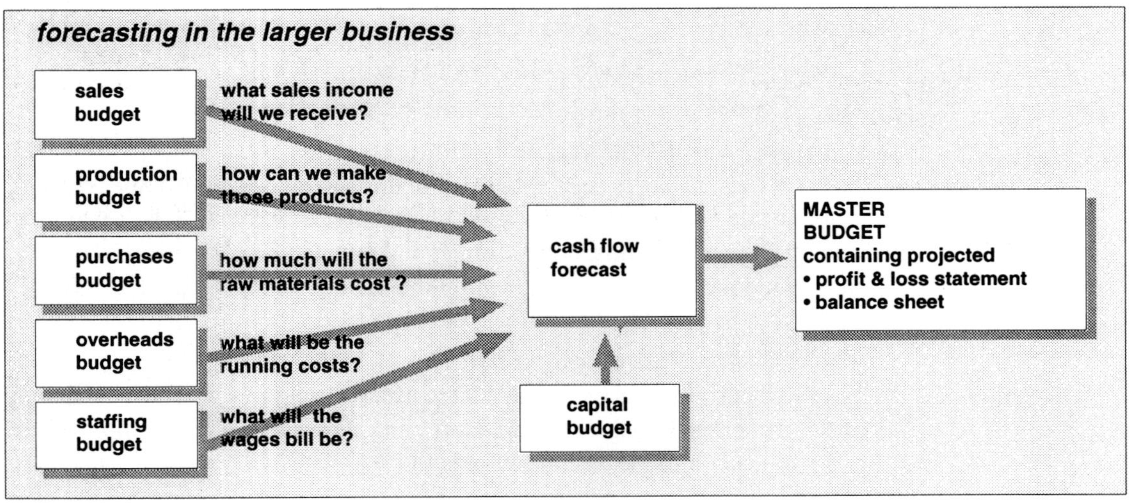

STUDENT ACTIVITY 9.1
performance criterion 7.2.1

business forecasting

situation

Carter Fine Foods is a small sole trader business run by Neil Carter. It manufactures a wide range of cakes and pastry dishes. Neil is currently planning next year's production, but has not yet got his figures into any form of forecast. He tells you:

"I want to expand next year by buying a new shop in March. I have my eye on one at the moment; it will cost £85,000. The following month I will need to buy new ovens, probably for £25,000. I also need a new delivery van for January, I doubt if the present one will get through its MOT. I reckon £10,000 will get me a good second-hand one.

As for sales, we are taking £8,000 a month now, and should average an extra 20% next year. Raw material purchases normally cost 50 per cent of sales. Our monthly expenses on average will be purchases £5,000; wages £1,500; other expenses £2,000 a month."

tasks

You are to draw up for the twelve month period January to December 1996:

1 an *annual* capital budget using the budget heads of premises, vehicles and equipment

2 an *annual* trading forecast using the budget heads of sales, raw material purchases, wages and other expenses (note: do not split the forecast into monthly periods)

When you have completed the two tables, devise spreadsheet masks for them both and input the figures from the two forecasts. Use the spreadsheets to check your calculations. Make sure that you save the two files for later use.

purpose of the cash flow forecast

pc 7.2.4

The cash flow forecast projects the amounts of money received into and paid out of the bank account each month.

A typical cash flow forecast sets out:

- the expected bank account receipts and payments
- on a month-by-month basis
- for a twelve month period

The cash flow forecast (also known as the cash budget) shows projections of *all* money received and money spent over the year (including VAT) passing through the bank account, eg sales income, runnning expenses, payment of tax, purchase of capital items. The 'bottom line' of each monthly column shows the forecast bank balance at the end of that month.

why draw up a cash fow forecast?

A business uses a cash flow forecast for a number of different reasons:

timing purchases

It will show the effect on the bank balance of buying *capital assets* (shown in the *capital budget)* at different times of year. It may prove that capital assets should be bought later in the year rather than earlier when there is little cash or expected income. It will also prove useful for a business which is subject to seasonal trends. A retailer, for example, which sells more at Christmas, will show greater sales income in November and December, but may need to pay for stock earlier than this. The figures here will come from the *trading forecast.*

supporting an application for finance

The cash flow forecast is arguably the most important financial statement in the Business Plan which is presented to a prospective lender in an application for finance. It shows *what* amount needs to be borrowed and *when.* If the figures show that the bank balance will move into credit, it provides the lender with *confidence* that borrowing can be repaid, and also gives the owner confidence that targets can be met.

monitoring performance

Many cash flow forecasts have extra columns each month so that the actual figures can be filled in as the months pass. Projected performance can then be compared with actual performance and any variations noted, and action taken. Sales income, for example may fall below expectation: the business would then probably have to reduce some costs.

format of the cash flow forecast

A simplified format of a cash flow forecast, with sample figures, is set out below. Study it carefully and read the commentary which follows.

Name ....Cash Flow Forecast for the .... months ending ....

	Jan £000	Feb £000	Mar £000	etc... £000
Receipts				
eg sales receipts	150	150	161	170
other receipts (loans, capital, VAT recovered)	70	80	75	80
Total receipts for month (A)	220	230	236	250
Payments				
eg to suppliers for raw materials or stock (creditors)	160	165	170	170
other payments (eg expenses, loans repaid, VAT paid)	50	50	50	60
fixed assets purchased		50		
Total payments for month (B)	210	265	220	230
Opening bank balance at beginning of month	10	20	(15)	1
add total receipts (A)	220	230	236	250
less total payments (B)	210	265	220	230
Bank balance (overdraft) at end of month	20	(15)	1	21

As you can see, the cash budget consists of three main sections:

Receipts are analysed for each month to show the amount that is expected to be received from sources such as cash sales, receipts from customers supplied on credit, sale of fixed assets, loans, capital introduced, VAT recovered, and any interest or other income received.

Payments will show how much is expected to be paid each month for cash purchases, to creditors (suppliers), running expenses, purchases of fixed assets, repayment of capital and loans, interest paid and VAT and other tax paid.

The **Bank** summary at the bottom of the budget shows the bank balance at the beginning of the month, to which all receipts are added (A) and payments deducted (B) resulting in the estimated closing bank balance at the end of the month. An overdrawn bank balance is shown in brackets, or by a minus sign.

timing and the cash flow forecast

pc 7.2.5

The main difficulty in the preparation of cash flow forecasts lies in the *timing* of receipts and payments – knowing which figure to enter for which month. For example, if a business sells goods in January, it is likely to be paid for them in February or March. The problems of timing affect a number of areas:

credit periods

As mentioned above, the cash flow forecast must take credit periods into consideration and show for each month:

- the amount *expected to be received* for sales for the month
- the amount *expected to be paid* for purchases during the month

bills and loan repayments

Some bills are payable *in arrears* – an electricity supply company will send you a bill *after* the end of the charging period. Some bills are payable *in advance* – water rates, for example, are often payable six-monthly in advance. BT bills contain *both* types: line rental is payable in advance and call charges in arrears! Loan repayments also need to be timed carefully: they can be made monthly, quarterly or even annually.

VAT payments

If a business is registered for VAT (Value Added Tax), it must record:

- the amount of VAT charged to customers on products it sells (this is known as 'output VAT')
- the amount of VAT it is charged on the goods and services it buys (this is known as 'input VAT')

Normally every three months a business will send a form (a VAT return) to HM Customs & Excise (the VAT authorities) *either*

- enclosing a cheque for the excess of output VAT (VAT on sales) over input tax (VAT on purchases), *or*
- making a repayment claim for the excess of input tax (VAT on purchases) over output tax (VAT on sales)

You may well ask how a business can pay more VAT on purchases than it charges on sales. The answer is that some goods (eg books, food, childrens clothes) are *zero-rated* – no VAT is payable on them. Therefore a business like a bookshop will be able to claim back most of the VAT it pays. How does VAT affect the timing of the cash flow forecast? As we saw above, every quarter a VAT registered business will either send a cheque for VAT with the VAT return or receive a refund of VAT onto its bank account via the BACS. This will normally happen in the month after the end of the VAT quarter.

constructing the cash flow forecast

pcs 7.2.6 - 9

We will now explain the various *headings* which appear in the Receipts and Payments sections of the cash flow forecast by means of a Case Study. This shows how the forecast is constructed and where the figures come from. Note that all figures include VAT where it is charged.

CASE STUDY

pcs 7.2.6 - 9

Merry-go-round Limited – a cash flow forecast

situation

Merry-go-round Limited is a small private limited company. It is a family business which makes outdoor toys for children – slides, swings, climbing frames, trampolines and so on. It operates in a leased factory unit on an industrial estate in Broadfield. It supplies stores throughout the UK and also operates a successful factory shop which has the benefit of a cash sales income.

Tom Merry, the Managing Director, is looking to expand the company by purchasing in January new machinery which will enable the business to manufacture its own moulded plastic products. The machinery will cost £50,000 and will be financed partly by a bank loan for £25,000 and partly by new capital of £25,000 introduced by the shareholders (the Merry family). Tom realises that the expansion will also mean that extra working capital is required, and will probably need to be financed by a bank overdraft. The question is, how much cash will the company need?

With the help of his accountant he draws up:

- a *capital budget* showing the purchase of the new machinery in January of the following year
- a *trading forecast* showing the increased sales and costs for the year

He now needs to construct a cash flow forecast to include in the Business Plan which he will take to the bank when he applies for finance. He uses a computer spreadsheet to set out the forecast, with a number of different headings in the receipts and payments sections.

As you read the following descriptions, refer to the cash flow forecast on pages 192 and 193.

receipts

cash sales — The factory shop is likely to take £8,000 per month in January and February, and then £9,000 a month when the new products are introduced (figures include VAT).

credit sales — Money received from credit sales is normally received in the month following issue of the invoice. Tom reckons he will receive £18,000 a month in January, February and March, and £25,000 a month for the rest of the year, following the introduction of the new products.

capital — The shareholders (the Merry family) will introduce £25,000 in January to help finance the new machinery.

loans — The bank is being asked for a £25,000 business loan to help finance the new machinery in January.

payments

raw materials — These are paid for a month after the invoice date. It is estimated they will cost £15,000 a month for the first four months of the year and £17,000 a month after that.

capital assets — The new machinery costing £50,000 will be bought and paid for in January.

wages — The wages bill for the company averages £10,000 a month.

water rates — Water rates for the year have to be paid for *in advance* in April. The company's water rates are £1,457.

telephone — Telephone bills, on the other hand, are paid for quarterly *in arrears*. On the basis of the previous year's bills they are likely to average £565 a quarter, paid in January, April, July and October.

heat and light — Gas and electricity bills are also paid for in arrears. They will average in total £650 a quarter, paid in January, April, July and October.

insurance — The company's comprehensive insurance premium of £7,500 is due *in advance* in June.

other costs — Other costs such as office expenses and advertising average £615 a month, paid monthly.

interest costs — Tom calculates that interest on his borrowing, including any overdraft will be £680 (March), £720 (June), £650 (September), £630 (December).

Loan repayments — Repayments on bank borrowing are £4,000 a quarter (March, June, September, December).

VAT — The company is registered for VAT and will have to send a cheque off with the VAT return every quarter. The amount each time will be VAT charged on sales less VAT paid on expenses over the previous three months.

totalling up the forecast

When the figures have been entered in the appropriate columns (see the next two pages), the following totals will be calculated by Tom's computer spreadsheet in the far right-hand column and the bank summary at the bottom of the forecast. If a computer spreadsheet is not used, these totals will have to be calculated manually – which is hard work! The figures are:

- totals for each category of receipt or expense in the far right-hand 'total' column (total across each row)
- total receipts for each month, and the far right-hand 'total' column, ie work down the columns
- total payments for each month, and the far right-hand column, ie work down the columns
- cross check the totals for both receipts and payments – ie the total of the monthly columns and the totals in the (far right) total column
- lastly, total monthly receipts and total monthly payments should be entered in the bank position on the appropriate line at the bottom of the forecast

the bank position

The bank position can now be calculated. Refer to the cash flow forecast on the next two pages as you read this section.

opening bank balance	Insert the bank balance at the beginning of January in the row marked 'Opening bank', the figure is £125 in this case.
add receipts	Add total receipts for the month.
deduct payments	Subtract total payments for the month.
closing bank	This is the projected month-end bank balance of the business. It is an overdraft of £4,455 in January. This figure should then also be written in as February's 'Opening Bank' balance. The process is then repeated for February, and so on.

The bottom line of the cash flow forecast shows the all-important figure of the closing bank balance (the expected balance at the end of each month). A minus figure (or a figure in brackets) indicates an overdraft – ie the business will be borrowing from the bank on its current account (subject to the bank' agreement!) A positive figure means there is money in the bank account. In this case Merry-go-round Limited will be borrowing on overdraft for most months until August when the borrowing will be repaid.

Merry-go-round Limited: cash flow forecast

	A	B	C	D	E	F	G
1	CASH FLOW FORECAST						
2	Name: Merry-go-round Limited						
3	Period: January - December 199-						
4							
5		Jan	Feb	Mar	Apr	May	Jun
6		£	£	£	£	£	£
7	RECEIPTS						
8	Cash sales	8000	8000	9000	9000	9000	9000
9	Credit sales	18000	18000	18000	25000	25000	25000
10	Capital	25000					
11	Loans	25000					
12	VAT receipts						
13	Interest						
14	Other income						
15	TOTAL RECEIPTS	76000	26000	27000	34000	34000	34000
16							
17	PAYMENTS						
18	Raw materials	15000	15000	15000	15000	17000	17000
19	Capital assets	50000					
20	Wages	10000	10000	10000	10000	10000	10000
21	Water rates				1457		
22	Telephone	565			565		
23	Heat & light	650			650		
24	Insurance						7500
25	Other costs	615	615	615	615	615	615
26	Interest costs			680			720
27	Loan repayments			4000			4000
28	VAT payments	3750			3885		
29	TOTAL PAYMENTS	80580	25615	30295	32172	27615	39835
30							
31	Opening Bank	125	-4455	-4070	-7365	-5537	848
32	Add Receipts	76000	26000	27000	34000	34000	34000
33	Less Payments	80580	25615	30295	32172	27615	39835
34	Closing Bank	-4455	-4070	-7365	-5537	848	-4987
35							

H	I	J	K	L	M	N
Jul	Aug	Sep	Oct	Nov	Dec	TOTAL
£	£	£	£	£	£	£
9000	9000	9000	9000	9000	9000	106000
25000	25000	25000	25000	25000	25000	279000
						25000
						25000
						0
						0
						0
34000	34000	34000	34000	34000	34000	435000
17000	17000	17000	17000	17000	17000	196000
						50000
10000	10000	10000	10000	10000	10000	120000
						1457
565			565			2260
650			650			2600
						7500
615	615	615	615	615	615	7380
		650			630	2680
		4000			4000	16000
4150			4150			15935
32980	27615	32265	32980	27615	32245	421812
-4987	-3967	2418	4153	5173	11558	125
34000	34000	34000	34000	34000	34000	435000
32980	27615	32265	32980	27615	32245	421812
-3967	2418	4153	5173	11558	13313	13313

using a computer spreadsheet

pcs 7.2.6 - 9

the benefits of a spreadsheet program

The calculations on a cash flow forecast are not particularly difficult, but they do take a long time if you are tackling the task with only pencil, paper and calculator. The task is, of course, made simple when you have input the worksheet onto a computer spreadsheet program. You will be able to change any figure, and the computer will do all the recalculations automatically, for example:

- projections of different levels of sales – optimistic, realistic and pessimistic
- projections of different levels of expenditure
- the effect of buying an asset at different times

In each case you will be able to see the effect on the critical figure of the closing bank balance which indicates the amount of money the business may have to borrow.

use of formulas in the spreadsheet – column C

Extensive use is made in cash flow forecasts of the adding together of a range of cells. You will need to check your computer manual to find the formula to use for your own program. The formula used here is =Sum(C8:C14) where all the cells between C8 and C14 are added together. The formulas for column C are as follows:

- Rows 15 and 32 – Total Receipts =Sum(C8:C14)
- Rows 29 and 33 – Total Payments =Sum(C18:C28)
- Row 31 – Opening Bank =B34

  – ie the closing bank balance of the *previous month.* Note that B31 is a value cell into which is entered the opening bank balance for the period.
- Row 34 – Closing Bank =C31+C32–C33
- Column N – Total column

  Each row is totalled, eg cell N8 is =Sum(B8:M8) and N29 is =Sum(N18:N28). Column N is also totalled vertically, in the same way as the other columns, except that cell N31 is =B31 and cell N34 is =M34. N32 is =Sum(B32:BM32) and N33 is =Sum(B33:M33).

STUDENT ACTIVITY 9.2
performance criteria 7.2.5 – 9

cash flow forecasts on computer spreadsheet

tasks

The tasks in this Activity should be carried out using a computer spreadsheet program. If you are unable to gain access to a suitable system, you should set up the forecasts using pencil and paper (clearly a more laborious and less flexible alternative). If time and opportunity permit, show the Case Study and completed spreadsheets to a bank lending officer to find out how a lender would react to the proposal.

1 Set up a computer spreadsheet for Merry-go-round Limited and input the figures from the Case Study. Print out the forecast and check the figures against those shown in the Case Study.

2 The accountant of Merry-go-round Limited is unhappy about presenting a single cash flow forecast to the bank and asks that a "best view" and "worst view" scenario are forecast on the following basis:

(a) The best view assumes that:

- cash sales receipts increase to £11,000 per month from March
- credit sales receipts increase to £28,000 per month from April

(b) The worst view assumes that the new machine fails to work and that the monthly sales receipts for the year stay at their January level.

You are to set up two new spreadsheet files based on (a) and (b). Amend the sales receipts figures only. For the sake of simplicity do not attempt to adjust any other figures. Print out the two new files.

3 (a) What do the three forecasts show, and what would be the likely reaction of a lender such as a bank? How would the "best view" and "worst view" alternatives affect the proposed bank loan?

(b) In the case of the "best view" and "worst view" scenarios, discuss the effect the increase and decrease in sales would have on raw materials purchases, VAT payable and interest payable.

the consequences of incorrect forecasting

pc 7.2.10

It must be appreciated that cash flow forecasts are only informed *estimates* of what the cash position of a business is expected to be over a given period. If a business seriously overestimates the inflow of cash, it is likely to have problems when that cash does not materialise. The major problem is *depletion of working capital.*

As you will have seen in your studies, working capital is the lifeblood of a business, being the excess of current assets (money in hand and due in the short-term) over current liabilities (bills which have to be paid in the short-term). A business which underestimates the need for working capital may experience problems with the money cycle (see page 16). Cash flow problems and working capital shortages may result in the business becoming insolvent (bankrupt) – the definition of insolvency being the inability to pay debts as they fall due. A worst view scenario might run along the following lines:

- cash due from debtors does not come in – a major debtor may have become bankrupt
- there is pressure on the bank account as important creditors and wages have to be paid – the bank manager is distinctly unhappy as the overdraft rises above the limit set by the bank, even though the borrowing is secured by a charge (mortgage) over the business premises
- the bank refuses to pay a cheque to a major supplier to whom the business owes money – the supplier refuses to supply any further goods on which the business depends for its production
- the business is unable to fulfil some important orders, so sales income falls further
- employees find that their wages are not being paid
- the bank decides that it is unlikely to be repaid and so it appoints an Administrative Receiver under its mortgage
- the business is closed down by the Receiver and the assets of the business sold off to repay the bank overdraft
- the employees lose their jobs and the owners lose their business

This is an extreme situation, although regrettably it is all too common. The point here is not so much that you will become bankrupt if you get your cash flow forecast wrong but rather that forecasting and control of cash flow are critically important for the management of any business.

EVIDENCE COLLECTION ASSIGNMENT 9

Compumail Ltd – financial forecasting

Element 7.2

introduction

This assignment tests your understanding of

- the way in which a small business uses financial data to draw up a capital budget, a trading forecast and a cash flow forecast
- how a computer spreadsheet can be used to make forecasting easier
- how a business will use the forecasts it makes
- what could happen if a business did not make accurate forecasts

situation

Rashid Singh runs a limited company – Compumail – from home. He does mailshots for businesses. His customers provide him with promotional material such as catalogues together with a list of addresses on computer disk. Rashid prints address labels from the disk on his computer system, inserts the promotional material in envelopes, franks them and arranges for them to be posted. He does the computer work himself and relies on part-time help for handling and franking the envelopes.

He now wants to increase his turnover by building a 'mailing room' onto his house, buying a machine which will wrap catalogues in plastic film, ready for mailing, and then buying a small van for collecting material from clients. He states that his house extension will cost £10,000 and will have to be paid for in April; the machine will cost £5,000 and will have to be paid for in May. The van (second-hand) will be bought in August for about £7,500.

task 1 – the capital budget

pcs 7.2.1 & 3

You are Rashid's financial adviser. You are to set up a capital budget for Compumail on a computer spreadsheet, using the following headings :

- premises
- machinery and equipment
- vehicles

Add explanatory notes setting out what a capital budget is and why it is useful. Use the current year and assume that the first month is January.

task 2 – the trading forecast

pcs 7.2.2 & 3

The projected figures for Compumail for the next year are set out below. You will notice that some of the figures increase in May; this is because the new machine and mailing room will become operational then. For the sake of simplicity VAT is ignored in this Task. Assume that the figures shown below exclude VAT, ie use them as they stand.

Cash sales	£2,000	per month
Credit sales	£10,000	per month (January to April)
	£15,000	per month (May to December)
Materials	£6,000	per month (January to April)
	£8,000	per month (May to December)
Wages	£5,000	per month (January to April)
	£6,200	per month (May to December)
Water rates	£450	annual (advance) payment in April
Telephone	£200	quarterly in arrears (January, April etc)
Heat & light	£305	quarterly in arrears (January, April etc)
Insurance	£2,500	annual premium paid in June
Other costs	£425	per month

You are to:

(a) Set out an annual *trading forecast* for Compumail on a computer spreadsheet. Remember that the monthly figures for sales and purchases ignore any credit periods – in other words the sales and purchases totals for the year are the totals of the figures shown above.

(b) Write notes for the owner explaining what a trading forecast is and what it shows.

(c) Comment on the forecast profit made by the business and explain to the owner how it could (or should) be used. Compumail is a limited company business.

task 3 – the cash flow forecast

pcs 7.2.4 – 10

You are now in a position to construct a cash flow forecast for Compumail.

Remember the following points:

- A cash flow forecast records actual receipts and payments which pass through the bank account
- Credit sales and purchases of materials are paid for here *in the month following the actual sale*: eg credit sales were £15,000 in May, but the money will be received in June.
- All other expenses are paid in the month in which they are incurred.
- The cash flow forecast also records capital purchases (see capital budget)

Note also:

- The opening bank balance of Compumail is £2,500
- Assume for the sake of simplicity that all figures now *include* VAT.
- VAT payments are due to be made as follows; January £2,625; April £2,625; July £3,000; October £3,000.

You are to:

(a) Construct a cash flow forecast for Compumail on a computer spreadsheet, entering all the figures given. Print out your results and comment on the state of the bank account during the year. What do you think might solve the problem?

(b) You learn that Rashid's uncle is prepared to lend him £10,000 which he will have available in April. Rashid himself has £10,000 which he plans to invest in the business in April. He says that he will go to the bank for a loan to cover any more money that is needed when he buys the new van in August. Amend the spreadsheet to show these new investments and save as a new file. How much money is Rashid likely to want from the bank, and for how long? Print out a copy of the new spreadsheet to support your comments.

(c) One of Rashid's cousins says that he thinks the cash flow forecast is a waste of time because it is impossible to be precise about future events. He says that if it were his business he would not bother to go to the bank for money for the van because the business would be earning so much more then anyway, and he could easily afford the van. Comment on these views and amend the spreadsheet, assuming that credit sales receipts fall to £10,000 per month from August onwards. Explain step-by-step what could happen to the business as a result.

chapter summary and key terms

- A forecast is a financial plan for a set time period (often 12 months).
- Forecasting is an important element of the business planning process, and financial forecasts form an essential part of the Business Plan produced by the business to support an application for finance.
- Forecasts also enable a business to assess future courses of action, to set targets, and to monitor performance against those targets.
- The capital budget plans for the purchase of fixed assets such as premises, machinery and vehicles, normally over a twelve month period.
- The trading forecast projects sales income and expense items such as raw materials, wages, water rates, telephone bills and other running costs, normally over a twelve month period.
- The cash flow forecast projects the amount of money in the bank account month-by-month; it brings together the capital budget and the trading forecast. It highlights the importance of the timing of payments. It also shows a lender such as a bank how much finance is needed, and when.
- The consequences of incorrect forecasting (or lack of forecasting) can be serious for a business. In extreme circumstances they can lead to business failure.

key terms

Business Plan	the formal written plan prepared by the business to present to a lender when it is asking for finance or assistance – it is covered in full in GNVQ Unit 8
components of forecasts	the different types of forecast include the capital budget, the trading forecast and the cash flow forecast
budget heads	these are the different categories of income and expenses which make up the budget statements, eg sales, purchases, wages etc
timing of payments	the timing of when an income item will be received and when an expense item will be paid – this can make all the difference to the state of the bank account of a business

multiple-choice questions

1 A capital budget is
- A a forecast of the capital assets a business intends to buy
- B the total of the capital contributed by the business owners
- C a forecast of capital coming in and out of the bank account
- D a spending allowance given to sales reps when they visit London

2 A trading forecast
- A advises a business which customers to trade with
- B sets out the likely level of sales in any given industry
- C sets out the likely level of sales and expenses
- D advises a business about the level of finance needed

Questions 3 – 5 relate to the following information:

In a cash flow forecast
- A the bottom line shows the monthly bank balance
- B the purchase of all assets is shown
- C changes in sales figures can affect cash flow

Which of the above statements applies to the following?

3 A cash flow forecast enables a business to work out the financing of capital items.

4 A cash flow forecast helps to support an application for finance.

5 A cash flow forecast is an ideal application for a computer spreadsheet.

6 Decide whether each of these statements is True (T) or False (F)
- (i) a cash flow forecast will show sales as they are invoiced
- (ii) the sales figures in a cash flow forecast include VAT

- A (i) T (ii) T
- B (i) T (ii) F
- C (i) F (ii) T
- D (i) F (ii) F

10 Monitoring the performance of a business

GNVQ SPECIFICATIONS

Element 7.4

Identify and explain data to monitor a business

performance criteria – a student must:

1 identify users of accounting information

2 explain the reasons for monitoring a business

3 explain the use of comparisons and variance in monitoring a business

4 Identify and explain key components of information required to monitor a business

5 explain the implications for the performance of a business from a given set of accounting information

6 explain the use of solvency ratios, profitability ratios and performance ratios in the interpretation of accounting information

what this chapter covers

Earlier in this book we investigated the ways in which accounting information is recorded and presented. In this chapter we look at the different types of people who will need this accounting information, and the ways in which they will analyse it to assess business peformance.

what you will learn from this chapter

- the people who will want to see accounting information from a business are the owners (including shareholders), managers, employees, providers of finance (such as the banks), the tax authorities and the public
- they need to see the information for a variety of reasons: making sure the business is in a healthy and profitable state, making sure that it is performing to target, assessing it for the amount of tax that is due, and ensuring that it will be able to repay any borrowing
- the types of accounting information assessed include forecasts, profit and loss statements, balance sheets, and aged debtor and creditor schedules
- the business can be assessed by extracting ratios from key figures in the profit and loss statement and balance sheet; these ratios cover the areas of solvency, profitability, and performance

who needs to monitor a business?

pcs 7.4.1 & 2

In this section we describe the *users* of accounting information and the reasons *why* they monitor a business.

the owners

Whether the business is a small sole trader enterprise or a public limited company (where the owners are its shareholders), the owner(s) will want to know how the business is performing in terms of sales and profitability, and whether it is *solvent*, ie it can repay its debts.

the managers

The management of a business will want to know the financial state of the business as they will have to take day-to-day decisions on the basis of the information. Managers will therefore look at:

- performance against *forecast targets* – sales, expenses, profit
- ways in which they can *improve* that performance
- control of the *money cycle* – paying debts and getting customers to pay

providers of finance

Lenders such as banks will want to be reassured that any money lent to the business will be repaid when due. They will be particularly interested in:

- *profitability* – can borrowing be repaid in the future?
- *liquidity* – can short-term borrowing be repaid now?

the tax authorities

The tax authorities will need to have financial information so that they can assess or check on how much tax will have to be paid. For example:

- VAT due to HM Customs & Excise is based on VAT charged on sales
- income tax for individuals in business (and corporation tax for limited companies) due to the Inland Revenue is based on business profit

the public

The public will be interested in the financial performance of a business, either as *investors* looking for dividends in that business, or for political or ethical reasons – is the business making *too much* profit?

employees

The employer will want to motivate the employee and instil loyalty by showing that the business is doing well, particularly in terms of profitability.

comparisons and variances

pc 7.4.3

Users of accounting information will make comparisons which will highlight variances. *Comparisons* involve comparing figures in a general sense. *Variances* refer to financial forecasts and measure the difference between actual and forecast figures.

comparisons

Comparisons involve:

- comparing actual figures with those forecast in the budgets produced by the business and calculating *variances*
- comparing this year's figures (eg for profit, costs or sales) with those from previous years
- comparing figures (eg profit, costs or sales) from one business with those from another business in the same industry

We will now illustrate these points.

comparing actual and forecast figures – variances

Set out below is an extract from a sales budget report for a business. You will see that it shows sales for the current period (October in this case) and the sales for the year so far. Look at the report and then read the text that follows.

BUDGETARY CONTROL REPORT –SALES

budget centre Sales Dept date 07.11.1995
month October 1995

	current period			*Year-to-date*			*trend*
	budget £000s	actual £000s	variance £000s	budget £000s	actual £000s	variance £000s	
PRODUCT A	200	250	+ 50	2,750	3,125	+ 375	FAV
PRODUCT B	225	200	– 25	1,275	1,150	– 125	ADV
PRODUCT C	425	450	+ 25	4,025	4,475	+ 450	FAV
etc . . .							

There are three columns under 'current period' and 'year-to-date', each of these showing:

- the budgeted (forecast) sales figure for each product
- the actual sales figure for each product
- any difference between the two – ie any *variance*

The final column shows the trend:

- FAV (favourable) means sales are better than forecast
- ADV (adverse) means sales are worse than forecast.

The management of the business would examine this report critically and investigate variances: "Why is product B not doing so well? Does it need more promotion? Are there any faults in the product?"

year-to-year comparisons

It is common practice to show the year-to-year trends in accounting data, eg the profit figures or sales figures. This enables owners, managers, employees, shareholders and the public to see how the business is progressing.

These financial trends lend themselves to diagramatic representation in the form of graphs and bar charts.

Look at the example shown below.

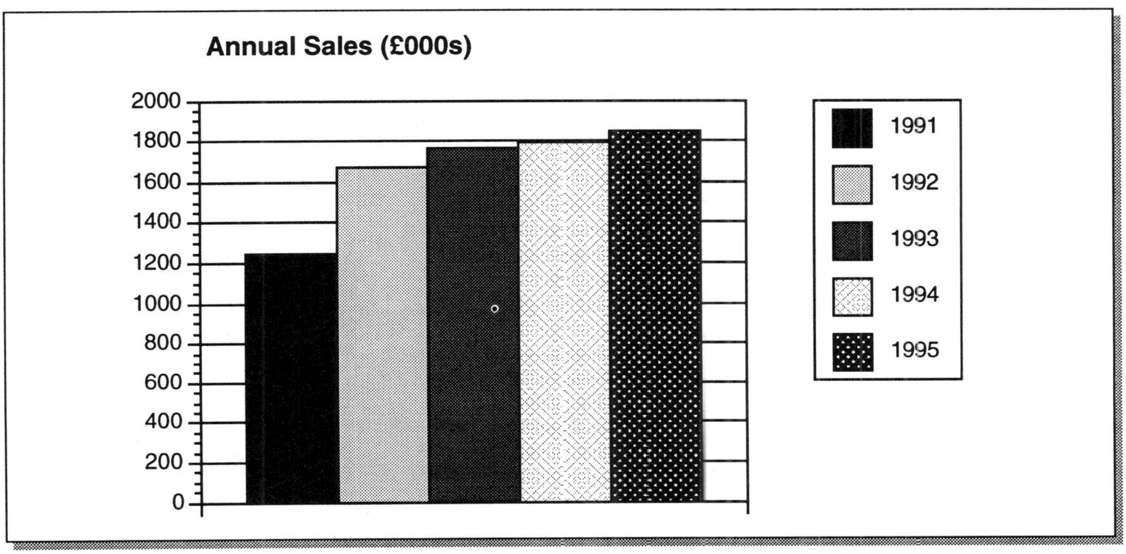

inter-firm comparisons

It is often useful to compare the performance of a business with that of other businesses in the same industry. Comparisons of this sort can be found in newspaper reports and also in published statistics. Look at the examples shown on the next page.

The first illustration is the sort of table that would appear in a newspaper's financial section – it will be of particular interest to shareholders (who own the shares) and the public (who generally do not like banks to make a big profit!). The second illustration shows average gross profit percentages in the catering trade. These statistics will be of use to owners of businesses in the trade who will want to see if their type of business is performing as it should. The figures will also be of interest to the tax authorities who be able to spot if a trader is understating profits in order to fiddle the amount of tax payable!

Banks report half-year profits

Figures for the first six months of 1994

Bank	Pre-tax profit (£M)
Barclays	1,036
NatWest	767
Lloyds	605
Abbey National	423

The Catering Trade
Gross Profit percentages

Trade	1992	1988
	%	%
Hotels and guesthouses	82.5	51.8
Holiday camps and caravan sites	77.0	54.8
Restaurants and cafes –food eaten on site	71.0	43.3
Fish and chip shops & other takeaways	67.6	42.6
Public houses	61.4	33.7

information for owners and managers

pc 7.4.4

We will now look at the types of accounting information – the *components* of accounting information – used by the owners and managers of a business in order to monitor its performance.

trends over time

Accounting information relatingto areas such as sales income, profit, and expenses can relate to three different time periods:

1. the *past* – trends can be identified by looking at what has happened in the past, possibly over a number of years, eg an increase in sales, an increase in profitability
2. the *present* – a business can see what is going on at the present time and relate it to the past and what it thinks is going to happen in the future through budget monitoring (see the next page)
3. *the future* – a business, as we have seen in Chapter 9 can forecast financial performance, using figures from the past and the present as a guide to what is likely to happen as a result of its planning processes

components used to provide information

You will already have studied the main components (financial statements) used by a business in the planning and monitoring process. They are:

- the *profit and loss statement* – showing business profitability and enabling the business to monitor income and expenses
- the *balance sheet* – showing how solvent the business is and what it owns and owes
- the *cash flow statement* – showing the money flows in and out of the bank account over a given future period

Clearly the profit and loss statement and balance sheet can be of use to the business as guides to past performance, as a statement of the current situation and also as a basis for a forecast. In Chapter 9 we looked at forecast profit and loss statements in the form of trading forecasts. The cash flow forecast is also, by definition, a statement of what is expected to happen in the future.

financial statements and business planning

All three financial statements discussed above will help owners and managers to think through the financial development of their business. They will also form an integral part of a *Business Plan* (see Chapter 11) and should give a provider of finance such as a bank sufficient information to enable an informed lending decision to be made.

business planning and monitoring

The diagram below shows four stages in business planning and monitoring. Study it carefully and note how it involves

- profit and loss statement and balance sheet
- cash flow forecast

Note that a continuous cycle is involved: what has happened in the past affects both the present and the future

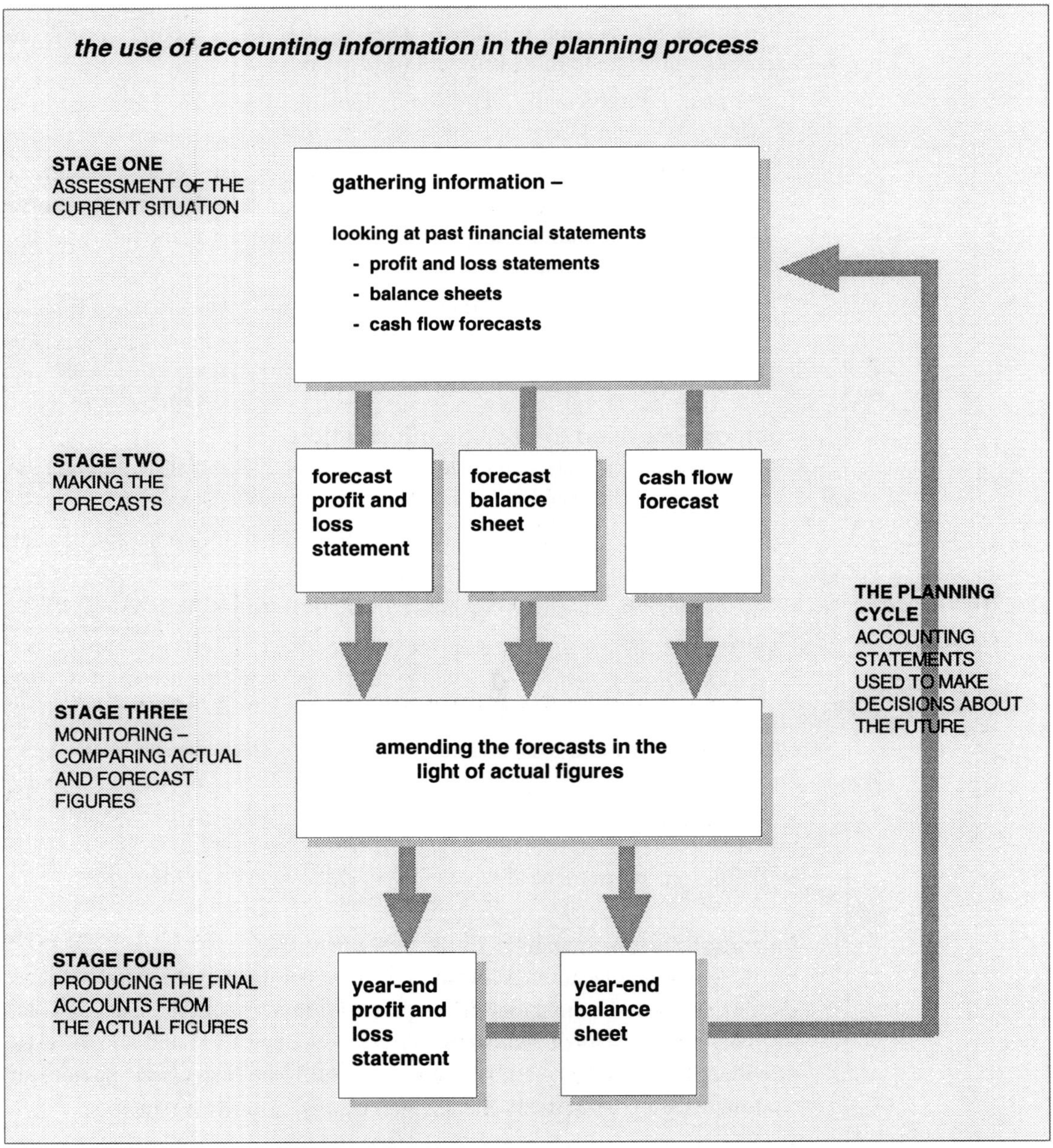

aged debtor schedule

The management of a business will need to ensure that customers who buy on credit pay up promptly. In this way a steady supply of funds will be received into the *money cycle.*

Credit control involves monitoring the sales ledger and chasing debtors for money. The management is kept informed each month about the bad payers by means of a report known as an *aged debtor schedule.* This is a list of individual debtors (customers), the amounts they owe, and the period of time the debts have been outstanding. The list can be extracted by hand from the sales ledger, or printed out automatically by computer if a computer accounting system is used.

The aged debtors schedule will enable a business to take decisions to follow up overdue amounts, and recover money which might otherwise become bad debt.

Study the example set out below.

JR CATERING LTD — SALES LEDGER - AGED DEBTORS SCHEDULE

A/C	Account Name	Turnover	Credit Limit	Balance	Current	30 Days	60 Days	Older
201	Merrion & Co	370.00	1000.00	164.50	164.50	0.00	0.00	0.00
202	Kingfisher Ltd	320.00	750.00	376.00	376.00	0.00	0.00	0.00
204	I Marcos	1730.00	1000.00	1632.75	799.00	0.00	833.75	0.00
205	Compusoft Ltd	2025.00	2000.00	1926.88	1880.00	46.88	0.00	0.00
208	R Weinberger	425.00	750.00	499.38	499.38	0.00	0.00	0.00
	Totals :	4870.00	5500.00	4599.51	3718.88	46.88	833.75	0.00

Note that:

- *turnover* is the total amount of sales to the customer during the accounting period (usually a year)
- *credit limit* is the maximum amount that the business is willing to allow a customer to owe at any one time
- the *balance* is the amount owing by a customer at the date of the schedule
- the remaining columns show how the balance is made up: 'current' means that the amount is not yet due, '30 days' means 'over 30 days', '60 days' means 'over 60 days' and so on
- it will be up to the business to decide what debts are chased up, when and how – by statements, letters, telephone calls, or even legal action

aged creditor schedule

An *aged creditor schedule* may be prepared manually, or printed out by a computer accounting system, on a monthly basis. It is based on the same principles as an aged debtors schedule and shows what debts are due to whom, and when. It will ensure that debts are not paid before time, thus benefiting the *money cycle* (money not paid is money that can be used in the business). It will also ensure that debts *are* paid and that no problems are encountered with suppliers. A schedule is illustrated below.

JR CATERING LTD — PURCHASES LEDGER - AGED CREDITORS SCHEDULE

A/C	Account Name	Turnover	Credit Limit	Balance	Current	30 Days	60 Days	Older
601	Alpha Foods	1200.00	1000.00	164.50	164.50	0.00	0.00	0.00
602	Nova Meats Ltd	4562.50	3000.00	350.00	350.00	0.00	0.00	0.00
604	Tuscany Wines	750.75	1000.00	124.75	0.00	124.75	0.00	0.00
605	Bennets	2025.00	2000.00	345.26	0.00	45.26	300.00	0.00
608	Zeta Supplies	425.00	750.00	0.00	0.00	0.00	0.00	0.00
	Totals :	8963.25	7750.00	984.51	514.50	170.01	300.00	0.00

STUDENT ACTIVITY 10.1
performance criteria 7.4.1 – 3

presenting accounting information

tasks

1 Examine the two tables of figures on page 206 and set them out diagrammatically in the format which you consider *best* illustrates the comparison between

(a) the profits of the individual banks

(b) the two years of gross profits in the catering trade

If resources permit, use a suitable computer program to construct the charts. You may find it useful to collect examples of similar graphs from the financial press.

2 State *whom* you think would be interested in the statistics you have prepared, and *why* they will want to see the figures.

information for the public and employees

pc 7.4.4

We will now look at the types of accounting information that is presented by a business to the public and to its employees. We will take the *public limited company* as an example, largely because the published Report and Accounts of plcs are widely available and offer a interesting variety of methods of presentation of accounting information. They also provide information about issues such as environmental and social policy, which are becoming increasingly important. There are, of course other organisations which will present financial information to the public and employees: local authorities and public sector businesses, for example.

annual Reports and Accounts

Public limited companies quoted on the Stock Exchange produce each year:

- *Annual Report and Accounts* – a formal report sent to to shareholders in the form of a booklet containing a profit and loss statement and balance sheet (both with detailed notes) plus other information required by company law. Companies are normally willing to send copies to students and any other interested people.
- *Summary Financial Statement* sent to all shareholders – this is less formal and less detailed than the Report and Accounts and is intended to be easier to read and understand

You will see that these reports contain a full or summary financial statement, the *Cash Flow Statement*, (which is not covered by your studies). This is only required of larger companies, and sets out *how* money has been received and spent during the financial year. It should *not* under any circumstances be confused with the Cash Flow Forecast which is a budget, and quite different in format. Extracts from the Report & Accounts of The Body Shop International PLC are reproduced with kind permission on pages 148 and 221 of this book.

the public and employees

The public will be interested in company financial statements as

- *shareholders* – they may already own shares in the company
- *investors* – they may be interested in buying shares

Many large companies encourage employees to invest in their shares, and so the financial reports will also be intended to provide information to *employees*.

We will now turn to the way the financial statements of businesses are analysed by means of accounting ratios which indicate to the business owner and lenders how the business is performing.

business performance – solvency ratios

pcs 7.4.5 & 6

solvency

In basic terms a business is *solvent* when it is not bankrupt:

- it can pay its debts when they fall due
- its assets exceed its liabilities

We have seen when looking at the money cycle, that a business needs either cash or the ability to realise cash (eg a bank overdraft) as working capital in order to pay bills, wages, and other pressing expenses.

who is interested in solvency?

The *owner(s)* of a business will want to be reassured that the business is solvent. If the owner is a sole trader or partner and the business becomes insolvent (bankrupt), their possessions may have to be sold off to pay creditors. *Lenders*, too, will want to know how solvent a business is; if there are problems they will want their money back.

measuring solvency: the current ratio

current ratio = current assets : current liabilties

Using figures from the balance sheet, this ratio measures the relationship between current assets and current liabilities. Working capital (calculated as current assets minus current liabilities) is needed by all businesses in order to finance day-to-day trading activities. Sufficient working capital enables a business to hold adequate stocks, allow a measure of credit to its customers (debtors), and to pay its suppliers (creditors).

Although there is no ideal working capital ratio, an often accepted ratio is about 2:1, ie £2 of current assets to every £1 of current liabilities. However, a business in the retail trade may be able to work with a lower ratio, eg 1.5:1 or even less, because it deals mainly in sales for cash and so does not have a large figure for debtors.

measuring solvency: acid test ratio

acid test ratio = current assets minus stock : current liabilties

One of the problems with the current ratio is that it includes stock in the current assets as a possible source of cash. Stock, of course, may be unsaleable or obsolete – shell suits or out-of-date cans of beans, for example. The *acid test ratio* (also known as the quick ratio or liquid capital ratio) includes the current assets and current liabilities from the balance sheet, *but stock is omitted.* This is because stock is the *least liquid* current asset: it has to be sold first, turned into debtors, and then eventualy into cash .

The balance between liquid assets, that is debtors and cash/bank, and current liabilities should, ideally, be about 1:1, ie £1 of liquid assets to each £1 of current liabilities. At this ratio a business is expected to be able to pay its current liabilities from its liquid assets; a figure below 1:1, eg 0.75:1, indicates that the business would have difficulty in meeting pressing demands from creditors. However, as with the working capital ratio, certain types of business are able to operate with a lower liquid capital ratio than others.

The acid test ratio may also be expressed as a percentage:

$$\frac{\text{current assets minus stock}}{\text{current liabilties}} \times 100$$

Thus an acid test ratio of 1 : 1 becomes 100%

how are the ratios used?

With both the current and the acid test ratios, trends from one year to the next need to be considered, or comparisons made with similar organisations.

STUDENT ACTIVITY 10.2
performance criteria 7.4.5 & 6

solvency ratios

The following figures have been extracted from the balance sheets of Businesses A, B & C

Business	*Total Current Assets*	*Stock*	*Current Liabilities*
A	£20,000	£5,000	£10,000
B	£20,000	£15,000	£10,000
C	£20,000	£15,000	£15,000

1 Calculate the current and acid test ratio for all three businesses.

2 Comment on how solvent the businesses are.

3 Why would it be misleading to rely on just the current ratio for one of the businesses?

profitability ratios

pcs 7.4.5 & 6

profitability

Most people dealing with businesses will want to know how profitable they are:

- *owners* – because it will affect the return they get
- *managers* – because they will see how close to target they are
- *lenders* – they will know that money is being generated to repay them
- the *tax authorities* – they will be able to assess the amount of tax due
- the *public* – they will want to know if they are getting 'value for money'
- *employees* – they will be reassured that their jobs are safe

a large profit or a small profit?

Is it good policy to be seen to be making a large profit? Generally speaking, the answer is 'yes'. There are, however, one or two exceptions. A business is taxed on its profits, and many businesses will try to bring the profit figure (and the tax bill!) down by deducting as many expenses as possible from profit.

Also, the public do not like businesses making big profits at their expense. You may be able to think of businesses such as BT which dominate the market and have actually *reduced* their prices following large profits.

measuring profitability – return on net assets (RONA)

The *net assets* figure is the total at the bottom of a balance sheet. It is the value of the assets less all external liabilities – it shows the owner(s) investment in the business and what the business is worth to the owner(s). The *return on net assets* is the percentage return in the form of net profit that the owner(s) will receive in terms of the value of the net assets. It is calculated by the formula

$$\frac{\textit{net profit}}{\textit{net assets}} \times 100 = \textit{return on net assets (RONA)}$$

Thus if a sole trader makes a net profit of £15,000 and his net assets are £100,000 he will be making

$$\frac{£15{,}000}{£100{,}000} \times 100 = 15\% \textit{ return on net assets}$$

In other words he will be doing much better than if his money was tied up in a building society account giving him a 7.5% return. You should also note that he gets a better return because he is taking a greater *risk* with his money. It could be safer in a building society.

measuring profitability – gross profit percentage

You will know from your study of the profit and loss statement that the *gross profit* of a business is the profit made after deducting from the sales figure the cost of making a product – the 'cost of sales'. The gross profit percentage is calculated using the formula:

$$\frac{\textit{gross profit}}{\textit{sales}} \times 100 = \textit{gross profit percentage}$$

This expresses, as a percentage, the gross profit in relation to sales. For example, a gross profit percentage of 50 per cent means that for every £100 of sales made, the gross profit is £50. The gross profit percentage should be similar from year-to-year for the same business. It will vary between organisations in different areas of business, eg the gross profit percentage on jewellery is considerably higher than that on baked beans.

profit margin – net profit percentage

You will know from your study of the profit and loss statement that the *net profit* of a business is the profit made after deducting *all* the expenses, ie the cost of sales and overheads such as insurance, advertising, business rates, fuel, and so on. The formula is:

$$\frac{\textit{net profit}}{\textit{sales}} \times 100 = \textit{net profit percentage}$$

As with gross profit percentage, the net profit percentage should be similar from year-to-year for the same business, and should also be comparable with other firms in the same line of business. Any significant fall should be investigated to see if it has been caused by an increase in one particular expense, eg wages and salaries or advertising.

STUDENT ACTIVITY 10.3
performance criteria 7.4.5 & 6

profitability percentages

The following figures have been extracted from the accounts of Businesses A, B & C

Business	*Net Assets*	*Sales*	*Cost of sales*	*Other expenses*
A	£100,000	£500,000	£250,000	£200,000
B	£200,000	£800,000	£600,000	£160,000
C	£200,000	£600,000	£480,000	£100,000

Calculate the Return on Net Assets, Gross profit percentage and Net profit percentage for all three businesses. Comment on your findings, assuming that they all manufacture the same type of product.

performance ratios

pcs 7.4.5 & 6

We have seen that the solvency and profitability indicators are of particular interest to outside bodies . The *owners* and *managers* of a business, on the other hand, will be anxious to know how a business is performing. They are *responsible* for that level of performance:

"Are our administration costs increasing too much?"

"Are our overheads being kept under control?"

"Is the stock moving as quickly as it should?"

"Are our customers paying up on time?"

There are a number of *performance ratios* which will provide answers to these questions.

administration costs

A business will want to know if the money it is spending on administration is resulting in an acceptable level of sales. The formula is:

$$\frac{\text{administration costs}}{\text{sales}} \times 100 = \text{administration cost percentage}$$

Clearly if this percentage rises over a period of time, it means that the business is not efficient in its selling.

overhead costs

Overheads are the normal running expenses of a business. They include items such as insurance, business rates, electricity bills and so on. The money a business spends on its overheads is to an extent 'dead' money: it is not producing anything. Businesses therefore look very carefully at the ratio of overhead costs to sales. This relationship is normally expressed as a percentage:

$$\frac{\text{overheads}}{\text{sales}} \times 100 = \text{overheads percentage}$$

If this percentage rises over time it means that the business will have to look closely at the items which make up the overheads, and trim expenses where possible. It is also possible to look at a *specific expense* in relation to sales. For example, the relationship between advertising and sales might be found to be 10 per cent in one year, but 20 per cent the next year. This would probably indicate that an increase in advertising had failed to produce a proportionate increase in sales. Again, the business will need to investigate.

asset/sales ratio

A business may want to know the value of sales generated from each £1 of net assets. This is calculated by the formula

$$\frac{\textit{sales (£)}}{\textit{net assets (£)}} = \textit{value of sales generated by £1 of net assets}$$

This figure will give an indication of how *efficiently* the net assets are being used. Remember: net assets are total assets less external liabilities.

stock turnover

Stock turnover measures the speed with which stock 'moves' (ie is replaced because it has been sold). Clearly the more quickly it moves the better. Stock turnover can vary with the type of business. For example, a market trader selling fresh flowers who finishes each day when sold out will have a stock turnover of one day. By contrast a furniture shop may have a stock turnover of 90 days, the average length of time for which an item of furniture is held in the shop before being sold. The lower the stock turnover, the more efficient the organisation, for the same type of business. Stock turnover can be measured using figures from the profit and loss statement:

$$\frac{\textit{sales for the year}}{\textit{stock}} = \textit{stock turnover (ie number of times stock is replaced)}$$

Some businesses measure stock turnover in *days*, using the formula

$$\frac{\textit{average stock}}{\textit{cost of sales}} \times \textit{365 days} = \textit{stock turnover (in days)}$$

The danger signs for a business are when the stock turnover period gets longer: it indicates that stock is not selling, and this in turn will hold up cash flow.

debtors' collection period

The debtors collection period shows how long, on average, debtors (ie the customers of a business) take to pay for goods sold to them on credit terms. The formula is:

$$\frac{\textit{debtors}}{\textit{sales for year}} \times \textit{365 days} = \textit{debtors' collection period (in days)}$$

The sales figure is taken from the profit and loss statement and the debtors figure from the balance sheet. The debtors collection period can be compared with that for the previous year, or with that of a similar business. In the UK, most debtors should make payment within 30 to 60 days. A comparison from year-to-year of the collection period is a measure of the business' efficiency.

STUDENT ACTIVITY 10.4

performance criteria 7.4.5 & 6

performance ratios

The figures shown below have been extracted from the balance sheets and profit and loss statements of a business for two years' trading. The owner is rather concerned about the situation. Examine the figures and then answer the questions set out below. If resources permit, discuss your answers with an accountant.

	Year 1 (£)	Year 2 (£)
Balance sheet extract		
Net assets	150,000	150,000
Debtors	12,500	25,000
Profit and loss statement extract		
Sales	100,000	100,000
Purchases	50,000	60,000
Opening stock	15,000	17,500
Closing stock	17,500	30,000
Cost of sales	47,500	47,500
Selling costs	7,500	10,000
Overheads	14,500	15,000

1 Calculate the following performance indicators for both years of trading:
- selling costs/sales percentage
- overhead cost/ sales percentage
- net assets/sales return
- stock turnover (days)
- debtor collection period (days)

2 Comment on the significance of the figures you have produced (do not just say they have 'gone up' or 'gone down'). Identify any problems you can see and suggest possible solutions.

3 What effect will the situation have on the money cycle/working capital position of the business?

EVIDENCE COLLECTION ASSIGNMENT 10

monitoring business performance

Element 7.4, pcs. 1 – 4

introduction

This assignment tests your understanding of

- the different formats in which accounting data can be presented
- the different types of people who might be interested in them

tasks

pcs 7.4. 1 – 4

Examine the examples of accounting data set out on the next three pages and then answer the questions which follow.

extract 1

	A	B	C	D	E	F	G	H	I	J	K	L	M	N
1	CASH FLOW FORECAST													
2	Name: Merry-go-round Limited													
3	Period: January - December 199-													
4														
5		Jan	Feb	Mar	Apr	May	Jun	Jul	Aug	Sep	Oct	Nov	Dec	TOTAL
6		£	£	£	£	£	£	£	£	£	£	£	£	£
7	RECEIPTS													
8	Cash sales	8000	8000	9000	9000	9000	9000	9000	9000	9000	9000	9000	9000	106000
9	Credit sales	18000	18000	18000	25000	25000	25000	25000	25000	25000	25000	25000	25000	279000
10	Capital	25000												25000
11	Loans	25000												25000
12	VAT receipts													0
13	Interest													0
14	Other income													0
15	TOTAL RECEIPTS	76000	26000	27000	34000	34000	34000	34000	34000	34000	34000	34000	34000	435000
16														
17	PAYMENTS													
18	Raw materials	15000	15000	15000	15000	17000	17000	17000	17000	17000	17000	17000	17000	196000
19	Capital assets	50000												50000
20	Wages	10000	10000	10000	10000	10000	10000	10000	10000	10000	10000	10000	10000	120000
21	Water rates				1457									1457
22	Telephone	565			565			565			565			2260
23	Heat & light	650			650			650			650			2600
24	Insurance						7500							7500
25	Other costs	615	615	615	615	615	615	615	615	615	615	615	615	7380
26	Interest costs			680			720			650			630	2680
27	Loan repayments			4000			4000			4000			4000	16000
28	VAT payments	3750			3885			4150			4150			15935
29	TOTAL PAYMENTS	80580	25615	30295	32172	27615	39835	32980	27615	32265	32980	27615	32245	421812
30														
31	Opening Bank	125	-4455	-4070	-7365	-5537	848	-4987	-3967	2418	4153	5173	11558	125
32	Add Receipts	76000	26000	27000	34000	34000	34000	34000	34000	34000	34000	34000	34000	435000
33	Less Payments	80580	25615	30295	32172	27615	39835	32980	27615	32265	32980	27615	32245	421812
34	Closing Bank	-4455	-4070	-7365	-5537	848	-4987	-3967	2418	4153	5173	11558	13313	13313
35														

extract 2

J R CATERING LTD – BUDGETARY CONTROL REPORT

budget centre Sales Dept date 07.11.19-5

	current period			*Year-to-date*			*trend*
	budget £000s	actual £000s	variance £000s	budget £000s	actual £000s	variance £000s	
PRODUCT A	200	250	+ 50	2,750	3,125	+ 375	FAV
PRODUCT B	225	200	– 25	1,275	1,150	– 125	ADV
PRODUCT C	425	450	+ 25	4,025	4,475	+ 450	FAV

JR CATERING LTD SALES LEDGER - AGED DEBTORS SCHEDULE

A/C	Account Name	Turnover	Credit Limit	Balance	Current	30 Days	60 Days	Older
201	Merrion & Co	370.00	1000.00	164.50	164.50	0.00	0.00	0.00
202	Kingfisher Ltd	320.00	750.00	376.00	376.00	0.00	0.00	0.00
204	I Marcos	1730.00	1000.00	1632.75	799.00	0.00	833.75	0.00
205	Compusoft Ltd	2025.00	2000.00	1926.88	1880.00	46.88	0.00	0.00
208	R Weinberger	425.00	750.00	499.38	499.38	0.00	0.00	0.00
	Totals :	4870.00	5500.00	4599.51	3718.88	46.88	833.75	0.00

JR CATERING LTD PURCHASES LEDGER - AGED CREDITORS SCHEDULE

A/C	Account Name	Turnover	Credit Limit	Balance	Current	30 Days	60 Days	Older
601	Alpha Foods	1200.00	1000.00	164.50	164.50	0.00	0.00	0.00
602	Nova Meats Ltd	4562.50	3000.00	350.00	350.00	0.00	0.00	0.00
604	Tuscany Wines	750.75	1000.00	124.75	0.00	124.75	0.00	0.00
605	Bennets	2025.00	2000.00	345.26	0.00	45.26	300.00	0.00
608	Zeta Supplies	425.00	750.00	0.00	0.00	0.00	0.00	0.00
	Totals :	8963.25	7750.00	984.51	514.50	170.01	300.00	0.00

extract 3

Group Five Year Summary

28 February 1994

	1994 £m	1993 £m	1992 £m	1991 £m	1990 £m
	Years ended February				
Summary of turnover and profits					
Turnover – UK	**91.1**	83.5	86.0	73.4	56.2
– USA	**50.4**	37.9	23.4	13.3	5.8
– International	**53.9**	46.9	38.0	28.9	22.5
Total	**195.4**	168.3	147.4	115.6	84.5
Operating profit	**30.1**	24.3	27.9	22.0	16.9
Disposal of subsidiary undertaking	**1.1**	–	–	–	–
Interest payable	**(1.5)**	(2.8)	(2.7)	(2.0)	(2.4)
Profit on ordinary activities before taxation	**29.7**	21.5	25.2	20.0	14.5
Dividends	**3.8**	3.2	3.0	2.3	1.6
Transferred to reserves	**15.6**	10.6	13.4	9.8	7.0
Ordinary dividends per share (adjusted for capitalisation issues)	**2.0p**	1.70p	1.60p	1.22p	0.913p
Earnings per share	**10.3p**	7.4p	8.8p	6.7p	5.0p
Weighted average number of shares in issue (adjusted for capitalisation issues) (millions)	**187.8**	187.2	186.3	180.3	170.6
Number of outlets – UK	**239**	233	210	173	139
– International	**814**	667	517	406	318
	£m	£m	£m	£m	£m
Summary of balance sheets					
Tangible and intangible fixed assets and investments	**71.6**	70.0	58.7	45.6	31.4
Net current assets	**61.1**	51.7	20.9	24.6	1.5
Other provisions and long term liabilities	**(35.8)**	(39.0)	(5.1)	(3.5)	(6.0)
Minority interests	–	(0.5)	(0.3)	(1.6)	(0.9)
Shareholders' funds	**96.9**	82.2	74.2	65.1	26.0

questions

extract 1

1 Identify the financial forecast set out here. Where are you likely to find it?

2 Who would be interested in the forecast, and why?

3 Using a computer (if available) produce a chart or graph showing the most significant line of figures on the forecast.

4 What does the graph or chart say about the performance of the business?

5 Collect examples of this type of forecast from other sources and compare them. What differences can you find? Is there anything missing from the forecast shown here?

extract 2

6 Identify the reports set out here. Who in an organisation would use them?

7 How would their use benefit business performance?

8 If you were monitoring the performance in JR Catering Limited, what action might you take as a result of these reports?

extract 3

9 Identify the financial statements set out in summary form here.

10 Who would be interested in them, and why?

11 Find out what is meant by "dividends per share" and "earnings per share". Who would be interested in these statistics?

12 Using a computer (if available) draw appropriate charts or graphs to illustrate the five year trend for:

(a) total sales (turnover) over the five years

(b) the split between UK, USA and International sales

(c) profit before tax

(d) shareholders' funds

Comment on what is shown by the charts and graphs.

EVIDENCE COLLECTION ASSIGNMENT 11

analysing accounting data

Element 7.4, pcs. 5 & 6

introduction

This assignment tests your understanding of

- the analysis of financial statements using accounting ratios
- how different types of business can produce very different ratios

tasks

pcs 7.4. 5 & 6

You work as a trainee accountant and come across, in your firm's files, the following information relating to two businesses, A and B. One business operates a chain of grocery supermarkets, the other is a heavy engineering company.

1 Study the extracts from the profit and loss statements and balance sheets of A and B shown on the next page.

2 Calculate the following ratios/percentages for the two businesses:

profitability ratios
- net profit percentage
- gross profit percentage
- return on net assets

solvency ratios
- current ratio
- acid test ratio

performance ratios
- overheads/sales
- sales/net assets
- stock turnover (use the stock figure from the balance sheet)
- debtors collection period

3 State which business is the supermarket chain and which is the heavy engineering company. Give reasons for your choice, supported by observation of the financial statements and the ratios extracted from them.

4 Comment on the profitability of the two businesses. Why should the gross profit percentage in particular be so different? Try to find gross profit percentages for other businesses in similar industries.

5 Comment on the solvency of the two businesses. Would you be concerned about business A? If not, why not?

6 Comment on the performance of the two businesses. Why is the debtor's collection period for Business A such an odd result?

7 What do your answers tell you about the use of ratio analysis in general?

	BUSINESS A		***BUSINESS B***	
	£000s	£000s	£000s	£000s
profit & loss statements				
Sales		3,057		1,628
Cost of goods sold		2,647		911
Gross Profit		410		717
Overheads		366		648
Net Profit		44		69
balance sheets				
Fixed Assets		344		555
Current Assets				
Stock	242		237	
Debtors	6		269	
Bank/cash	3		1	
	251		507	
Less Current Liabilities	195		212	
Working Capital		56		295
NET ASSETS		400		850
FINANCED BY				
Capital		400		850

chapter summary and key terms

- The parties that need to monitor the peformance of a business are the owner(s), the managers, providers of finance, the tax authorities, the public and employees.
- Outside parties will monitor a business for a number of reasons. These include looking at its solvency, profitability, tax liability and its ability to repay finance.
- Owners and managers will monitor a business by setting forecasts, comparing actual performance withthe forecasts and taking appropriate action to improve its performance. Comparisons can also be made with performance in previous years and by other businesses in the same industry .
- The financial statements used for comparative purposes include the profit and loss statement, the balance sheet and the cash flow forecast.
- The performance of a business can be assessed by extracting ratios and percentages from key figures in the profit and loss statement and balance sheet.

key terms

variances	the difference between forecast and actual figures in a budget report
aged debtors schedule	an internal business report taken from the sales ledger showing amounts owed by debtors, when they are due to be paid, and what amounts are overdue
aged creditors schedule	an internal business report taken from the purchases ledger showing amounts owed by the business, when they are due to be paid, and any overdue amounts
Report and Accounts	a formal report produced annually by a public limited company making public its financial results and other details such as its environmental policy and a review of its operations, also available in summary form
accounting ratios	relationships betwen figures in the financial statements of a business – expressed in the form of ratios, percentages and time periods (days)
solvency	the ability of a business to pay debts as they fall due; asituation where assets exceed liabilities
performance	the way in which a business meets, fails to meet or exceeds its targets – eg sales, costs, stock levels

multiple-choice questions

Questions 1 – 3 relate to the following information:

The following are reasons for monitoring a business

A assessing its solvency

B assessing its tax liabilities

C assessing its ability to repay a loan

Which of the above can be analysed from the following financial statements?

1 Cash flow forecast

2 Balance sheet

3 Profit and loss statement

4 An aged debtor schedule shows

A which customers have become bankrupt

B which bills a business will have to pay

C which bills a business will have to chase

D which customers have had accounts for the longest time

5 The acid test ratio

A includes stock

B excludes stock

C includes capital

D excludes debtors

6 Decide whether each of these statements is True (T) or False (F)

(i) a business with a low profit margin should turn over its stock quickly

(ii) a rise in gross profit will always mean a higher tax bill for a business

A (i) T (ii) T

B (i) T (ii) F

C (i) F (ii) T

D (i) F (ii) F

SECTION

3

GNVQ UNIT 8
BUSINESS PLANNING

introduction to content

This section is based on the business planning process and the production of a formal business plan, a document which will be required by any business approaching a lender or investor for finance. The section can be seen as the culmination of the GNVQ Business award, combining as it does, marketing, production, human resources, financial statements and forecasts. The first two chapters of the section cover the preparation of the plan and the writing of the plan. The final chapter is a more personal one, looking at your own aspirations – do you want to go into employment, or do you want to be self-employed?

This section is essentially practical in nature. You should investigate business plans from organisations with which you have made contact; you should also co-ordinate the activities with any Young Enterprise or mini-business project in which your school or college may be involved.

assignments

You should draft your own business plan and carry out a self-assessment exercise, but where possible work can be done in groups to find information and discuss progress. The assignments should be seen as a progression of tasks through the Unit rather than self-contained 'blocks' of work. They are:

11 Preparing for the business plan

GNVQ SPECIFICATIONS

Element 8.1

Prepare work and collect data for a business plan

performance criteria – a student must:

1 explain the purposes of a business plan

2 identify the business objectives and collect supporting information for the business activity for which a plan is to be prepared

3 identify the legal and insurance implications of the business objectives

4 discuss the feasibility of proposals with others

5 estimate resource requirements to design, produce, promote and sell the goods or service

6 produce a flow chart illustrating estimated timescales

7 identify potential support for the plan

8 prepare an action plan identifying actions to be taken to finalise the business plan for presentation

what this chapter covers

This chapter should be approached as an introduction and preparation for the Assignment on the opposite page. The object is to decide on a business idea and prepare a business plan as if you intended to approach a lender for finance. Much of the activity will involve discussing ideas with your colleagues, tutors and advisers, and carrying out preparatory tasks.

what you will learn from this chapter

- what a business plan is
- what the objectives of your business will be, and what sort of information you will need before you start
- the legal and insurance implications of starting a business
- the resources you are going to need in terms of people, finance and physical resources such as premises, equipment and stock
- how to plan the timescales needed for starting a business
- identifying potential support – the sources of support and advice

EVIDENCE COLLECTION ASSIGNMENT 12

preparing for the business plan

Element 8

introduction

This assignment brings together all the information gathering and planning activities you will be undertaking for this Element.

You will be working together as a class or in smaller groups under the supervsion of your tutor. You may also be taking part in a Young Enterprise scheme. The work for this assignment, however, will be *individual* work.

Sources could include the 'sources of help' listed on page 259.

tasks

pcs 8.1.1-8

Each student will:

1 Set out in a single paragraph the *purposes* of producing a business plan.

2 Decide on a *product* for the business – a manufactured item or a service. Discuss this choice with your Tutor.

3 Choose a *form* of business – ie sole trader, partnership, limited company. Discuss this choice with your Tutor.

4 Draft an *outline* business plan setting out:

- a description of the product and its market
- notes on the legal and insurance implications of the chosen business
- estimates of resource requirements in terms of people, physical resources (premises, equipment and materials) and finance
- rough financial estimates: the price of your product, the costs involved, the likely sales income, an outline trading forecast, cash flow forecast and breakeven analysis
- notes on your business objectives – draft a Mission Statement
- a list of your sources of support
- a chart showing the planned timescales for planning, production, marketing, selling, and an estimated date when you might breakeven
- action points for *what to do next*

It should be stressed that this is only a draft plan. It could take the form of notes (or data on computer disk). It should be seen as part of an on-going discussion with the Tutor rather than the fully completed plan which will be presented in the Assignment in the next chapter.

the purposes of a business plan

pc 8.1.1

definitions

A business plan could be defined as:

> *A plan presented to a bank or other provider of finance, describing what the business intends to do, explaining what its costs will be, what it expects to earn, how it will repay money it has borrowed, and how soon it will make a profit.*

In other words it is a confident statement to a lender or investor of what a business is, where it plans to go, and how much money it needs to get there.

Try to obtain a copy of a business plan, if you have never seen one. It normally comprises some form of presentation folder – an A4 ringbinder for example – with its contents clearly set out in word-processed or 'Desk Top Published' form. It is often illustrated with pictures of the product or with publicity material.

what are the purposes of the plan?

The writing of a business plan is a very useful exercise . . .

for providers of finance

A business plan will help to persuade a lender such as a bank or venture capital company to lend money. Providers of finance need financial information about the business – a cash flow forecast and final accounts – set out in a clear and detailed way.

for the management of the business

A business plan will help the management of a business to see clearly where the business is going. All too often a person running a business does not have time to see further than the next week; a business plan will make the business owner sit down and think through business objectives and financial requirements.

monitoring the business

Once a business is up and running, the regular writing (or re-writing) of a business plan will enable the management of a business to *monitor* its progress; it will also enable a provider of finance to see that repayment of loans and overdrafts will take place on schedule.

STUDENT ACTIVITY 11.1
performance criterion 8.1.1

business plan? why bother?

situation

A friend of yours who thinks he 'knows it all' is setting up in business, having just been made redundant. You tell him that it would be a good idea to draft an outline business plan; you comment that the banks often have useful free booklets describing how to write one. He says he does not want to go to this trouble. "I can't be bothered with all this 'red tape', and besides, I haven't got time to write out all these fancy plans. I have got a good product – it should sell like 'hot cakes'. The bank will lend me the money anyway."

task

Discuss in your class how you would deal with a character like this. Write down in short paragraphs at least three reasons why you think a business plan is a good idea.

business objectives

pc 8.1.2

If you are starting a business, the type of business will depend on your objectives. Most people go into business to make money. The profit motive remains the most important goal of any business organisation, although there are, of course, other motives. The Body Shop, for example, has a very firm commitment to environmental issues. The main business objectives can be summarised as follows:

goods or services?

One of the early choices facing a person wanting to set up in business is whether to produce a *manufactured product* or to provide a *service*. As you will have seen when studying business, the manufacturing (secondary) sector in the UK is in decline, whereas the service industries (tertiary sector) are increasing in size. As we will explain shortly, it is essential that a person setting up in business investigates what is 'on the up' – eg high technology products – and avoids areas of business which are in terminal decline!

breakeven/subsidy

Businesses aim to *breakeven* – to cover their costs. As we will see when we look at the business plan, a business must be financially viable if it is to continue trading. The only exceptions to this is where a *subsidy* is involved. This could be a government subsidy to an assisted area, where the aim is to create employment and encourage techological innovation. A subsidy could also be involved where a large business such as a pharmaceutical company invests in a new area which will only breakeven and generate profit after a long period of development.

profit making

Profitability means success and wealth creation for the owners of the business, and indirectly for the employees. But the drive for profitability also has its downside; it inevitably means a cutting of costs, which could affect the workforce or the environment.

market share

One aim of a business may well be to achieve power and influence in its market sector. The business plan often contains a projection of the percentage market share a business will aim to achieve.

business objectives – the mission statement

If you are starting or expanding a business you should have very specific objectives – targets which you hope to achieve. These objectives can be short-term and long-term. The current phrase for a summary of these objectives is the "Mission Statement".

short-term objectives

For example, the owner of Express Pasta, an Italian fast-food store, might have the following short-term objectives:

In the next twelve months I intend Express Pasta:

- to offer the best standard of customer care in Stourminster High Street
- to turn over £100,000 of business
- to achieve a profit after all expenses and deductions of £15,000

long-term objectives

A long-term objective might be:

Within three years, I intend Express Pasta:

- to open a further two branches in St Martins and in Wimbury
- to increase annual turnover to £300,000

mission statement

These objectives might be summed up in a mission statement:

> **Express Pasta will provide the best quality Pasta, offer the best service, and be the most profitable fast food outlet in Stourminster High Street.**

Objectives and the mission statement are normally set out in a business plan.

what business?

There are two major problems in starting a business:

1. Deciding *what* business you are going to start
2. Choosing the *right* business

If you are taking part in a school or college enterprise/mini-business you will cope with the first problem in the initial stages. The second problem – choosing the right business – will determine whether or not it is successful. In the school or college context this will be an interesting learning process; in the actual business world it will make all the difference between making money and business failure. This is why it is important to 'get it right' in the early stages of planning.

STUDENT ACTIVITY 11.2
performance criterion 8.1.2

business ideas and business objectives

task 1

This Activity should help you to get some ideas for a product for your business. It can be used for the Assignment in this chapter or for helping you formulate ideas for a Young Enterprise or mini-business scheme.

Divide up the whole class into smaller groups of approximately four students. Elect a secretary and a spokesperson for each small group. Conduct a "brainstorming session" for ideas for products or services which the eventual mini-business could provide. The secretary should record the suggestions, and the group should select up to five ideas.

When the groups have come to the end of their discussions (or arguments!) the class should re-assemble and the spokesperson from each small group should present the ideas. The class as a whole can then debate the suggestions and add further ideas which emerge.

task 2

If you are setting up a business in your school or college or doing the Assignment

(a) discuss in your class the objectives of your business in terms of the factors outlined in this chapter

(b) produce a written statement of your business objectives

(c) draft a mission statement for your business – bear in mind that it may have to be amended when you have produced the final version of your business plan

Note: if you are not taking part in a mini-business scheme or doing the Assignment, but are doing work experience or a part-time job

(d) identify the objectives of the business or organisation in which you work

(e) produce a written statement of those aims, and discuss it with your adviser in the workplace.

obtaining information for the business plan

pc 8.1.2

If you are starting a business you will need to collect *supporting information* which will help in your decision-making. If you are considering manufacturing a product or providing a service you will need to look at a number of critical questions . . .

is there a demand for the product?

There is no pointing launching a new product for which there is no demand, or for which you cannot create a demand. Fashion clothes, for example, are notoriously subject to changes in demand.

what is the competition?

If you are going to market a product you will need to research the competition. As you will know from your marketing studies, it is always more difficult to launch a new product in a market which is already congested with existing products. It is possible, however, to do so by cutting your price ('penetration pricing') and by heavy advertising.

who are your customers?

Another aspect of marketing policy is to decide *which group(s)* of customers your business is going to target. This will in turn enable you to calculate *how many* customers you will be selling to, and whether you think they will be *repeat* customers who will buy from you again.

what are the financial implications of this information?

When you have worked out the number of customers to whom you will be selling and have assessed the market, you can then:

- fix a price for your product
- estimate the number of items you will be able to sell in a year
- estimate your annual sales figure (turnover)
- estimate annual profit (once the costs are known)

STUDENT ACTIVITY 11.3
performance criterion 8.1.2

information for the business plan

task

If you are taking part in a Young Enterprise project or doing the Assignment, set out in the form of short notes:

(a) who your competitors are
(b) who your customers are
(c) how you can keep those customers and get them to buy repeatedly
(d) approximately how many items (product or service) you can sell in a year
(e) what price you could charge for the product
(f) what your approximate annual sales income could be

what other information will be needed?

The points we have mentioned in this section are clearly only part of the information you will need for a business plan. You will also need to find out about:

- financial requirements
- production requirements (for a manufacturing business) – raw materials, machinery
- staffing requirements
- timescales
- sources of assistance
- legal and insurance implications

We will deal with these points in the remainder of this chapter, starting with the legal and insurance implications.

legal and insurance implications

pc 8.1.3

If you are starting a business, as we have just seen, you will first decide upon the *type* of business and then define its *objectives*. There then remains the question of the *legal and insurance implications* of your decisions. The type of questions that a person starting a business will ask are:

- can the proposed business function in the premises we have in mind?
- do we need to issue contracts of employment to our staff?
- can we employ sixth-formers as casual workers?
- do we need a first aid officer?
- what guarantee will our customers have if our goods are faulty?
- what insurance do we need to cover our premises?

These areas can be a potential minefield to the unwary business owner, and it is essential that professional advice is sought before trading starts. Help can be given by Enterprise Agencies, solicitors, accountants and insurance brokers.

legal implications

These include:

- the legal form a business can take – sole trader, partnership, limited company – and the name a business adopts
- the legal implications of taking on premises
- the legal implications of employing staff
- the legal implications of providing goods

insurance implications

- insuring premises, machinery and stocks
- insuring against accidents which happen to employees and the general public on your premises
- insuring your product

the legal form of the business

You will have to decide the legal form will your business will take – sole trader, partnership or limited company. In this chapter we will look at some of the legal implications of each of these types of business.

sole trader and partnership

A sole trader is an individual trading in his or her name, or under a suitable trading name.

A partnership is a group of individuals working together in business with a view to making a profit.

The legal implications of being a sole trader or a partner are:

unlimited liability

A sole trader or partner is personally liable for business debts – if the business 'goes bust' he or she will have to pay off the creditors (bank, suppliers, tax authorities) from his or her personal assets and any remaining business assets. This is known as *unlimited liability.*

no registration needed

A sole trader or a partnership business can trade as soon as it wants to. It does not have to register the legal formation of the business anywhere.

Partnerships are regulated by the Partnership Act 1890 and any written Partnership Agreement which exists. This will state what money is being invested by each partner, how profits are split, and what will happen if there is a dispute. It is an unfortunate fact that partners can argue, and if you are entering into a partnership you will have to make sure that you can get on with and trust your co-partners – they may be spending your money and running up business debts for which you will be liable.

limited company

A limited company is a separate legal body, owned by shareholders, run by directors.

limited liability

A limited company is quite different from a sole trader or partnership in that it has a legal identity separate from its owners. If you are taking part in a Young Enterprise scheme you will be well aware of how a limited company is set up. The owners – the shareholders – are *not* personally liable for the business debts (the company's debts). They are said to have *limited liability.* If the company becomes insolvent ('goes bust') the shareholders will not normally have to 'dip' into their pockets to pay off the creditors. This is seen by many to be a substantial advantage!

registration needed

A company must be registered at a central office known as Companies House, which will issue to the directors a Certificate of Incorporation, the 'birth certificate' of a company. An annual return and financial statement must be sent each year to Companies House by the directors. The rules for running the company must be set out in documents known as the 'Memorandum and Articles of Association' which must also be sent to Companies House. As you will see there is much paperwork and 'red tape' involved in establishing and running a limited company. Paperwork and 'red tape' clearly mean extra expense.

STUDENT ACTIVITY 11.4

performance criterion 8.1.3

limited or unlimited liability?

task

A friend of yours is unsure about the difference between limited and unlimited liability. Explain to him/her in your own words (face-to-face) what this difference is and how it could affect the owner of a business which 'goes bust'. Your Tutor will play the part of the friend.

the legal implications of premises

If a business plans to operate from premises, there are a number of legal obligations that the owner(s) of the business must consider. These include:

planning permission

There must be planning permission for the type of business carried on at the premises – for example, you could not open up a retail outlet on an industrial estate, or set up a 'heavy' industrial process in a unit given 'light' industrial usage. If you are using your own house for your business, planning permission may be required, depending on the use. You must also check (with the help of a solicitor) to see if there are any covenants (restrictions which apply to the property) or local by-laws which might restrict what you are planning to do. You must also ensure that your premises comply with Local Authority *building regulations.*

licences

Certain types of business need a licence to trade; these include: restaurants, food manufacturers, ice cream and mobile food stalls, sellers of alcohol and tobacco, nursing homes, child nurseries and scrap metal dealers.

checking the lease

If you are taking on a lease (ie renting the property for a set period of time rather than buying it), have you checked any restrictive terms and conditions in the lease? Have you checked how long the lease has to run and how often the lease payments can be reviewed (ie increased), eg every five or seven years?

environmental restrictions

The law places strict controls on the emissions which a business can make into the atmosphere, into drainage systems, and into rivers and streams. Offenders can (and are) prosecuted for breaking these regulations.

STUDENT ACTIVITY 11.5
performance criterion 8.1.3

legal implications of premises

What legal implications relating to premises are involved for:

(a) a graphic design consultancy operating from home – a sole trader who designs publicity leaflets, brochures, packaging, book jackets and so on, using a computer and a drawing board in a spare bedroom?

(b) a car mechanic who decides to operate an engine tuning service from the garage in his house?

(c) an ice cream salesman who plans to operate a "Mr Creamy" van in the main shopping street in the town?

(d) a scrap metal dealer who wants to buy an old redundant school building and use the playground as a scrap metal yard?

(e) a printer who wants to move into a leased building on an out-of-town industrial estate?

(f) a skip rental firm which wants to take over an old quarry in which it plans to dump waste?

legal implications of employing staff

age limits

The normal minimum age for an employee in industry is 16, and there are restrictions on the part-time working hours for the under-16s in other occupations. The normal retirement age is 60 for women and 65 for men, although it has been proposed that the retirement age for everyone should be 65. There is nothing, of course, to prevent a person from retiring early or working beyond normal retirement age; the legal restrictions apply to those under age and aim to protect young people from exploitation.

contracts of employment

By law all employees working sixteen or more hours a week must be given within thirteen weeks a written statement of the terms of employment. This may take the form of a formal written contract, but it does not need to. The statement must include

- the name of the employer
- the date when the job starts
- the name, job title and job description of the employee
- the hours of work
- holiday entitlement (and pay where appropriate)
- details of pay and when it is paid
- grievance, sickness and injury procedures (ie whom to go and see)
- pension schemes
- length of notice required for termination of employment

discrimination

It is illegal for an employer (or an employer advertising for a job) to discriminate against any person on the grounds of race, sex or religion: eg "Required for work in bar: white girl. No Roman Catholics". The only exception would be if the nature of the business demanded discrimination (eg wet nurses).

Health and Safety at Work

Health and Safety at Work is becoming an increasingly complex area of regulation, particularly with the influence of EC directives. A person starting a business would be well advised to approach the local Environmental Health Office which will be able to provide literature and advice about Health and Safety in the workplace. The Health and Safety Executive publish through HMSO an excellent and inexpensive booklet "Essentials of Health and Safety at Work". The main legislation affecting the workplace is the Health and Safety at Work etc Act 1974. This Act requires an employer to look after the health and safety of employees and people visiting the premises. It states specifically that the employer must provide:

- safe machinery and equipment – and maintenance of that machinery and equipment
- safe operating systems for the machinery and equipment
- safe and healthy methods of using, handling, storing and transporting of items and substances: these can include solids, liquids and gases which may be harmful to health

- information, instruction and training in safety procedures
- supervision of employees
- safe and healthy premises – adequate toilets, canteen facilities, heating, lighting and ventilation
- safe access to the premises
- a safe environment for visitors to the premises, eg maintenance contractors, sales representatives

If the employer employs more than five people, he or she should issue a written Statement of Policy to the employees, giving details of the safety procedures in force on the premises. This policy may be given to the employees personally, or it may be placed where it can be read – on the notice board, for example.

Other Acts of Parliament relating to Health and Safety at Work include the Factories Act 1961, and the Offices Shops and Railway Premises Act 1963.

payroll

An employer must by law deduct income tax and National Insurance Contributions from employees on its payroll who earn over a certain amount. This PAYE (Pay As You Earn) system requires the employer to pay these deductions to the Inland Revenue, together with a contribution from the employer for National Insurance. It is a requirement that an employer must keep accurate and full records of pay and deductions, and make an annual return to the tax office.

STUDENT ACTIVITY 11.6
performance criterion 8.1.3

employing staff?

task

Write short notes on the legal implications for your planned business if:

(a) a person interviewed by you stated "I must have a written contract of employment."

(b) you were opening a Chinese restaurant and asked in the job advert for "waiters, preferably Chinese."

(c) you decided that you did not want (or did not have time) to issue a written Statement of Policy relating to Health and Safety at Work.

(d) a new recruit told you that he wanted to be paid "in cash, because you won't have to pay any National Insurance".

the legal implications of providing goods

The subject of consumer law will be covered in detail if you take the "Business Law" option unit. For the purposes of business planning you should appreciate that manufacturing and selling a product (or in some circumstances providing a service) brings with it three basic legal obligations:

faulty products

If a product is faulty a customer will have a right to a refund or a replacement. There are no grounds for a manufacturer or a retailer disclaiming responsibility or putting up a notice stating "no refunds". The consumer's right is enshrined in law.

products as described

Products must be sold as described in advertising material, and must as far as is reasonably possible fulfil the claims made for them. A "waterproof jacket" should withstand a shower of rain, but the manufacturer could dispute a claim, if, for example the jacket were worn in a tropical storm and let in water. If goods are labelled with a false description (eg a gold-plated ring advertised as "solid gold"), a criminal prosecution could result.

safety standards

Products must meet with safety standards. The children's toys market, for example, is subject each Christmas to the usual influx of highly dangerous cheap foreign imports: teddy's eyes which come off and are swallowed, poisonous paint, and so on. Products which do not meet with the safety standards can result in prosecution for the business concerned.

Manufacturers normally take out product liability insurance to safeguard against claims as a result of faulty goods (see next section on insurance). Many products now carry safety marks (see below).

BSI kitemark

This symbol appears on products which comply with safety standards set down by the British Standards Institute (BSI).

BEAB safety symbol

This symbol appears on household electrical products. BEAB stands for British Electrotechnical Approvals Board.

insurance needs of a business

pc 8.1.3

the need for sufficient insurance

Another aspect of business planning is the provision of sufficient insurance. Insurance is an essential protection for a business: a warehouse fire or a computer theft can force a business to stop trading, lose its customers and even result in a trading loss.

what type of policy?

A business would normally approach a firm of insurance brokers which would be able to obtain quotations from a number of insurers, and so provide the 'best deal'. It is possible to obtain different types of cover, eg fire cover and computer insurance, from different insurers, but it is becoming increasingly common to obtain a 'combined' insurance policy to cover all the appropriate risks from a single insurance company. These policies often operate on a 'pick and mix' basis – you pick the cover you need to cover your particular needs.

what type of cover?

The list below sets out the most common types of cover. Clearly not all businesses will want all types of cover: the insurance broker will be able to advise.

asset insurance – insurance of assets, eg premises and stock

fire cover

This type of cover insures premises and its contents against damage by fire and other disasters such as lightning, explosions, aircraft, riots, vandalism, earthquake, storms, floods. The premises are normally insured for their rebuilding cost.

theft

This insurance covers the removable assets of the business, eg machinery, computers, office machines, stock, money. The cover is normally for assets both on the premises and also off the premises, eg goods in transit, money being taken to the bank. These assets are normally insured for their replacement value and not their value in the books of the business.

business interruption

Another form of cover related to asset insurance is business interruption cover. This reimburses financial loss which happens as a result of the business coming to a halt following a fire or any of the other disasters covered under fire insurance. This cover can be extended to insure against problems caused by a failure of the utilities, eg a long-term power cut, or contamination of the water supply.

employer's liability insurance

employer's liability

This type of cover insures the employer against claims from employees who have been injured at work. 'Employee' includes a person on the payroll, self-employed people contracted to work for the business (eg a consultant brought in for a specific job) and, in some instances, students on work experience!

public liability

This type of cover insures against claims from members of the public who may be injured as a result of something which happens in connection with the business, eg a person who visits a workshop and is injured by a machine which topples over. The cover also extends to assets of the public, eg a parked car which is damaged by a falling roof tile from the business premises. If you have access to your home insurance policy, you will see that household insurance also normally includes public liability cover.

product liability insurance

An extension of public liability cover is insurance against claims arising from people who have suffered injury or damage from faulty products which they have purchased. This type of insurance will cover legal costs in defending claims made under consumer protection law.

STUDENT ACTIVITY 11.7
performance criterion 8.1.3

insurance needs

questions

What type of cover would you need to insure for the following risks:

(a) your warehouse roof blowing off in a storm?

(b) theft of your computer workstations from your office?

(c) your employee being mugged on the way back from the bank, and the wages cash being stolen?

(d) a loose coping stone falling off your office building and damaging a visitor's car parked nearby?

(e) an employee's foot being crushed by a fork-lift truck?

(f) a customer suing you after being electrocuted by a faulty hair dryer you have manufactured?

(g) your business being put out of action by a fire at the factory, resulting in a financial loss from lost income?

resource requirements

pc 8.1.5

When planning a business you will need to work out what resources you are going to need:

- *human resources* – ie the skills and experience of the owner(s) and the staff that will be needed to carry the plan through
- *physical resources* – the premises, machinery, computing equipment, stock, and materials that the business will need
- *financial resources* – the capital that the owner(s) of the business can contribute, and the external finance that may be needed

planning for human resources – objectives

A business will need to choose and use people so that

- the productivity and output of the business is efficient
- the profit is maximised
- people working in the business are motivated and satisfied

These objectives will inevitably result in some form of compromise!

planning for human resources – looking for skills

A business start-up will involve one or more entrepreneurs who have to provide *skills* in a number of areas:

- administration and management
- marketing and selling
- finance/book-keeping/payroll skills
- production and operations
- research and development – the "ideas" person

It may be that the sole trader has all these talents, or the partners/directors share these abilities between them. It is more likely, however, that the business starting up will have to "buy in" help in one or more of these areas. This can be done by:

- bringing in a new partner/director with a particular skill who may be willing also to put in capital and share in the success of the business
- using self-employed specialists (eg for accountancy services or marketing) on a contract basis
- employing temporary staff from an agency
- employing one or more general assistants who can be on the permanent payroll of the business

The first option (new partner/director) can be a risky proposition. The personal factor may be a problem: can the new director get on with the existing management? Employing self-employed specialists or agency staff can be expensive, but it is also flexible: a business only pays for what it wants done, and no employer's National Insurance is payable. A general assistant may cost less in terms of £'s per hour, but there is little flexiblity in terms of hours worked, and the employees may need training.

short-term human resources planning

In the human resources section of this book we looked in detail at the responsibilities of a personnel manager. As far as business planning is concerned, the owner(s) of a new or expanding business ought to bear in mind:

- Manpower planning – what are the staffing requirements likely to be?
- What training provision needs to be made?
- What industrial relations implications are there? Will the new employees be joining a Union?
- What facilities will need to be made available for staff welfare? – Is there a rest room?
- Have the wages levels been fixed?
- Have Health and Safety requirements been planned out?

STUDENT ACTIVITY 11.8
performance criterion 8.1.5

human resources planning

task

You are starting up a new business as a sole trader making picture frames. You are giving some thought to human resource planning:

(a) What would be your main objectives in human resource planning?

(b) You are very good at making picture frames but have had less experience in financial matters and in selling. What options are open to you in solving this problem? State what option you would choose, and why.

(c) You are moving into a small workshop owned and subsidised by the local authority. What practical human resource planning will be necessary, bearing in mind that you may be employing other people to work on the premises?

physical resources planning

pc 8.1.5

Planning for physical resources is essential when starting up or expanding a business, and much of the detailed planning will be included in the business plan. We will look at :

- planning for premises
- acquiring machinery and equipment
- buying and planning for stock and raw materials

premises – can I work from home?

Many small businesses operate very successfully from home. These businesses are mainly sole traders who either provide a service to the public by travelling away from home, or who deal with the public over the telephone. Examples include electricians, photographers, designers, and insurance sales representatives. Business people who use the home as a base can charge a proportion of their expenses (telephone, electricity, heating) to their business – ie the business will pay rather than the expense falling on the household budget. The major disadvantage of using the home for business use is that the rooms used will be subject to Non Domestic Rate, a tax on business property collected by the Local Authority. Another practical disadvantage is keeping the business and private life separate: the problems of confidentiality and keeping small children at bay!

should I buy or lease premises?

If the business needs to deal with the public face-to-face as part of its everyday operations, it needs premises – commercial property. Information about premises can be obtained from

- local Enterprise Agencies (some produce registers of vacant premises)
- the commercial property offices of estate agents
- the commercial property pages in the local press

You will see when you look at this information that premises can be classified in a terms of office space and warehousing and production space. This distinction is self-explanatory: certain businesses will only need offices, others will need a combination of office space and warehousing.

The principal concern when choosing premises will be whether you wish to *buy* or *lease* the property. If you have the capital you may wish to buy the premises, possibly with the help of a commercial mortgage. If, as is more likely, you do not have much spare money to invest, you will plan to lease a property, ie pay a 'rental' to the owner of the property.

what are the other considerations when taking on premises?

Non-Domestic Rate

Central Government taxes business premises and property by means of the Non-Domestic Rate. All business property has been valued for taxation purposes by the Inland Revenue and given a rateable value expressed in £s. The Non-Domestic Rate is collected by the Local Authorities, and is normally paid in ten monthly instalments.

valuation and survey

It is important when taking on premises to make sure you are not paying too much, either in terms of purchase price (the buy option) or in monthly rental (lease option). A Chartered Surveyor will (for a fee) undertake a valuation of the property and also look at it for structural problems. If you are borrowing money, on commercial mortgage for example, the lender will want to see the survey and valuation report. The surveyor will also assess a fair rent, if you are taking on a lease. The surveyor's fee is therefore money well spent.

insurance

The cost of insuring business premises can be high (eg £4,000 per year for a £100,000 warehouse) because, as we saw in the last chapter, there are many risks against which to insure.

location

A number of questions need to be answered:

- Can your staff and clients get to you easily? Is there sufficient parking?
- Do delivery and collection vehicles have clear access?
- Do you have sufficient office space?
- Do you have sufficient warehousing for the future?

All these considerations can appear overwhelming if you are starting up in business for the first time. It is therefore essential that you obtain professional advice:

- a Chartered Surveyor for valuation of property and help with negotiating a lease (if you are leasing a property)
- a solicitor for conveyancing (carrying out the enquiries and paperwork when a purchase is made)
- an accountant for the financial aspects – helping with the business plan and approaching the bank with a request for finance
- an insurance broker for a competitive quotation for the required insurance (no fee charged in this case)

STUDENT ACTIVITY 11.9
performance criterion 8.1.5

planning for premises

task

You run a business which is looking for a 2,500 square feet warehouse with office facilities. Obtain through your tutor details of up to five suitable vacant premises in your locality. Assess each of them in terms of

- price per square foot (if they are freehold)
- annual rental per square foot (if they are leasehold)
- accessibility and parking facilities
- the annual Non Domestic Rate (if you can find this out)
- general condition (from an external inspection, if this is possible)

Note: be guided by your tutor in what you can and cannot assess.

Write a brief report comparing the alternatives and giving your recommendation – with reasons – as to which warehouse is the best.

additional task

Carry out the same exercise as in Task 1 above, but this time looking for an office of 1,500 square feet for an insurance broker.

planning for machinery, equipment and vehicles

When a business acquires machinery or equipment or vehicles – which we will for convenience call "equipment" – a number of critical decisions will have to be made:

- should the equipment be acquired now?
- should the equipment be bought or leased?
- which supplier should be chosen?

Other factors include affecting the choice will be payment terms (ie when payment can be made), after-sales service, and (possibly) environmental considerations.

The equipment which a business may need includes a wide range of items including telephones, computers and photocopiers, vehicles, and machinery used in the production process. Clearly every business has its own particluar needs, but the same principles apply in the decision-making process. We will now consider these principles in detail.

should the equipment be acquired now?

When a business starts up for the first time, it is easy to fall into the trap of making a 'shopping list' for physical resources, assuming that they all have to be acquired at once. This is not always the case, and great care should be taken in the planning process. A business will have to list all the items it wants to acquire, cost them, and compare them with the available financial resources. It can then decide which items have to be acquired immediately (eg telephones, delivery van) and which items can wait (eg a new car for the Managing Director).

should the items be bought or leased?

You will be aware that if you have a telephone line installed in your house or premises, you can choose either to rent a handset (and be charged regularly on your bill), or to go to a retail outlet such as Dixons or Boots and buy a handset, and pay immediately. The same choice exists for a wide range of business assets – computers, photocopiers, machinery, cars and vans for example – buy now and pay up front, or pay regularly over a period of time. The term 'lease' is often used when a piece of equipment is rented: payments are made by the business using the asset, but ownership always remains with the firm 'leasing' it out.

There are a number of factors which will be involved in the decision to buy or to lease. The most crucial of these is the availability of capital or finance. If neither of these is available, the business cannot buy the asset, and the decision to lease will be made. If capital is available, the choice is normally based partly on financial considerations (how much tax can be saved) and also how soon the equipment will get out of date. There is little point buying an expensive piece of new technology if next year the price will have fallen, or the technology will have been superseded.

STUDENT ACTIVITY 11.10
performance criterion 8.1.5

a mobile telephone

task

You are setting up in business and have decided that your sales manager needs a mobile telephone (the type that can be used outside the car – ie anywhere). Investigate the various methods and costs of obtaining a mobile telephone and write a brief report concluding with a shortlist of two models together with the cost of the various alternatives.

purchasing stock and materials

Purchasing has traditionally been defined as

buying goods and services of the right quality, in the right quantity, at the right time, from the right supplier, at the right price

This may seem all very well in theory, but as most people in business will tell you, purchasing often gets a low priority in comparison, say, with selling. The task may be easier for the larger business which has a purchasing department and senior purchasing staff, but for the smaller concern or sole trader, purchasing very often means choosing the supplier that sends you a brochure, or always choosing the same supplier, a far from ideal situation. When you are starting a business, there are so many decisions to be made that planning for purchasing often gets a low priority, and wrongly, as the example below shows.

the right price – the importance of efficient purchasing

The price of materials and stock purchased is an important factor for a business which wants to make a profit. Achieving a price cut for raw materials and stock can have a dramatic effect on profitability : "a penny saved is a profit made" as the saying goes. Look at the following example taken from a business which is already trading:

A manufacturing company makes garden gnomes. The financial details are as follows:

Annual sales	£500,000
Annual spending on materials	£250,000
Other expenses	£200,000
Net profit	£50,000

The management want to increase profit by £5,000. How can they achieve this? There are two alternatives:

1. Increase sales by £50,000 – the business makes £5,000 profit from £50,000 of sales
2. Reduce costs by £5,000 – this will bring about an increase in profit without the need for an increase in sales

The second alternative appears by far the more attractive. If they spend £250,000 a year on materials, a saving of £5,000 is only a 2% reduction in material costs. To achieve the same increase in profit by increasing sales will require a 10% increase in sales. An increase in profitability is clearly more easily achieved by 'shopping around' for cheaper materials (a cut of only 2%) than by trying to increase sales of gnomes by 10%. £50,000 saved by efficient purchasing is a £50,000 increase in profit!

methods of obtaining lower prices

How are these lower prices to be found? Various suppliers must be approached, and prices obtained from price lists, telephone enquiries and written requests for prices. If suppliers realise that a business is 'shopping around' it may be prepared to drop a price to gain a customer. Businesses must also be aware of discounts offered for

- early payment (cash discount), often 2.5% of the purchase price
- large quantity orders
- trade customers (trade discount) – this is discount given to customers 'in the trade' who are likely to give repeat orders

A new business must 'shop around' as a matter of course, and existing businesses should do so on a regular basis; it is all too easy for an established business to fall into a state of inertia when buying, and always buy from the same supplier, regardless of price.

quality and purchasing

The quality of an item means in very basic terms "how good is it for the job?" For example a "poor quality" audio tape means that it gets chewed up in the car stereo and wobbles in pitch – it is inadequate for the job. If an item is described as a "quality" item, it should do its job well: in fact the term "quality" is used in advertising to attract the customer to a product.

As far a business is concerned, purchasing for quality means balancing cost and performance: the item must do the job well, but at the lowest obtainable cost (see above). There is no point buying a superior brand of cement powder for making garden gnomes when a standard brand achieves the desired result – hardness, frost resistance, and so on.

timing of purchases

A supplier must be able to keep to specified schedules. Any unreliability in supply could lose valuable sales for the buyer: for example, a shop which is let down by a wholesaler and runs out of a popular item, or a manufacturer which is unable to obtain a vital component because the supplier has failed to deliver. A buyer must take careful note of the time it takes for an order to be processed by the supplier and the delivery time quoted.

Just-in-Time (JIT)

A mention must be made here of Just-in-Time (JIT) ordering, a Japanese technique which involves ordering the materials and stock only as and when they are needed. This system is used to effect by large retailing chains and by some manufacturers. The object is to reduce stockholding to an absolute minimum, and to cut costs.

planning financial resources

pc 8.1.5

Financial planning means asking three basic questions

> *"How much money are we going to need?"*
>
> *"How much money have we got?"*
>
> *"How much external finance – loans and investment – are we going to have to raise?"*

A business plan traditionally includes financial forecasts and financial statements which answer these questions. We have already looked in detail at these documents earlier in the book and at the planning process in Chapter 8 "Financing of business". If you need to refresh your memory you should re-read this material.

calculating timescales

pc 8.1.6

We will now look at some specific techniques used when a business is undertaking a project which involves planning to acquire physical resources in the form of fixed assets, eg premises, plant and machinery and current assets eg stock and materials. Examples of this type of situation are the business start-up, relocation of a business, and expansion of an existing business. These techniques are based on two types of flow chart:

- critical path analysis
- bar charts known as Gannt charts

It should be stressed that these will form part of the *operations plan* of a business, and *will not form part of the business plan* . The results obtained from the planning process – for example how long it will take to complete a project – will *contribute* to the business plan. The prospective lender who reads a business plan will be interested in *when* a project becomes operational rather than *how* it is completed.

critical path analysis

Critical path analysis is a technique for working out the minimum time a project is likely to take. It is a form of what is termed 'network analysis'. Critical path analysis operates by examining all the individual actions which contribute to the project, eg ordering, constructing, testing, and determining the minimum time the project will take. The process can be very complex, and may be introduced by looking at a simple operation such as making a cup of instant coffee, eg "Take the kettle, fill it up, plug it in, take a cup" ... and so on. This form of analysis is presented in visual form by a network of arrows. Each arrow represents an individual activity, and is normally labelled with the activity and the time it takes (in, say, weeks) to carry out the activity, for example:

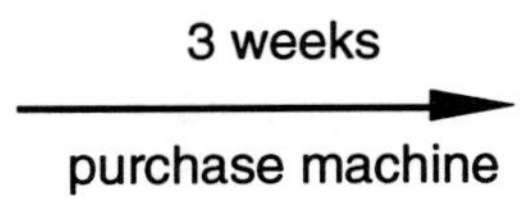

Arrows start and finish in circles known as *events* or *nodes*. Activities shown by arrows pointing into a circle (event) must be completed before any activity shown on an arrow coming out of an event can be started. For example:

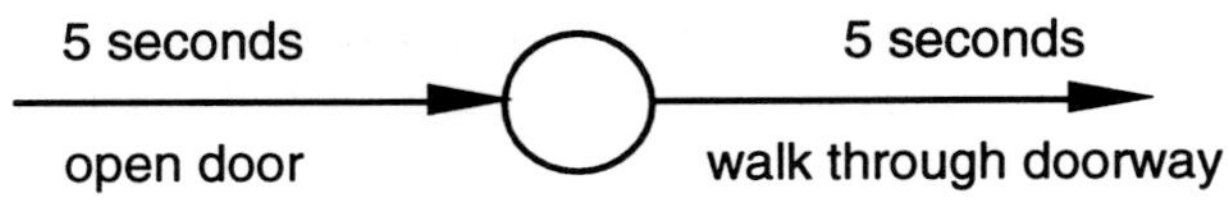

Here the door has to be opened before someone can walk through the doorway; to attempt to walk though the doorway before the door is opened would clearly not be advisable.

It is common for a number of activities to take place *simultaneously*. If you are making a cup of instant coffee, the kettle will be boiling while you are getting a spoon and putting the instant coffee in the cup. In this case the there will be arrows denoting these parallel activities, and these arrows will converge on the event which marks the pouring of the water into the cup. It is important to note that all activities on the converging arrows must be completed before any activity on any arrow leaving the circle can be started.

the critical path

You will know that if you are making a cup of coffee that you will have to wait for the kettle to boil before you can make a decent cupful. You therefore have to wait the longest time of the two alternative arrows before completing the event – the steaming cupful of coffee. In critical path analysis the activities which take the longest time to complete are known as *critical activities*, and are shown with a thicker arrow.

In an analysis of a complex project, the *quickest* time the project will take to complete will be the *sum of the time taken for the critical activities in sequence.* In visual terms there will be a thick black line runing through the network of activities: this will be the critical path, shown in the illustration below.

labelling the network

In critical path analysis, there are certain labelling conventions:

- The circle (event) is often annotated with numbers to show the stage in the project which has been reached. The number is the event number.
- The arrows (activities) are also given abbreviated labels:
  - the time taken for the activity is shown as a simple number which could stand for minutes, days, weeks as appropriate
  - the activity itself may be given a letter which is explained in a separate list (this would give clarity to the network when the activity descriptions are long and involved)

A critical path analysis is illustrated below. Note how the sum of the numbers on the critical path (the thicker arrows) indicates the activities which take the longest time – a total of 13 as opposed to the other route, which totals 8.

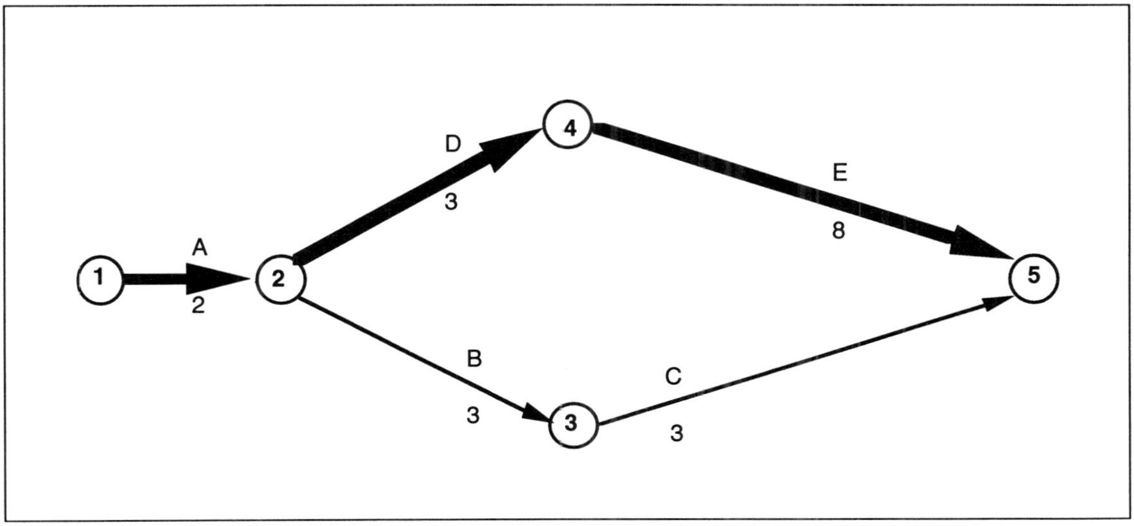

Now read the Case Study which sets out how critical path analysis can be used by a business planning to relocate its premises.

CASE STUDY

pc 8.1.6

Hermes Bureau – relocation of premises

situation

You run a computer bureau – Hermes Bureau – which provides accounting, payroll and other computer services to a wide range of commercial customers. You are planning to relocate your premises shortly, and have taken a lease on a new and larger office in the town, and will be able to move in six months' time.

You are taking the opportunity when moving to update your computer hardware and software (program) systems. There are a number of important tasks to carry out before you move, and after consultation with your colleagues you have made the list set out below. Your software needs updating and customising for your bureau by programmers, and this will be the task which will take the most time. You see that all the tasks will have to be completed before you can become operational, and the obvious fact that the ordering of software and hardware can only take place after full assessment. You allow yourself a clear two weeek planning period before starting the process. You are very busy at the moment. When should you start planning?

Task A	time available for detailed planning	2 weeks
Task B	assessment of computer hardware	2 weeks
Task C	ordering new computers	2 weeks
Task D	assessment of new software	4 weeks
Task E	ordering software	10 weeks
Task F	obtaining quotes from removal firm	3 weeks
Task G	ordering the removal van	3 weeks

solution

The planning process can be carried out using critical path analysis, which will set out the different activities in the form of a network and will determine the maximum time, and thus the project time. The procedure is as follows

step one

List the activities and the times which they will take, and give them a code letter. This has already been done (see above)

step two

Draw a sketch setting out the different activities in the forms of arrows, starting on the left, making sure that

- the arrows are annotated with the activity coding and the time taken (in weeks)
- all activities follow Task A – the planning process
- C follows B, E follows D, G follows F

step three

Set out the 'events' which mark the completion of activities in the form of circles, and give them consecutive numbers

step four

Add up the time taken by each alternative route taken by the arrows. This produces the result:

- planning and ordering software 16 weeks (2 + 4 + 10)
- planning and ordering new computers 6 weeks (2 + 2 +2)
- planning and arranging removal van 8 weeks (2 + 3 + 3)

step five

Draw up a final neat copy of the network, marking in the critical path – the 16 week software upgrading – in heavy ink. The final version appears below.

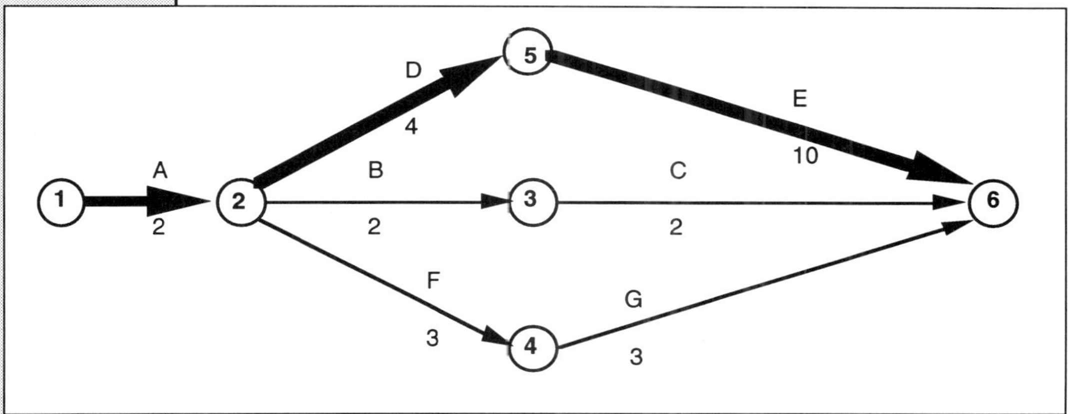

using a Gannt chart

Your colleagues are impressed by this planning technique, but say that they cannot easily 'work from the diagram. You therefore set out the activities on a planning bar chart, known as a Gannt chart.

This chart shows

- the activities on a weekly schedule (the weeks are numbered across the top)
- the critical activities as black bars
- the activities which are not on the critical path as grey bars
- float times for non-critical activities, ie times during which a delay can occur which will not hold up the project

This chart is useful because each week it can be consulted to see what is due to start, to finish or to continue. Note that the chart shows the activity letters allocated to the critical activities.

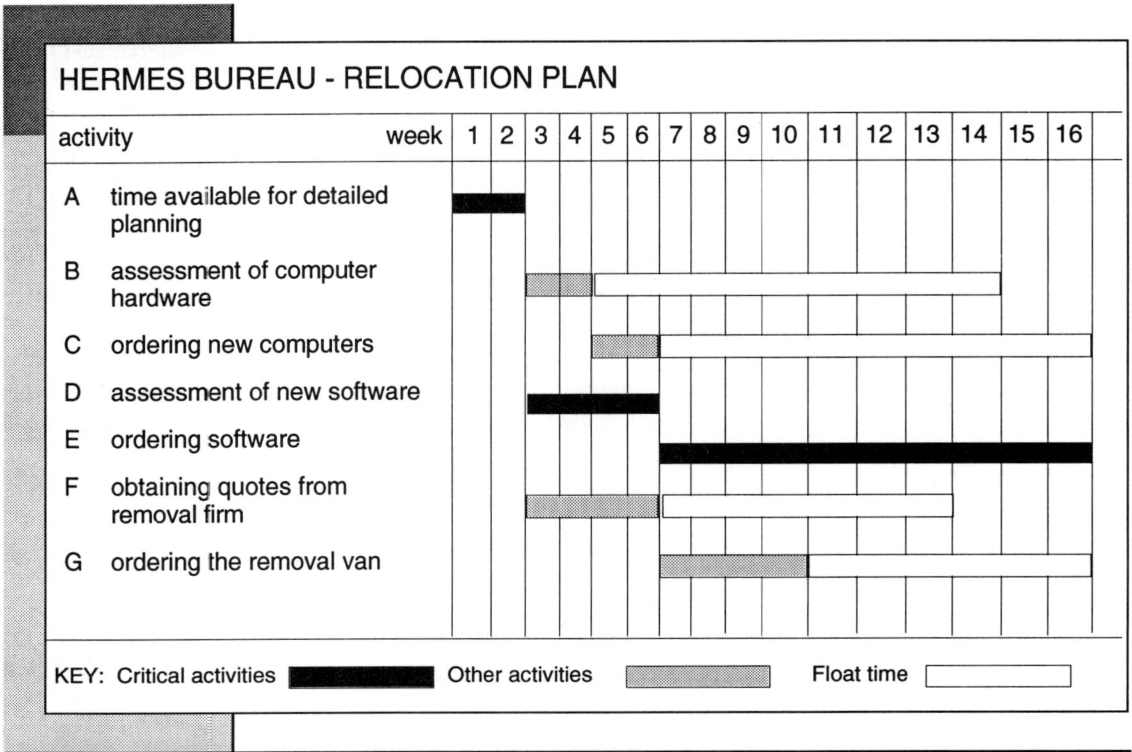

STUDENT ACTIVITY 11.11
performance criterion 8.1.6

Gannt chart planning

situation

A friend of yours runs a small printing shop in Stourminster. He has decided to expand his operations into computer typesetting and colour copying. He works from a small shop in the city centre, and considers that he has room for

- a new desktop computer
- a colour photocopier which will also scan and print customers' colour pictures

He is concerned, however, that the introduction of the new machinery and the need to move an old printing machine to a new position will disrupt his everyday work-flow. He is anxious to reduce the disruption to a minimum. He wants to open for business with all his new equipment up and running on 1 November.

You question him and establish the following facts:

- he wants to spend one whole day planning what equipment he is going to buy, and also thinking up a new name for the business
- the new machinery will be delivered 10 days after order and will take one day to install

- the owner will be given 3 days training on the new equipment after installation and before 1 November
- he will need paper and toner for the new machinery – delivery time is 7 days
- he will need new invoices and stationery as he is changing his business name – delivery time 14 days
- he will also need a new sign for the shopfront – delivery time is 7 days after order, installation time is one day
- the old machine will take one day to move and two days to refit
- everything must be finished by 1 November!

You are to produce for him a Gantt chart (as shown in the Case Study in this chapter) to help him work out the minimum time needed for the introduction of the new equipment, and for moving the old equipment.

sources of help for the business plan

pc 8.1.6

Like any person in business you will need *help* when you are compiling information and writing the first draft of your business plan. Sources of *potential support* include:

your tutors

You may find that there are qualified accountants, lawyers, bankers, insurance experts on the Business Studies staff – you can but ask!

educational advisers

If you are taking part in a Young Enterprise scheme, make the most of the knowledge and experience of the Advisers. If your school or college is taking part in an educational/industry link, talk to the people you meet.

the professionals

Make contact, if you can, with professional people such as accountants, lawyers, bankers, marketing consultants and insurance brokers. Ask them to your school or college to 'sit in' on your discussions about starting a business.

outside bodies

Talk to your local TEC (Training and Enterprise Council), Business Link office, Chamber of Commerce and bank 'business centres'.

chapter summary and key terms

- A business plan explains to a lender what the business is, what its costs are, how much money it needs, and how any borrowing will be repaid.
- The purposes of a business plan are to provide information to lenders, to help the management of the business to see where the business is going, and to enable progress to be monitored.
- A business plan enables a business to clarify its objectives: these normally include breaking even and making a profit, and achieving an acceptable market share.
- Compiling a business plan means that much information has to be collected and sources of assistance identified.
- A business must appreciate and deal with the legal and insurance implications of starting trading and day-to-day operations.
- Resource requirements must be identified: these include human resources (staffing), physical resources (premises, equipment and materials) and financial resources (the money needed).
- Timescales must be calculated for planning and implementing plans.

key terms

business objectives	what you want to achieve by running a business
mission statement	a simple summary of business objectives
unlimited liability	the situation where a sole trader or partner is personally liable for business debts
limited liability	the situation where the owners of a limited company – the shareholders – are *not* liable for business debts
lease	where the owner of an asset – eg premises, cars – 'rents' out the asset to someone else
liability insurance	cover against claims from - employees injured at work (employer's liability) - the public injured at work (public liability) - the public injured by products (product liability)
critical path analysis	a graphical technique for working out the minimum time a project is likely to take
Gannt chart	a planning chart set out in the form of a bar chart

multiple-choice questions

1 A mission statement

A a list of the sources of information for the business plan

B a summary of business objectives

C a summary of the financial forecasts

D a plan of the areas to be covered by sales reps

2 Limited liability means

A a sole trader cannot normally be made liable for business debts

B a partner cannot normally be made liable for business debts

C a shareholder cannot normally be made liable for business debts

D a leaseholder cannot normally be made liable for business debts

Questions 3 – 5 relate to the following information:

A business plan often contains

A a production plan

B financial projections

C a marketing plan

Which of the above will be of *most* interest to the following?

3 The bank manager

4 The purchasing manager

5 The sales manager

6 Decide whether each of these statements is True (T) or False (F)

(i) all employees must be given a formal written contract of employment

(ii) a business which has a faulty product which causes injury to a consumer should be covered by public liability insurance

A (i) T (ii) T

B (i) T (ii) F

C (i) F (ii) T

D (i) F (ii) F

12 Producing and presenting a business plan

GNVQ SPECIFICATIONS

Element 8.2

Produce and present a business plan

performance criteria – a student must:

1 describe and explain business objectives for a business enterprise
2 outline a marketing plan for a business enterprise
3 outline a production plan for a business enterprise
4 outline the resource requirements for marketing and production
5 produce financial data and forecasts to support the business plan
6 identify monthly profit and loss and balance sheet monitoring and review procedures for the business plan
7 present and explain business plan to an audience

what this chapter covers

This chapter is based around the Assignment on the opposite page. The aim is to present your business plan to an audience. In short you will have to 'sell' your idea and proposals to a provider of finance such as a bank.

what you will learn from this chapter

- the structure and contents of a business plan
- how to formulate your business objectives
- how to write the marketing section of the business plan
- how to write the production section of the business plan
- how to present your requirements for human, physical and financial resources in the business plan
- the importance of the financial data to the plan – the cash flow forecast, profit and loss statement and balance sheet
- the need to set up a system to monitor progress – to compare actual results with the figures projected in the business plan

EVIDENCE COLLECTION ASSIGNMENT 13

presenting the business plan

Element 8.2

introduction

In this assignment you will use the information you have gathered about your proposed business and you will draft a formal business plan.

The aim of the assignment is to give a formal presentation of the plan to an 'audience'. This could include your Tutor, outside advisers and preferably a lending officer from one of the banks.

You can *either* compile a written plan in an A4 ring-binder, *or* produce the data on computer file (on disk or on a file server). This plan should be assessed by your Tutor. Whichever format you choose, you should extract visual aids from the plan to show to the audience, either in the form of OHPs or hand-outs. These visual aids will then form part of your portfolio.

task 1

pcs 8.2.1 -7

Each student will give a formal presentation of the business plan to an 'audience' which should ideally include a lending officer from a bank. The presentation should be clearly structured to cover the following areas:

- *Introduction and objectives* – including a description of the product
- *Marketing* – a statement of how, where and to whom the product will be marketed. Areas covered should include pricing, packaging, promotion and distribution. A clear indication of sales targets and breakeven should be given.
- *Production* – this should include product design, production processes, quality control and production targets. If the product is a service, the presentation should be designed to show how the service is 'put together'.
- *Resource requirements* – staffing, premises/equipment/materials, finance needed.
- *Financial data* – a cash flow forecast, a projected profit and loss statement and balance sheet, plus the system for monthly review of targets.

task 2

pcs 8.2.1 -7

Each student should undergo a question and answer session with the Tutor to test underlying knowledge of the business planning process as seen in the business plan submitted for assessment. Areas covered will include the marketing, production and financial aspects of the plan.

business plan format

pcs 8.2.1 -7

This chapter looks at the *practicalities* of writing a business plan. In this book so far we have looked at the preparatory work in terms of defining objectives, financial planning, resource and production planning, market research and marketing planning. All these processes culminate in the business plan, a written document – often in ring binder or similar format – which will be presented to any potential lender of money or investor in the business. The object of the plan is to convince the reader, who may know nothing about the business, that the proposition is viable and that money invested in it will be safe and will grow.

It is dangerous to assume that there is a set format for a business plan. The structure and contents of a plan may vary widely from business to business, depending on the nature and size of the project and the expertise of the writer. If you are undertaking a Young Enterprise or mini-business scheme, there may well be a specified format for you to follow.

the case study – Sonic Deco Limited

To help you in the writing of your own plan we will set out the format and an example of a five-part plan, which is a fairly typical structure. The business is Sonic Deco Limited, a loudspeaker manufacturer. The five sections, which we will deal with in turn, are as follows:

- setting of objectives
- marketing plan
- production plan
- resource requirements
- financial support data

You will see that much of this material has been covered in earlier chapters. We will refer to the earlier text where appropriate and concentrate here on the practicalities of selecting the appropriate information and presenting it in a persuasive way. As we mentioned above, a business plan is about *selling a business idea*. The effective use of communication skills is vital to the plan's success.

how should a plan be written?

A business plan, as we will see in this chapter, is a highly technical document, calling for the combined expertise of a marketing executive, an accountant and a production or operations manager. If the business owner is confident in all these aspects, there are books on the market and pamphlets from the banks which will give guidance. If the business owner needs assistance, an accountant or management consultant will be able to help, although, of course, at a price. If you are undertaking a Young Enterprise or mini business scheme, you should consult your documentation. It is recommended that the plan be produced on a word processor so that it can be printed out in a presentable format.

CASE STUDY

pcs 8.2.1 - 6

Sonic Deco Limited – compiling the business plan

In this Case Study we set out the five part business plan compiled by John Eliot and Edward Gardiner, the owners of Sonic Deco. They are forming a limited company to manufacture hi-fi loudspeakers. The product, the "Presence" loudspeaker, has already been successfully launched on the market by John Eliot working as a a sole trader; he is now being joined by Edward Gardiner. A large increase in production is planned, and the two directors need to approach the bank for finance of £110,000.

You should now read the notes set out below and study the relevant sections of the business plan which follows. The notes refer to the specific sections of the business plan in the order of presentation in the plan.

introductory page

A business plan, like any document, needs careful thought about the order in which material is arranged. The first page is critical. It should include:

- the name and address of the business
- a summary setting out the business idea positively and clearly, quoting appropriate detail
- a list of contents – so that the reader can find the information he or she wants without having to thumb through pages of material

business objectives and mission statement

The nature of the business and its legal status (here a limited company) should be set out, together with the objectives of the business. The short-term (12 months) objectives should state:

- the type of product – whether it be a manufactured item or a service
- the expected sales volume (number of items sold)
- the sales value (the amount of income to be received from sales)
- the projected market share
- the profit target, eg net profit figure

It is common practice to summarise these objectives in a clearly-expressed sentence known as a "Mission Statement".

personnel

An important determining factor of the the success of a business is the people that it employs. It is customary to list in a separate section the management of the business, showing their qualifications and experience. If necessary their CVs can be attached as an Appendix. The extent of the other staff of the business should also be listed, although in less detail.

marketing plan

As we have seen in the marketing section of this book, a successful business should invest time and money in marketing. The business plan should convince the reader that the product or service will fulfil a specific need. The plan should set out details of:

- the product and its price (sales brochures could be included in the Appendix)
- the present market and the expected market share
- the competition, and why the proposed product is better
- promotion plans – showing timings
- distribution and sales
- the marketing budget (brief details)
- break-even calculations

It should be stressed that the marketing plan which appears in the business plan is an abbreviated version of the internal marketing plan of the business.

production plan

The production will set out details of the physical resources needed for the production of the manufactured item. It will contain:

- a summary of the production method
- the premises used, showing full details of cost, valuation, whether freehold or leasehold
- the machinery and vehicles required, together with details of cost, valuation and expected life
- raw materials needed, stating cost, supplier details and expected stock levels
- labour and training requirement
- quality control procedures

You should note that if the plan is presenting a service, the appropriate details will be listed, although there will obviously be no raw materials requirement.

resource requirements

This section summarises in financial terms:

- the resources that will be needed
- the amount of money being contributed by the owner(s)
- the amount of finance required
- the assets available for security

This section summarises for a potential lender the essential questions of

- how much finance is being requested in proportion to the capital sum being invested by the owner(s)?
- what assets are available for security?

financial data

This section will contain for a new business:

- a twelve month cashflow forecast
- the balance sheet at the beginning of the twelve months
- projected profit and loss statement for the first twelve months
- projected balance sheet at the end of twelve months

If the business is already trading, the financial data should also include past financial statements, normally over a three year period.

When looking at the figures in the financial statements in this Case Study, remember that the cashflow forecast will include VAT, and the profit statement will not.

You should also note that the financial projections contained in the plan will enable the business to **monitor and review performance** during the course of the year.

Specifically the business will be able to look at:

- *cashflow* – the business can compare the projected cash flow forecast figures with the actual figures on a monthly basis; if the figures are going widely adrift, the cashflow forecast can be redrafted
- *monthly profit and loss statement* (a standard report if the business has its accounts on a computer) – against the projected figures in the plan (normally divided by twelve)

It will be useful for the business each month to produce *cumulative* (year-to-date) figures for the profit and loss statement. This will show any adverse or positive trend much more accurately.

NOW STUDY THE EXAMPLE BUSINESS PLAN WHICH FOLLOWS – NOTE THAT IT SHOWS THE POSITION BEFORE THE BANK IS APPROACHED FOR FINANCE.

BUSINESS PLAN

name Sonic Deco Limited

address Unit 1b Severnside Industrial Estate
Link Road
Stourminster ST2 4RT

summary

Sonic Deco Limited is a hi-fi loudspeaker manufacturing business founded by John Eliot and Edward Gardiner in 19-1. John Eliot has fifteen years' experience of loudspeaker design and has pioneered as a sole trader a new Deco'Presence' speaker which is now in production in rented premises, and has already sold 500 units in six months to hi-fi dealers in London and the West Midlands. There is proven market demand for an estimated 5,000 units a year.

The new company proposes to takeover and expand the sole trader business. It will purchase an industrial unit, machinery and delivery vehicle. Total cost of assets will be £219k. The owners are contributing £125k of capital, and the company seeks a further £110k from the bank: £50k by way of commercial mortgage on the premises, £20k by way of business loan for the machinery, and £40k by way of overdraft for working capital purposes.

contents

business and objectives

name Sonic Deco Limited

address Unit 1b Severnside Industrial Estate
Link Road
Stourminster ST2 4RT

legal status Limited company
Shareholders:
John Eliot 50%
Edward Gardiner 50%

business Hi-fi loudspeaker manufacturer

start date 1 January 19-1

mission statement

"Sonic Deco Limited will become a leading manufacturer of quality loudspeaker systems and a household name in the UK"

short-term objectives

Sonic Deco will within the first twelve months of trading:

- produce and sell 4,800 units (pairs) of loudspeakers
- achieve sales turnover of £480,000
- achieve a pre-tax profit of over £45,000
- supply over 50 major hi-fi retailers throughout the UK
- take 10% of UK market in similar units

long-term objectives

Sonic Deco will within the first three years of trading:

- increase the product lines to six loudspeaker models
- increase annual turnover to £1,000,000
- establish sales through agents in the EC, USA and Japan

personnel

key personnel

name	age	qualifications	position	annual salary
John Eliot*	35	BSc. MSc	Managing Director -responsible for production, sales and R & D	£24,000
Edward Gardiner*	45	BA.MBA.ACCA	Finance Director Company Secretary - responsible for finance and administration	£24,000

* CVs attached

other personnel

job description	number	expected weekly wage
production line workers	3	£175
despatch clerk/driver*	1	£150
part-time packer*	1	£50
clerical assistant	1	£150

*to be recruited

marketing plan

product

Sonic Deco "Presence" loudspeakers (sold in pairs):

- matched pairs in high density chipboard laminate with moulded fascia
- attractive modern styling
- two colourways - black ash and light oak finish
- price £100 per pair (excluding VAT)

The product specifications and price have been arrived at following market research among existing customers:

- questionnaires sent with products and mailings
- customer comments made during telephone conversations

A copy of the brochure for the "Presence" loudspeaker is included in Appendix 1.

the market

- domestic use, supplied by hi-fi retailers and mail order houses
- total UK sales in 19-0 of £45m for similar units
- expanding market (10% in 19-0) - especially B, C1, C2 social groupings
- further growth in market (forecast 7% p.a. to 19-5) stimulated by demand by consumers for CD-play and CD-record systems

Sonic Deco Limited realistically expect to take 10% of the UK market in 19-1.

the competitors

Major names in the market are BEF, Rosedale, Session, M&W who take 80% of current total UK sales. Their weaknesses are:

- staid image
- high unit price -an average of £115 for similar units
- slow delivery

We can gain market share by

- our bright "modern" image
- price-cutting to £100 per unit
- rapid delivery to suppliers
- responsive after-sales service

We also have the advantage of being a small company which is able to offer a more "personal" service to our customers.

- 4 -

marketing plan (continued)

promotion

Promotion is by way of

- monthly advertising in the hi-fi magazines
- mailshots to existing suppliers (quarterly from January 19-1)
- purchase of product-related mailing lists (January)
- John Eliot visiting retailers and mail order houses
- sending the speakers for review to the Hi-fi magazines

distribution and sales

Distribution of the speaker units is in sealed cartons direct to hi-fi retailers and mail order houses. No wholesaler is involved.

Sonic Deco Limited is purchasing a van for local and urgent deliveries. It also has a contract with a carrier, SpeedDirect, which offers a 24 hour and three day delivery service within the UK.

marketing budget

In the first twelve months the marketing budget has been estimated at £12,000. This will cover

- advertising costs in magazines
- mailings
- purchase of mailing lists
- postages related to mailings

In addition, £1,800 has been budgeted for postage and delivery costs.

sales projections

Expected turnover for the first 12 months, based on the sale of 4,800 units: £480,000

sales break-even figures:

$$\frac{\text{£145,275 (total overheads)}}{\text{42\% (gross profit margin\%)}} \times 100 = \text{£345,892}$$

sale of units needed for break-even = 3,459

Sonic Deco Limited is confident of achieving this level of sales (72% of annual projected sales) in view of the existing good name of the speakers and the current demand shown in the order books.

production plan

production

Sonic Deco Limited will manufacture pairs of "Presence" speaker units on a power saw and welding production line set up in their freehold premises. 3 production line workers will produce 400 pairs of speakers per month.

The units will be packed on site in double-walled cartons with high-density moulded filling pads.

The units will be despatched from the premises either in the company van or collected by carrier.

The business will be administered from the premises by the two directors and a clerical assistant. An office will be set up on the premises.

All Health and Safety at Work conditions will be met.

premises

freehold factory

Sonic Deco Limited will operate from:

Unit 1b Severnside Industrial Estate
Link Road
Stourminster ST2 4RT

Freehold premises of 2,500 square feet

Purchase price £125,000

Professional valuation £127,500 (December 19-0)

Business rates £2,900 p.a.

No mortgage currently outstanding

Financed by capital and proposed £50K bank commercial mortgage.

machinery

production line

Sonic Deco Limited will purchase power saws and other production machinery:

Cost: £45,000

Expected life 5 years (20% straight line depreciation)

Financing: from capital and proposed £20k bank business loan

office machines

Sonic Deco Limited will purchase a PC and other office machines:

Cost: £12,500

Expected life 5 years (20% straight line depreciation)

Financing: from capital

- 6 -

production plan – continued

vehicle

Sonic Deco Limited will purchase a delivery van. Cost: £12,500

Expected life 4 years (25% straight line depreciation)

Financing: from capital

raw materials

speaker units

Sonic Deco Limited purchase high quality bextrene cone individual speaker units for building into the "Presence" cabinets.

Supplier is R & T of Cambridge.

Cost of the individual units is £20 (£40 per pair).

At present terms are cash, but from February 19-1 terms will be 30 days.

speaker cabinets

Sonic Deco Limited purchase high quality chipboard laminates, internal bracing and filling from two suppliers.

Total cost of materials per pair of speakers is £20.

At present terms are cash, but from February 19-1 terms will be 30 days.

Total materials cost per pair of speakers: £60

Average stock to be held £10,000

labour costs

The total annual labour budget is £43,750, calulated on the basis of employing the following for a 50 week year:

3 production line workers @ £175 per week

1 part-time packer @ £50 per week

1 despatch clerk/driver @ £150 per week

1 clerical assistant @ £150 per week

quality control

Strict quality control procedures are at present in operation for materials purchased and for finished products in respect of physical finish and sound reproduction.

Sonic Deco is at present investigating its overall systems with a view to application for Quality Assurance registration through BS EN ISO 9000.

resources requirements

resources required

item	*cost (£)*
freehold premises	125,000
production machinery	45,000
office equipment	12,500
vehicle	12,500
materials and working capital	40,000
TOTAL	235,000

financial requirements

item	*finance(£)*	
freehold premises	50,000	commercial mortgage*
production machinery	20,000	business loan**
stock/working capital	40,000	overdraft
TOTAL FINANCE REQUIRED	110,000	
CONTRIBUTION FROM OWN RESOURCES	125,000	
TOTAL	235,000	

* commercial mortgage with annual repayments of capital and interest requested

** business loan with first year interest only repayments requested

assets available for security

security	*value (£)*
freehold premises	£127,000 (valuation Dec. 19-0)
other fixed assets	£70,000 (at cost)

- 8 -

financial data – cashflow forecast

Name of Business: Sonic Deco Limited								
Period: January - Dec 19-1								
	Jan	Feb	Mar	Apl	May	Jun	July	Aug
	£	£	£	£	£	£	£	£
RECEIPTS								
Cash sales								
Cash from debtors		47000	47000	47000	47000	47000	47000	47000
Capital	125000							
Loans	70000							
Interest								
TOTAL RECEIPTS	195000	47000	47000	47000	47000	47000	47000	47000
PAYMENTS								
Cash purchases	28200							
Credit purchases			28200	28200	28200	28200	28200	28200
Capital items	195000							
Wages	7645	7645	7645	7645	7645	7645	7645	7645
Rent/rates			290	290	290	290	290	290
Insurance	1500							
Services	200	200	200	200	200	200	200	200
Telephone				300			300	
VAT				7000			7000	
Vehicle expenses	200	200	200	200	200	200	200	200
Stationery	50	50	50	50	50	50	50	50
Postages	150	150	150	150	150	150	150	150
Bank charges			150			150		
Interest			500					
Loan repayments								
Advertising	1000	1000	1000	1000	1000	1000	1000	1000
Packaging	500	500	500	500	500	500	500	500
TOTAL PAYMENTS	234445	9745	38885	45535	38235	38385	45535	38235
NET CASHFLOW	-39445	37255	8115	1465	8765	8615	1465	8765
OPENING BANK	0	-39445	-2190	5925	7390	16155	24770	26235
CLOSING BANK	-39445	-2190	5925	7390	16155	24770	26235	35000

financial data – cashflow forecast

Sept	Oct	Nov	Dec	TOTAL		
£	£	£	£	£		
47000	47000	47000	47000	517000		
				125000		
				70000		
				0		
47000	47000	47000	47000	712000		
				28200		
28200	28200	28200	28200	282000		
				195000		
7645	7645	7645	7655	91750		
290	290	290	290	2900		
				1500		
200	200	200	200	2400		
	300			900		
	7000			21000		
200	200	200	200	2400		
50	50	50	50	600		
150	150	150	150	1800		
150			150	600		
			7000	7500		
			2000	2000		
1000	1000	1000	1000	12000		
500	500	500	500	6000		
				0		
				0		
38385	45535	38235	47395	658550		
8615	1465	8765	-395	53450		
35000	43615	45080	53845	0		
43615	45080	53845	53450	53450		

financial data – projected profit statement –

PROJECTED TRADING AND PROFIT LOSS ACCOUNT OF SONIC DECO LIMITED FOR YEAR ENDING 31 DECEMBER 19-1

	£	£
Sales		480,000
Purchases	288,000	
Less closing stock	10,000	
Cost of Goods Sold		278,000
Gross Profit		202,000
Wages	43,750	
Directors salaries	48,000	
Rates	2,900	
Insurance	1,500	
Services	2,400	
Telephone	1,200	
Vehicle expenses	2,400	
Stationery	600	
Postages	1,800	
Advertising	12,000	
Packing	6,000	
Bank charges	600	
Interest	7,500	
Depreciation	14,625	
		145,275
Net profit		56,725

Note:

The figures for purchases and sales on the cash flow forecast differ from those quoted above because the figures here *exclude* VAT.

financial data – opening balance sheet

PROJECTED BALANCE SHEET OF SONIC DECO LIMITED AS AT 1 JANUARY 19-1

	Cost	Dep'n	Net
	£	£	£
Fixed Assets			
Premises	125,000	0	125,000
Machinery	45,000	0	45,000
Vehicle	12,500	0	12,500
Office equipment	12,500	0	12,500
	195,000	0	195,000
Current Assets			
Stock		24,000	
Less Current Liabilities			
Overdraft		24,000*	
Working Capital			0
			195,000
Less Long-term Liabilties			
Bank Loans			70,000
NET ASSETS			125,000

FINANCED BY

Authorised Share Capital	
125,000 ordinary shares of £1 each	125,000
Issued Share Capital	
125,000 ordinary shares of £1 each, fully paid	125,000

*Note that the overdraft of £24,000 results from the initial stock purchase of £24,000. The full overdraft requirement of £40,000 shown in the Resources Requirement Section (p.8) will not be utilised until the end of the first month of trading.

financial data – year-end balance sheet

BALANCE SHEET OF SONIC DECO LIMITED AS AT 31 DECEMBER 19-1

	Cost	Dep'n	Net
	£	£	£
Fixed Assets			
Premises	125,000	0	125,000
Machinery	45,000	9,000	36000
Vehicle	12,500	3,125	9,375
Office equipment	12,500	2,500	10,000
	195,000	14,625	180,375
Current Assets			
Stock		10,000	
Debtors		40,000	
Bank		53,450	
		103,450	
Less Current Liabilities			
Creditors		34,100	
Working Capital			69,350
			249,725
Less Long-term Liabilties			
Bank Loans			68,000
NET ASSETS			181,725

FINANCED BY	
Authorised Share Capital	
125,000 ordinary shares of £1 each	125,000
Issued Share Capital	
125,000 ordinary shares of £1 each, fully paid	125,000
Profit and loss	56,725
	181,725

monitoring of financial results

CASHFLOW FORECAST

Monthly figures will be recorded and compared with forecast figures and inspected by the directors.

If results fluctuate significantly the situation will be investigated and the forecast redrafted.

PROFIT AND LOSS STATEMENT

Monthly figures will be extracted from the computer system and compared with the projected monthly equivalent from the forecast.

Year-to-date figures will also be calculated and compared with the forecast. The directors will investigate significant adverse and positive trends and take action accordingly.

All monitored figures will be supplied to a lender on request.

NOTE
THE APPENDICES ARE NOT ILLUSTRATED

13 Planning for employment and self-employment

GNVQ SPECIFICATIONS

Element 8.3

Plan for employment or self-employment

performance criteria – a student must

1 identify and give examples of types of employment or self-employment
2 identify statutory requirements for employment or self-employment
3 identify sources of information and collect information for employment or self-employment
4 identify opportunities for employment or self-employment
5 analyse and discuss skills to support employment or self-employment
6 propose a personal plan for employment or self-employment

what this chapter covers

This chapter will enable you to plan ahead for a job in business and to gain an appreciation of all the 'red tape' that is involved. You will also consider whether you are better suited to working for yourself (self-employment) or getting a job with an established organisation(employment).

what you will learn from this chapter

- the different types of job available – for both the employed and self-employed
- the statutory (legal) requirements for the employed and self-employed
- where to find information about jobs
- the job opportunities that are available in your area
- the skills that are needed for employment and self-employment
- the skills that you have or could develop
- how to make a personal plan for the type of job that would best suit you in both the short-term and the long-term

employment and self-employment

pc 8.3.1

definitions – what is employment?

Being *employed* means that you work for someone else; being *self-employed* means that you are in business on your own, running your own enterprise, making the decisions , running the risks and taking the profit.

types of employment

If you are considering getting a job – being 'employed' – there is a wide range of opportunities available:

- *private sector* jobs – working in industry, financial services, travel and tourism. for example
- *public sector* jobs – working for government agencies and public corporations, the Civil Service, Local Government
- *voluntary work* – working for a non-profit-making organisation, eg Voluntary Service Overseas or the Prince's Youth Business Trust

types of self-employment

If you want to work for yourself, there again many options available:

- being a *sole trader* – eg opening a music shop
- becoming a *partner* – eg going into practice as an accountant
- taking a *franchise* – eg opening a branch of Body Shop

Becoming self-employed can involve starting a *new* business (the shop), buying *into* a business (the accountant) or buying an *existing* business or business name (the franchise).

STUDENT ACTIVITY 13.1
performance criterion 8.3.1

investigating types of job opportunity

task

Investigate a range of job vacancies that are available in your area – you can use Job Centres, and local newspapers as your source. Classify the jobs according to:

- whether they involve employment or self-employment
- whether they are public or private sector
- how much they appeal to you (give them a 'rating' out of ten – ie a job you like will get a high number, a job you do not like will get a low number)

Compile your results on a computer database or spreadsheet. Get the computer to sort the data according to the various classifications and print appropriate reports.

STUDENT ACTIVITY 13.2
performance criterion 8.3.1

types of employment – the statistics

Study the statistics set out below and carry out the tasks that follow. Use computer charting facilities wherever possible to illustrate your findings.

employment and self-employment

Self-employed people	3.3 million
People employed in the private sector	15.6 million
People employed in the public sector	5.9 million

average weekly hours worked by employed and self-employed people

employed men	40.7
self-employed men	46.8
employed women	34.6
self-employed women	43.9

regional differences in employment

area	*employed 000's*	*self-employed 000's*
Greater Manchester	949	121
Inner London	866	163
Hereford & Worcester County	258	56
Powys County	35	14

tasks

1. Draw a pie chart showing the number of self-employed people, and people employed in the public and private sectors. Calculate percentages and show them as labels. What conclusions do you draw from your result?
2. Comment on the differences in the average working hours of employed and self-employed people? Show your results in the form of a bar chart.
3. What are the regional differences in the number of employed and self-employed people? Does the type of area make any difference? What reasons can you suggest for the difference?

statutory requirements

pc 8.3.2

A statutory requirement is something that is required by law.

An example of an everyday statutory requirement is the need for a car driver to have a driving licence. When you are employed or become self-employed there are a number of *statutory requirements* with which you (and your employer, if you have one) have to comply. We will summarise them below. On the pages that follow are two Case Studies which show how the statutory requirements work in practice.

paying tax on business profits

Business profits are taxed by the Inland Revenue (the Government-controlled tax authorities). Sole traders, partners and franchisees – the *self-employed* – have to pay *income tax*. They will have to complete a *tax return* form for the Inland Revenue setting out their business income and expenses. This 'self assessment' enables the Inland Revenue to calculate the amount of income tax they have to pay (normally in two six-monthly instalments). People who are employed also pay income tax, deducted from their pay by the employer through a PAYE (Pay As You Earn) system. Limited companies, on the other hand, pay *corporation tax* on their business profits, in the year following the financial year in question.

National Insurance and benefits

National Insurance is another form of taxation paid by the self-employed, the employed *and* the employer! National Insurance Contributions are paid to the Department of Social Security and help finance State pensions and benefits. If you are employed, your employer will deduct National Insurance Contributions; if you are self-employed you will have to register with the local *Benefits Office* and pay contributions at the special 'self-employed' rate. If you are low-paid or on an Enterprise Allowance scheme you may qualify for state benefits.

Value Added Tax (VAT)

VAT is a tax which is charged on the supply of most goods and services, and is paid to HM Customs & Excise by the seller. Businesses which sell more than a fixed amount each year (£44,000 in 1995) *must* register for VAT. VAT-registered businesses will send a VAT cheque and a 'VAT Return' form to HM Customs & Excise, normally every three months. This cheque represents VAT charged on their sales less any VAT paid on goods and services they have bought. Some small businesses are spared the quarterly VAT Return, and can complete an annual return. Some businesses can actually claim VAT back when the amount paid *exceeds* the amount charged.

rules and regulations for limited companies

If you set up a limited company business, you will encounter *statutory requirements* set out by the Companies Acts. A limited company in law is a separate body, owned by its shareholders and run by its directors. If a person sets up a small business as a limited company, with, say himself and his wife as directors, he and his wife are *employees* of the company, even though it is run like any sole trader or partnership business. A limited company is *registered* at Companies House (a Government-run office) in Cardiff, and given a number and a name. Details of the company are kept at Companies House and must be updated regularly. If you run a company you will have to send to Companies House each year:

- an Annual Return giving details of shareholdings, directors etc
- financial accounts including a balance sheet – the amount of detail required will depend on the size of company

keeping business records

Businesses are obliged to keep accurate records of financial transactions – the 'accounting system' covered in Chapter 6. Both the Inland Revenue and the VAT authorities are allowed to inspect these records so that any tax 'fiddles' taking place can be detected and action taken. A common tax 'fiddle' is a self-employed person working for cash (notes and coins) and not declaring the income (and therefore not paying tax on it!). As we have seen, limited companies must send audited accounts (accounts checked and verified by an accountant) to Companies House every year.

travelling and working abroad

If your business involves you travelling or working abroad you will need a passport and also possibly a visa, a work permit, or licence to export goods or services.

pensions

When you (and your employer if you have one) pay National Insurance Contributions you will be entitled to State benefits, including the State Pension after retirement age. If you are *employed* you will probably have an *occupational pension scheme* towards which which your employer will make contributions. You may (or may not) have to contribute to this scheme. If you are self-employed, you can set up your own *personal pension plan* and make contributions out of your business profit to provide a pension after you retire.

The two Case Studies which follow show the requirements placed on self-employed and employed people.

CASE STUDY

pc 8.3.2

Jane Willis – self-employed decorator

I set up my own decorating business two years ago on an Enterprise Allowance Scheme funded by the local TEC. My family has always been in decorating, so it seemed a natural step to take. I do all sorts of painting indoors and outdoors. It has been hard work – long hours and little holiday – but it is very satisfying working for yourself, especially when you get new business from existing clients recommending you to friends. I now have two assistants working for me, so our annual income (but not profit!) is £75,000. So I am now an employer as well!

There is a certain amount of red tape involved, but I have had a lot of help from the local Business Link office and my accountant.

I do all my accounts on the computer. The Sage accounting program is very easy to use – it will do invoices, statements, monthly trial balances and payroll. My accountant produces a profit and loss statement and balance sheet each year. I need these for the business plan I have to prepare for the bank who are giving me an overdraft.

I also need the profit statement for my annual tax return which I have to send off to the local Inland Revenue office. I am taxed on my annual profits and have to pay the tax in six-monthly instalments. I pay National Insurance Contributions at the self-employed rate.

I do all my payroll on the computer, too. I operate the Pay As You Earn system. This means that I deduct income tax and National Insurance Contributions from my assistants' pay and send the deductions off each month on a bank giro to the Inland Revenue. I also have to complete a summary of these PAYE deductions each May and send it to the Inland Revenue. The tax authorities insist on a lot of detail, so it is important to keep the financial records accurately, and make sure I have backup discs.

I am registered for VAT because my annual turnover is over the registration limit. This means I have to charge VAT (which customers don't like!) but it also means I get back all the VAT I pay on materials. I have to fill in a VAT return every three months and send a cheque off to Customs & Excise. Paperwork can be a bit of a pain, but the computer does help me here.

I have recently arranged a personal pension plan through my financial adviser. I can pay 17.5% of my annual income into this scheme – it saves tax and will provide me with a decent income when I retire.

CASE STUDY

pc 8.3.2

John Miller – running the family company

I am managing director of Miller Software Solutions Limited. We are a family-owned private limited company which has been trading for only three years. We act as consultants to other businesses, advising on the installation of computer hardware and software. We employ ten staff and have an annual turnover of £850,000. I run the business with my wife Alison. We each own fifty percent of the shares and are the only two directors. Fortunately we normally agree about things! Although we run and own the company, strictly speaking we are its "employees". It pays us through the PAYE system and provides us each with a company car and with a pension.

Setting up the business in the first place was reasonably straightforward. With the help of our accountant we established a limited company, drafted the necessary documentation, and registered it at Companies House. The paperwork of running the company is a little more complicated and time-consuming than if you were self-employed, but it runs fairly smoothly once you have got the hang of it. We have to send off an Annual Return to Companies House each December notifying them of any changes in shareholdings, directors, security given to the bank, and so on. Most of the details are preprinted by Companies House, so it is often just a matter of signing it and sending it back.

We have to keep accurate books of account. These are audited each year by the accountant who then prepares the 'final accounts' for sending off to Companies House. The company has to pay corporation tax to the Inland Revenue. Our accountant calculates the amount due, agrees it with the Inland Revenue, and we have to pay it within nine months of our financial year-end. Having a good accountant really is a plus!

We are, of course, registered for VAT, and settle with Customs & Excise every quarter. We had a VAT inspection last year – the inspector went through our financial records with a 'toothcomb', but fortunately we had a clean bill of health.

We process our payroll on the computer and have to complete and send an Annual Return (a P35) to the Inland Revenue each May. It summarises all the Income Tax and National Insurance Contributions made by the employees (including of course ourselves!).

Yes, running a limited company is no problem, once you know what you are doing.

STUDENT ACTIVITY 13.3
performance criterion 8.3.2

statutory requirements for jobs

task

You work in an agency which advises people setting up in business. Your boss sees the need for *two* simple checklists for:

- people wishing to become self-employed
- people wanting to set up a limited company

He asks you to design two suitable checklists. His instructions for each checklist are:

format

- it should be no more than 4 A4 sides in length
- it should be produced on a word processor or Desk Top Publishing package
- it should contain short paragraphs with headings and bullet points

registration

The checklists should explain if any registration of the business is necessary (eg VAT, Companies House), and provide the necessary addresses.

returns to be made

The checklists should explain what returns may need to be made, and to where (eg VAT return, company returns).

taxation

The checklists should outline:

- the tax liability of the self-employed and company employees
- how business profit is taxed
- the situation relating to National Insurance Contributions
- the situation relating to VAT

pensions

The checklists should explain about State pensions, occupational pensions and personal pension plans.

going abroad

The checklists should explain briefly what a business may need to do in order to send a representative abroad.

personal plan for a job

pc 8.3.6

The main activity for this Element is drawing up a *personal plan for employment or self-employment.* This is covered by the Evidence Collection Assignment at the end of this chapter. It must be stressed that you are unlikely to go straight into self-employment after leaving college (or Higher Education). You are most likely to get a job, and then possibly become self-employed later on when you have accumulated both experience and capital. The Evidence Collection Assignment therefore concentrates on employment opportunities and requires you to draw up a plan in four sections:

1. the time scale required for getting a job (or becoming self-employed)
2. the information you are going to need and where you are going to get it from
3. an action plan – what you are actually going to do
4. any statutory requirements you will need to fulfil

Before doing the Assignment, read through the following paragraphs. They outline the sources of information about jobs, and describe the skills and qualifications you are going to need for getting and doing a job.

sources of information about jobs

pcs 8.3.3 & 4

Sources of information about jobs can be divided into two types:

- advice and counselling about the *type* of job you are looking for
- information about *actual* job vacancies

career guidance – *types* of job available

One of the most difficult choices to make is what *type* of job you want to do, There are many people and organisations who will help with career guidance:

- school or college Careers teachers and resource centres
- local authority Careers Officers and Careers Centres

In addition, it is always worthwhile talking to people – family, friends, relatives – to see what they think about their jobs. You may also have the opportunity of going on work experience or work-shadowing (working alongside someone in a job). Another source of guidance is the computer: many Careers Centres and some schools and colleges have interactive computer programs such as 'Kudos'. These enable students to sit in front of a computer screen and answer questions about their likes and dislikes; the program then analyses the type(s) of job that would suit them and will print out a report.

job vacancies – employment opportunities

Job vacancies are advertised and publicised in a number of places:

- Job Centres
- recruitment agencies
- newspapers – local and national
- local authority employment officers

In addition, training vacancies are offered through the Training and Enterprise Councils (TECs) and local Chambers of Commerce.

information about self-employment

If you are looking for information about self-employment – setting up on your own – there are various sources of assistance and information:

- your local office of the Department of Trade and Industry (DTI)
- your local Training and Enterprise Council (TECs)
- Business Link offices
- booklets produced by the banks
- Chambers of Commerce
- Federation of the Self-Employed

the need for skills and qualifications

pc 8.3.5

Employers sometimes value skills more than knowledge. A student that can show initiative, solve problems, and take responsibility for his or her actions is often worth more than a student with any number of academic qualifications. Skills can be:

- *vocational* skills – particular skills *relating to the job being done*
- *core* skills – *general* skills which can be applied in any job

vocational skills

A vocational skill is a skill which can be used in a particular job. The following jobs, for example, all require very specific skills:

- accountant
- car mechanic
- brain surgeon

The skills required for these jobs are normally acquired 'on the job' – the employee is trained while working. Practical vocational skills will be acquired in the workplace, and the theoretical knowledge which backs up these skills will be acquired through college or correspondence courses. The important point about vocational skills is that they cannot easily be transferred from one profession to another: you would not be happy if your brain surgeon had trained as a car mechanic!

core skills

Core skills, on the other hand, are general skills which can be used in any job context. They therefore form a compulsory part of many educational courses such as GNVQs. They include:

Application of Number

This skill involves the use of *numbers*: gathering them, making sense of them, using them to solve problems, and presenting them.

Communication

This skill involves taking part in discussions, being able to prepare written documents, using illustrations and images, and being able to understand and respond to them.

Information Technology

This skill enables employees to be familiar with computers and to be able to use them for a variety of business tasks: word-processing, storing and handling data, and tackling business calculations.

Other skills which will be used in the workplace include:

- evaluating your own strengths and weaknesses
- working with others
- working independently
- planning and time management
- setting targets and reviewing progress
- decision making and problem solving
- information seeking and handling

what qualifications will you need in a job?

Qualifications can be:

- *vocational* qualifications – NVQs and GNVQs, for example
- *academic* qualfications – GCSEs, for example

We will now look at the difference between the two types of qualification.

vocational qualifications

'Vocational' means 'related to a particular job area', eg tourism, retailing, manufacturing. *National Vocational Qualifications* – or *NVQs* as they are called, are taken by employees as part of their job training.

General National Vocational Qualifications (GNVQs) were introduced by the Government so that vocational qualifications could be taught full-time *in schools and colleges.* GNVQs are therefore in 'vocational' (job) areas: art and design, business, health and social care, leisure and tourism, manufacturing, science and so on.

academic qualifications

The more traditional route of obtaining qualifications is to obtain GCSEs (and possibly A Levels) at school or college, and then apply for a job or for a place at college or university. GCSEs and GCSE A Levels are *academic qualifications.*

ACADEMIC AND VOCATIONAL QUALIFICATIONS

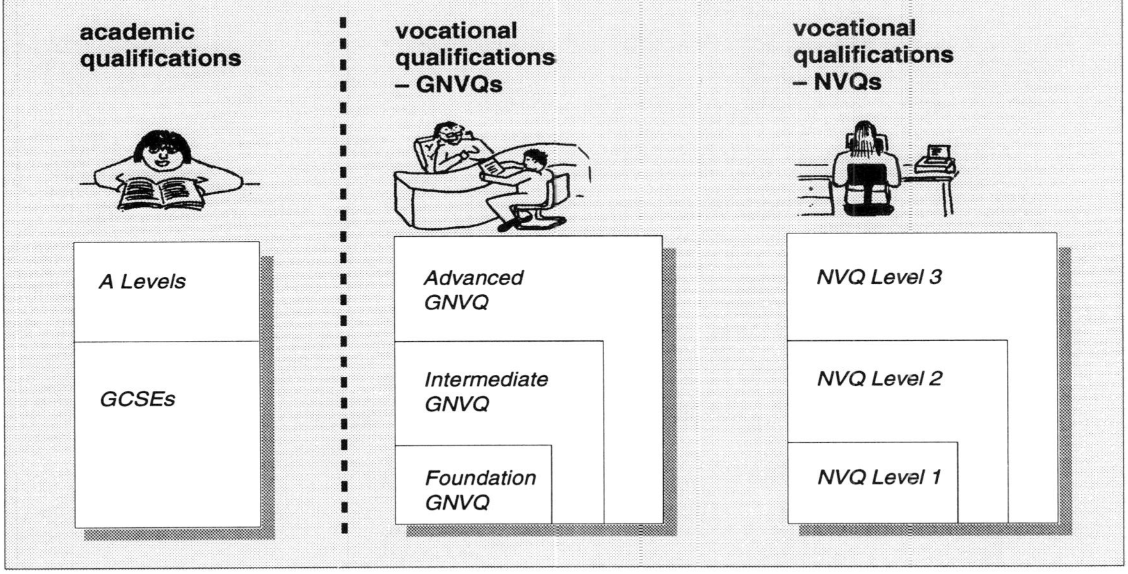

EVIDENCE COLLECTION ASSIGNMENT 14

job planning

Element 8.3

introduction

This assignment prepares you for getting a job or for becoming self-employed. It involves

- a self-analysis and discussion with your tutor about how suited you are to working for yourself or for working as an employee
- an investigation into *three* jobs which interest you
- an in-depth analysis of one of the three jobs
- a short-term and long-term action plan for getting a job

task 1 – self analysis

pc 8.3.5

Read through the list of personal qualities needed by someone who is considering becoming self-employed. In each box put either:

- a tick for "yes"
- a cross for "no"
- a question mark for "not sure"

You might find it useful to discuss the questions with someone who knows you very well – a close friend or a member of your family who will give you an honest opinion about your personal qualities!

1. I can work long hours. ☐
2. I am prepared to work seven days a week if necessary. ☐
3. I am in good health. ☐
4. I can cope under stress. ☐
5. I am a good decision maker. ☐
6. I am self-disciplined and organised. ☐
7. I am good at dealing with other people. ☐
8. I have a positive outlook and know my aims in life. ☐
9. I can learn from mistakes and take advice from others. ☐
10. I do not give up easily. ☐

Discuss the results of this questionnaire with your Tutor and decide:

(a) whether you are suitable for self-employment

(b) the types of employment in which you are interested

In relation to (b) you should decide on three jobs for investigation in Task 2.

task 2 – analysis of three jobs

pcs 8.3.1 - 4

Choose, following discussions with your Tutor, **three types** of employment which interest you (see your investigations in Activity 32.1 to start you off). In each case you should set down in writing:

(a) the type of organisation involved, eg PLC, charity, local authority

(b) the sector (eg public/private) to which it belongs

(c) the skills and qualifications you will need for the job

(d) a *brief* description of the type of work involved in each of the three cases for
- an employee who has just started work
- an employee at managerial (or equivalent) level

Lastly choose the **one job** which interests you most and **investigate**

- the sources of information you could use to obtain further information about the job, eg a Careers Centre and the professional body which deals with the job (eg Law Society, Chartered Institute of Bankers etc)
- any statutory requirements you will encounter (eg paying tax) and where you can find out about them (eg your local Inland Revenue office)
- actual job vacancies – list all the sources of information and cut out any adverts you find to support this Assignment

task 3 – a personal action plan

pc 8.3.6

Using the one job chosen for further investigation in Task 2 **or** the self-employed option (see Task 1), draw up a formal written action plan which will include:

1 A chart showing the time scale required for getting into the job and becoming qualified – this could include a HE course and professional training. The chart should show short-term targets (up to 12 months) and longer term objectives (up to 5 years).

2 A list of your sources of information – include contact addresses and telephone numbers.

3 A list of the actions you will need to take to get the job or become self-employed (this could accompany the time scale chart).

4 Any statutory requirements you will encounter in getting a job or becoming self-employed.

chapter summary and key terms

- There are job opportunities both for the employed and the self-employed.
- As a school/college/university leaver you are most likely to become employed – you will need capital and expertise to become self-employed.
- The are a number of statutory requirements for the employed and particularly for the self-employed. These include:
  - paying tax on income and business profits
  - paying National Insurance Contributions
  - registering and paying VAT
  - registering limited companies and sending annual returns
  - keeping business records
  - travelling and working abroad
- There is a wide range of information sources for both careers and jobs.
- Employment and self employment involve skills. These can be
  - vocational skills, which relate to the job being done
  - core skills, which are general skills which can be applied in any job

key terms

self-employment	working for yourself – you have control, take the decisions and run the risks
employment	being employed by someone else
statutory requirements	things you have to do which are required by law
income tax	a tax paid by *individuals* on income received
corporation tax	a tax paid by *limited companies* on business profit
National Insurance	a tax paid to the Benefits Agency by individuals and companies, employers and employees
State Pension	a pension provided by the Government and paid for out of National Insurance Contributions
occupational pension	a pension provided (in full or in part) by an employer
personal pension plan	a pension arranged by a self-employed person
vocational skills	skills which relate to the job being done
core skills	general skills which can be applied in any job

index